CONTRACT JOINERY

Contract Joinery

Ken Austin

Lp Linden Publishing
Fresno, California 93726

CONTRACT JOINERY
BY
KEN AUSTIN

First published 1981
Revised 1986

©International Thomson Publishing Ltd. and C.K. Austin.

ISBN: 0-941936-12-0

35798642

First United States publication August 1988.

Library of Congress Cataloging-in-Publication Data

Austin, C.K. (Cyril Kenneth)
  Contract joinery.

  Reprint. Originally published: Rev. ed. London,
England : International Thomson Pub., 1986.
  Includes index.
  1. Joinery. I. Title.
TH5662.A97 1988   694'.6   88-21571
ISBN 0-941936-12-0

Linden Publishing Co.
3845 North Blackstone
Fresno, California 93726 USA

Contents

Preface

Many books dealing with fine quality joinery tend to overlook basics: the continuing importance of hand tools in a machine tool world plus the need to be thoroughly familiar with all the tools and materials one uses.

The initial chapter of Ken Austin's excellent book on modern joinery covers hand tools, adhesives, assorted materials including plywoods and particle boards; and a section on wood identification and timber, showing methods of cutting to produce various figure and graining.

In chapter two, the author deals with a wide variety of portable and stationary power tools and their relationship to fine joinery. Good illustrations are provided. From there, the book goes into all important areas of contract and architectural joinery. There are informative sections on building doors, windows and stairs, as well as on veneering and lamination, all useful to woodworkers.

Originally published in Great Britain as a test for use in secondary and trade schools and in apprentice programs, "Contract Joinery" has rapidly become popular with all those interested in joinery and finish work. Occasional "Britishisms" add to the interest of this book.

Questions and answers at the end of each chapter enable the reader to test his understanding of the material presented. Directed toward the student preparing for testing or competition in the building trades, they range from straight-forward queries to problems requiring sketches and thoughtful geometrical reasoning. As a one-time teacher of apprentices, I can attest to the thought and preparation that went into these chapters. Most of the questions are taken from examinations offered by the Institute of Carpenters, and the City and Guilds of London Institute (CGLI) examination.

Ken Austin's book offers instruction on a wide spectrum of joinery and finish likely to be encountered, particularly on jobs requiring custom-type work. With the resurgence of upscale home building and the emphasis on "one-off" finish work in quality homes and other buildings, more and more of this sort of work is being recognized by architects and appreciated by the public.

Because of the excellent apprentice system and a reverence for wood and for "doing it right", British woodwork has long set a standard for the world. "Contract Joinery" continues that tradition.

Robert Ericson

CHAPTER 1

Tools and Materials

It is not intended to duplicate here the information easily obtained from popular textbooks on the names of tools and their common uses or to repeat details given in trade catalogues. Instead the principles behind the design of tools are considered and the factors stressed which influence their effective use.

Many tools have become redundant nowadays, the work being carried out by machine even for small quantities. However, the need for the efficient use of those tools which are left is still as great as ever. Only the main tools in common use will be considered here; any special tool is discussed with the work to which it is relevant.

Tools are commonly classified as marking or setting out tools, saws, planes (any tools which produce shavings), chisels and gouges, and assembly tools: e.g. mallet, hammer, screwdriver, etc.

MARKING-OUT TOOLS

The pencil
This should produce a firm line and should preferably be sharpened to a chisel edge at one end and a point, not too long, for pricking off dimensions at the other. If it is H or 2H hardness, it will last longer; but in any case an HB or B (softer pencils) should be used for writing instructions, making face marks, etc, which should be bold and easily seen.

The striking knife
The typical striking knife has a point at the opposite end to the blade; the point should be long and sharp, while the knife should be thin and bevelled at about 60 degrees with a keen corner at the long end. An old

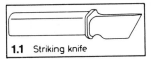

1.1 Striking knife

table knife with a bone handle cut off (**Fig. 1.1**) is better to use and control.

For scribing, I use a stiletto with a small handle

(used in needle-work) which easily gets into tight corners, marking dovetails, etc.

Straight-edges
Straight-edges, which are best made of Honduras mahogany (yellow pine does not wear as well), can be most accurately made in threes. The procedure is:

1. Shoot no. 1;
2. Shoot no. 2 to fit no. 1;
3. Fit no. 3 to no. 1;
4. Try no. 2 against no. 3.

The error will be half of that shown by the gap. Adjust no. 1 and repeat as necessary.

Squares, mitre squares, sliding bevels, etc
These should not be accepted as being dead accurate but should be checked. All blades and stocks should be parallel (this is easily tested with callipers). The square may be checked off a board with a shot

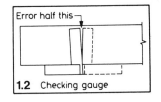

1.2 Checking gauge

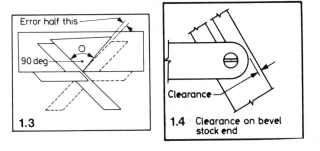

1.3

1.4 Clearance on bevel stock end

edge – not just off the planer (**Fig. 1.2**). The same process applies to a mitre square which also uses a set square (**Fig. 1.3**). Make sure the end of the sliding bevel stock is below the blade (**Fig. 1.4**).

Gauges

The stem of the gauges should be a hand-tight fit in the stock. Avoid over-tightening the screw when setting; this damages the stem. It is useful to have several marking gauges to avoid 'mid stream' resetting. It is a good idea if they are made of different coloured woods – beech, boxwood, rosewood, etc – so that each can be easily identified.

A pencil gauge can be made from a marking gauge as in **Fig. 1.5**. The points on marking gauges should be

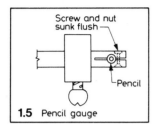

1.5 Pencil gauge

sharp and the projection should be about 3mm. The knife of the cutting gauge should have its edge splayed. It should be sharp and bevelled on the inside only to reduce the risk of running back with the grain. In use, several light strokes are better than one heavy one.

A panel gauge is useful for marking wide boards parallel: use either a pencil or a steel point. The rebated stock keeps the stem off the board surface (**Fig. 1.6**) and gives better control.

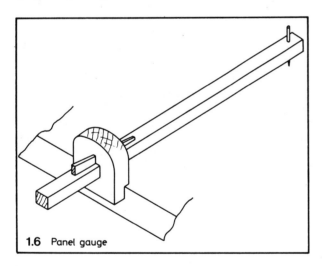

1.6 Panel gauge

SAWS

The saw is undoubtedly the most difficult tool to maintain and, in my opinion, the most important tool in the joiner's kit. It is the primary tool which is brought into use before all others. The greater the precision in its use, the greater the saving of materials and labour, and therefore time, in all subsequent operations. Time spent on the saw's careful maintenance is never wasted.

For efficient use, the saw should be sharp and capable of fast cutting without great effort. It should run easily in the cut without excessive clearance and should not drift or wander one way or the other.

The young craftsman apprentice should form the

habit when sawing, of always working carefully. His aim – not likely to be attained without some trouble – when cutting to a pencil line should be to cut half the line away on the waste side, and leave half the line showing. If the saw is working properly, it should be allowed to run free in the cut once started accurately. This is indicated by an even shadow along the side of the saw.

Saws are divided into two main types in relation to their action:

1. Rip saws for cutting with the grain.
2. Cross-cut saws for cutting across, or at an angle to, the grain.

The rip saw

The rip saw is seldom used in industry today, as most of the ripping is done by machine; but it may be useful to take out on a job for the odd operation when machines are not available. The rip saw teeth are sharpened nearly square to the blade giving chisel edges (**Fig. 1.7**) and nearly square (about 8 degrees less) to the line of cut.

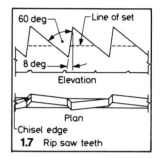

1.7 Rip saw teeth

A full rip saw is usually 66cm (26in) long with four to six points of teeth to every 25mm. It is held at an angle of about 60 degrees to the surface of the timber. If there is a tendency to kick, this angle should be lowered.

CROSS-CUT SAWS

Most other saws come in the category of cross-cut saws and vary from the handsaw (say 650mm long and six points to each 25mm) progressively down to a panel saw (500–550mm long at 10 points to each 25mm). The tenon saw is 300–350mm long with 12 points to 25mm and the dovetail saw is 250mm long at 18 to 20 points to 25mm.

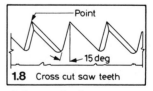

1.8 Cross cut saw teeth

The fronts of the teeth of cross-cut saws should be pitched at 15 degrees to the line of cut. When sharpening the file should be held at an angle of about 70 degrees to the blade. The file should point towards the handle and should file the front of the tooth pointing towards the operator. Reverse the saw to file in the alternate gullets, so producing points instead of chisel edges (**Fig. 1.8**). The actual angles are not so important as maintaining the same angle and keeping the teeth and gullets all the same size and shape.

The size of file used should be such that slightly less than half the depth of the file sits in the gullet. This avoids double wear in the middle when the file is

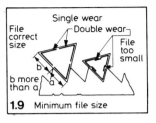

1.9 Minimum file size

turned (**Fig. 1.9**). Files generally recommended are given in **Table 1.1**.

Table 1.1

Saw points per 25mm	4	6	7–8	10–12	15–20
Taper saw (file length mm)		200	175	150	150	112

Setting the saw

The setting of the saw is usually done with a hammer on a steel block by the saw doctor, but the average craftsman uses a pistol grip saw set. In the best type, the level operates two plungers. The first comes out and holds the base of the tooth, while the second pushes the top over. It is best that the saw should be sharpened lightly and frequently, setting as required; but even so it will eventually need reconditioning. This involves four operations as follows:

1. Topping with mill file (**Fig. 1.10**).
2. Shaping with saw file: filing straight through and bringing all teeth to the same size (**Fig. 1.11**).
3. Setting: most of the set will be taken out of the teeth and they will need to be reset.
4. Sharpening: filing at an angle to the blade to put the cutting points on. In carrying out all filing operations the size of individual teeth should be watched constantly and corrected where possible.

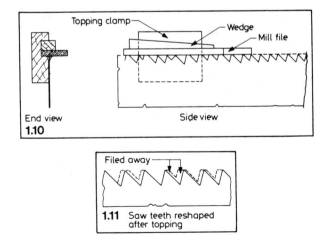

1.10

1.11 Saw teeth reshaped after topping

In setting the teeth, it is usually considered correct to set them to half the depth only. I prefer to put a little more set than is needed and then take this out

with a few light rubs of an oilstone slip along the side. This has the effect of putting minute flats on the sides of the points, gives a smooth cut face and enables the saw to be sharpened several times before resetting. The exaggerated sketch in **Fig. 1.12** illustrates this.

Dovetail saws have teeth which are so small that most craftsmen file them straight through and do not bother to set them. I prefer to do both. The teeth may be set with a fine nail punch on a block of hardwood with light blows, using an oilstone slip to remove any unevenness left on the sides. If a saw with plenty of set runs or leads one way, the set may sometimes be reduced with the slip on the offending side to correct this.

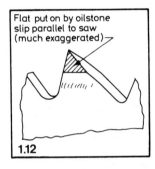

1.12

PLANES

The planes most commonly used by the joiner and left on the bench are the jack plane, try plane and smoother. The first of these, the jack plane, is for preparatory work and is designed to take comparatively heavy shavings. It should be sharpened with about 3mm of camber on the edge, so that the stout shaving produced comes off easily without making dig marks in the surface of the timber (**Fig. 1.13**).

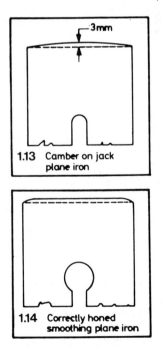

1.13 Camber on jack plane iron

1.14 Correctly honed smoothing plane iron

The try plane and smoothing plane must produce a smooth flat surface so the cutting edge of the iron is kept straight. To avoid making cutter marks, the corners are rubbed away (**Fig. 1.14**). The purpose of the back iron is to break the shaving and stop it from lifting just in front of the cut and tearing.

The closer the back iron is to the cutting edge, the less the surface will be torn but the thinner the shaving must be. It should be set about 3mm from the edge of the jack plane iron, and about 1½mm to 1 mm from the edge of the try plane and smoother irons.

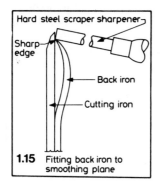

1.15 Fitting back iron to smoothing plane

If it is found that the shavings get under the back iron, this should be sharpened with a rocking motion to a sharp edge on an oilstone. It should then be fixed in position on the cutting iron and finally the polished end of a scrape sharpener should be drawn along it pressing the sharpened edge against the cutter as in **Fig. 1.15.**

CHISELS

Chisels are generally ground back to an angle of about 25 degrees and honed at 30 degrees. When they are reground after continuous honing, the tendency is to rub the new thin edge away excessively. It should only be necessary to use a few strokes on the oilstone. For the efficient use of chisels, it is important that the corners also should be kept sharp. Most people tend to sharpen out of square one way or the other. This tendency may be minimised if an eye is kept on the edge and an effort made to correct it each time it is rehoned.

Boring tools
Brace bits are obtainable in many varieties from spoon bits and shell bits for small screw holes, etc, to twist bits for larger and more accurate work. The general principle in all cases is to sharpen always from the inside. This is to avoid reducing the cutting circle to less than the bit's diameter.

It should be appreciated that the cutting parts of twist bits are small and will allow only of limited resharpening; they should therefore be well protected to reduce the need for resharpening to a minimum.

Care of oilstones and oilstone slips
These should be kept clean and covered when not in use. The oilstone should have its own case. It is essential that it should not be allowed to become hollow in order to produce straight cutting edges as for rebate and smoothing planes. When sharpening small tools, the edge of the stone should be used, rather than the middle. It is also an advantage to have two stones, one coarse and one fine.

ASSEMBLY TOOLS

These are tools used in fitting parts together or assembling: hammers, mallets and screwdrivers. Each person has his own preferences in regard to sizes, but Warrington and pin hammers are essential as well as a mallet for chisels and assembly.

The faces of hammers should be kept clean by rubbing them frequently on an old piece of glasspaper. A greasy hammer face will invariably turn a nail over. A screwdriver blade should be square and not chisel ended and should just fit the slot in the smallest of the range of screws for which it is designed.

ADHESIVES

The range of proprietary adhesives available to the joiner today is so wide that he can have some excuse for being confused by the many trade names he meets, and the particular qualities that each represents. However, if he looks for the descriptive chemical title, always shown somewhere in the instructional literature provided, he can (when he is familiar with this title and the qualities it stands for) at least start with a basic knowledge of the suitability of the product for the job in hand. Having selected the adhesive, the user will be provided with particular and detailed instructions as to its preparation and use. It is important that he should always follow these to the letter. In this chapter, trade names are deliberately omitted; only the types of adhesive are discussed.

ANIMAL GLUE

The original adhesive used by woodworkers over the ages, it has largely been superseded. However, it still remains highly satisfactory for work in dry positions, within its practical limits of application, when used by informed and skilled craftsmen.

Animal glues are covered by the British Standard BS745. Animal glue cannot be used in damp situations or where, due to its magnitude, a job cannot be assembled in a reasonably short time.

It is obtainable in powder, pearl or cake form. The cake should be soaked for 24 hours in three times its own weight of cold water before heating for use. It should be of a consistency to flow off the brush thinly but without breaking into drops. It should not be boiled or it will lose much of its strength.

Glued joints must be assembled while the adhesive is still warm and they must be a perfect fit to gain maximum strength. For example, a glued joint between two boards, thin to the point of invisibility, will be stronger than the timber itself, while a thick black joint may be broken with the finger and thumb.

POLYVINYL ACETATE ADHESIVES

These are produced in the form of white emulsions. There are two commercial types: one for glueing woodwork and the other for general use.

Woodworking pva

This is supplied ready for use and has the advantages that it is non-staining, easy to apply and non-abrasive to tools used to clean off the dry glue. However, not water-resisting. It is thermoplastic, which means that it softens and loses some of its strength when heat is applied. Although it is suitable for joinery it does not have the strength needed for structural carpentry as joints have a tendency to creep under permanent load.

General-use pva

This is available under several trade names. It has a multiplicity of uses and may be combined with cement, plaster, etc, to form or bond in screeds.

As far as the joiner is concerned, the glue may be diluted slightly and used for normal gluing; or it can be thickened, using one of the standard resin-based fillers, and used for bedding rigid panels to irregular surfaces such as brick walls. Where wall surfaces are porous they should be treated first with a weak solution of the glue (say, 1:5). This should be allowed to dry before the final gluing process.

This adhesive also loses strength through heat and under permanent load. This makes it unsuitable for structural work. It may be used for external joinery, provided prolonged immersion in water is not encountered. Pva glues are covered by BS4071.

CASEIN GLUE

This is produced in powdered form from skim milk. There are two qualities: one is slightly moisture resistant, the other is not. The powder is stirred into the correct quantity of cold water and allowed to stand for 20 minutes before use.

The period for which it may be kept before mixing, known as the 'shelf-life', is about one year. Once mixed it must be used within a given period known as the 'pot-life'. This varies with the working area's temperature and may be from seven hours at 16°C to three hours at 33°C.

The time between bringing the glued surfaces together and applying pressure, known as the 'close assembly time' (CAT), will vary with the temperature and the dryness of the timber. The maximum will be about 45 minutes.

When used for large or long joints, the clamping pressure should be applied methodically working from one end or each way from the centre so that joints are always free to slide together to fit. The maximum pressure should be just sufficient to bring the joint surfaces firmly together.

It may be necessary to carry out the cramping in two stages, but a cramp should never be applied hard and then partly released as this would starve the joint of glue. The ultimate pressure should always be the greatest.

The pressing time during which the cramps should remain in position is affected by the temperature as setting will be faster in warm weather. It may vary from four to 16 hours. If the joint is under stress, as in a curved laminated beam, the glue line may have to develop a higher strength; it may require 48 hours to reach maximum.

Casein glue may be used for joinery work in softwood but is liable to stain hardwood. It is gap-filling and heat-resistant above 39°C. Under dry conditions, it develops a high strength. It is therefore suitable for structural work in dry or hot situations, but loses its strength in wet or humid conditions. It is covered by BS1444.

SYNTHETIC RESIN GLUES

These are probably used more than any other today. They are all formaldehyde compounds and are classified as urea formaldehyde, resorcinal formaldehyde, phenol formaldehyde and melamine formaldehyde. They are covered by BS1203 and BS1204.

They are classified in terms of qualities under the following headings:

WBP (WEATHER- AND BOIL-PROOF): Highly resistant to weather, micro-organisms, cold, boiling water and dry heat.

BR (BOIL-RESISTANT): Good resistance to weather but fails under prolonged exposure. Will withstand cold water for many years. Resistant to attack by micro-organisms.

MR (MOISTURE-RESISTANT): Moderate resistance to weather. Will withstand cold water for long periods and hot water for short periods. Resistant to attack from micro-organisms.

INT (INTERIOR): Resistant to cold water, not necessarily resistant to micro-organisms.

All of these adhesives combine with a hardener to set. The shelf-life depends upon the particular type and may vary from six months to one year. The pot-life depends upon the type of adhesive, the hardener and the temperature. It may be from about one hour to nine hours. These conditions must be adjusted to suit the minimum operational time required.

The various adhesives described are placed under one or other of the above classifications. By this means their suitability for a particular purpose may be ascertained.

Urea formaldehyde

This adhesive is generally classified as **MR** but, with a percentage of melamine added, the standard may be raised to **BR** (more heat being required to set it). Urea formaldehyde may normally be used at room temperatures and, when used in favourable conditions, has a high strength value which makes it suitable for timber engineering work. It cannot be used in exposed positions or subjected to excessive heat.

The moisture content of the timber should not exceed 18 per cent or some loss of strength will occur. Urea formaldehyde is available in powder form with the hardener (also a powder) mixed in to the correct proportions. When stirred with the correct amount of water, reaction begins and the work must be glued (open assembly), put together (close assembly) and cramped up within the time (pressure time) available before setting takes place.

These details differ with the various proprietary makes and are always available from the manufacturer. Urea glues may be of the close-contact type; in which case the joints have to be well fitting (a problem with constructional carpentry). Alternatively they may have a gap-filler incorporated which makes them effective in imperfect joints to show gaps of up to 1½mm.

Another type of urea formaldehyde glue has a separate hardener to be added as required by the user (i.e. mixed in before use). Otherwise the hardener, in the form of a liquid, is applied to one side of the joint and the glue to the other; this is known as the separate application method. No reaction takes place until the two sides of the joint are brought together.

This gives a very long open assembly time. The close assembly and cramping or pressing times are still controlled by the hardener.

Resorcinal formaldehyde
This adhesive is classified as **WPB**. It is usually a dark wine-coloured fluid, is gap-filling and should not be used at temperatures below 16°C. The hardener, either a powder or liquid, is mixed in at the beginning of the gluing operation. This limits the pot-life from one to 10 hours according to conditions.

It has a high strength value and may be used on timbers with a moisture content of well over 18 per cent. It may be used in practically any situation and is eminently suitable for structural work in exposed positions.

Phenol/resorcinal formaldehyde
This is mainly a resorcinal resin with some phenol added. It retains the same general values, is a little cheaper but needs a slightly higher temperature for curing than resorcinal formaldehyde.

Phenol formaldehyde
It has the same general qualities as resorcinal resin but requires considerable heat to set. It is therefore most suitable for gluing work to be cured in presses, such as plywood.

Melamine formaldehyde
This is an extremely hard resin and is used primarily in the manufacture of laminated sheet plastics.

Epoxy resin adhesives
These are again resins which require the addition of a hardener to set them, but they have the special characteristic of not giving off any vapour when curing. This enables them to be used between two impervious materials, such as metal and glass. They have a tremendous bond strength but, in order to reach this, great care is needed in the preparation of the faces to take the glue.

The greatest enemy of these adhesives is any form of grease, and the contact surfaces must be either scrubbed in a solution of detergent and washed with hot water, or cleaned off with a volatile chemical known as trichlorethylene. Surfaces should be lightly abraded; glass may be scoured with normal silicon-carbon wet-dry abrasive paper. A general indication that any glued surface is chemically clean is given when the adhesive 'wets' the surface and does not gather in drops. Epoxy resins are expensive and have only a limited use in joinery work.

Impact adhesives
These are rubber- or synthetic rubber-based with a volatile or spirit vehicle and are therefore highly inflammable in use. The adhesive is applied to both faces with a toothed spreader giving an even coverage. Both surfaces are allowed to dry completely before bringing together.

Adhesion is then instantaneous, no adjustment being possible after first touch. It is therefore absolutely necessary to bring the joint surfaces accurately into position before making contact. After the adhesive is completely dry, a piece of paper may be laid on one surface (there will be no adhesion). The second surface may then be placed on the paper and the paper slid out. Alternatively, strips of plywood may be used.

Impact adhesives are liable to creep and are not suitable for general joinery work where any rigidity is required. Their most common use is applying laminated plastic tops to counters, tables, etc, when no method of cramping or weighting down is possible.

When impact adhesive is applied to wood, a great deal is absorbed. The result is that the adhesion is imperfect and the joint tends to open. This risk may be avoided by putting a preliminary coating along the edges of the glued surface and allowing it to dry before applying the final coat all over.

HEAT CURING

As already stated, the setting or curing of all the modern adhesives is accelerated by the application of heat. This enables the work to be removed from the jigs, etc, so that they can be used again. There are two ways of applying heat to small areas, such as glued lipping to doors: these are high frequency (or radio frequency) heating, and low voltage heating.

High frequency heating
This is an elaborate system of electric circuits incorporating transistors which create oscillating electric fields between two plates. The molecules in the glued joint oscillate in sympathy and generate their own heat (there is no question of heat conduction. Setting may take place in minutes or even seconds. The system is dangerous if not used properly and is beyond the scope of this series.

Low voltage heating
Low voltage heating is, by contrast, perfectly safe, as the voltage is reduced to well below that which can be conducted by the human body. The current is passed through a flat metal strip and raises its temperature to the required degree to complete the curing of the

glue. The metal strip is attached to the face of a long rail which is pressed or cramped against the lipping to close the joint which is then cured by heat from the strip.

Heat transference is, in this case, by conduction and a little time must be allowed for it to penetrate to the glue line. One of the problems with this system is that the metal strip will expand with the rise in temperature and is then likely to buckle. To prevent this the ends of the strip are spring-loaded as shown in **Fig. 1.16**. **Fig. 1.17** shows one end of the rail and a method of clamping it while **Fig. 1.18** shows the layout for cramping the lipping to one door.

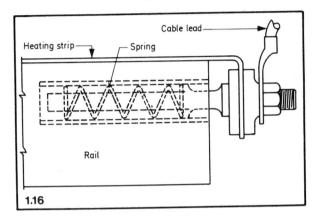

1.16

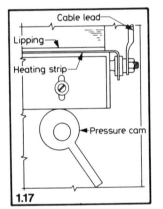

1.17

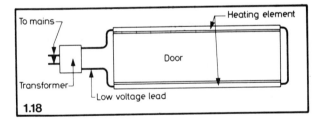

1.18

In some cases, work may be placed in a heated chamber to complete the curing. It is then essential that some steam should be introduced or the dry heat will cause some evaporation from the face of the timber. The result would be to set up some undesirable stresses.

Safety precautions
Most cements and adhesives are chemically active in use and care should be taken to ensure that they come into contact with the worker's hands and arms as little as possible. Protective sleeves and rubber gloves

should be used. If a barrier cream is rubbed into the hands at the start, this will minimise the effect of accidental contact with the glue.

It is important to use containers for the glue, the substance of which does not react with it. Brass, copper and, sometimes, steel vessels should be ruled out; plastic buckets are always safe.

Brushes; buckets, etc should be cleaned immediately after use with hot soapy water; once the glue has set it is usually impossible to remove it.

SHEET MATERIALS

Plywood
In this category of sheet materials comes blockboards, laminboard and batten board. Plywood proper may consist of three to nine plys or veneers. There is usually an odd number of plys but an American four-ply is available. In this, however, the inner plys have the grain running the same way so both outer plys are in balance.

The three main advantages of plywood over solid timber are

1. It provides a broad jointless surface,
2. It has almost equal strength in all directions, and
3. The long grain of each ply or veneer restrains the shrinkage or swelling across the grain of the other plys adjacent to it, thus producing a stable material.

Tests made on 4mm three-ply, when subject to a range of humidities from 30 to 90 per cent, showed a movement of 0.27 per cent across the grain and 0.18 per cent along the grain of the outer plys due to the swelling of the one ply stretching the other along the grain. This range of movement may be considered negligible.

The water-resistance of plywood depends largely upon the cementing materials between the plys and, with regard to such, it is classified in the same way as the adhesive used, i.e. **WBP**, **BP**, **MR** and **INT**.

Although the interior plys in the sheet are largely protected, plywood, being a natural material, is still liable to attack from various micro-organisms. When used externally, **WBP** or **BP** qualities should be used but the surface should still be treated. It is also necessary to seal the edges, otherwise the wetting and drying of the alternate exposed end grains which will set up movement stresses and cause the breakdown of the wood, despite the fact that the adhesive may be impervious.

All veneers in standard plywood are produced by turning off the log, thus producing continuous jointless sheets with a very wide tangential grain appearance which is commonly called 'blister'. If a normal wood grain is required, the outer veneers must be obtained by slicing straight off the log. They will then be of limited width and will have to be jointed in the width of the board.

Softwood plywoods, commonly of Douglas fir, mostly fall into three categories, each available in various exterior or interior grades. They are also classified according to surface finish: these being interchangeable on either side of any one board. They are as follows:

GOOD: Means that there are no knots and small defects have been neatly patched.

SOLID: Indicates also the presence of a few small knots but the surface is still considered suitable for painting.

SHEATHING: Indicates that this surface is not suitable for finished work.

Douglas fir
This is not really suitable for highly finished work. The grain is too wild for normal tastes, while the hardness of the summer wood will still show through a painted surface. Common sizes are 1800 by 1200mm and 2400 by 1200mm.

Finnish birch plywood
This is made entirely from birch. Qualities are graded down from 'A' quality (free from knots and discoloration and suitable for a clear finish) to 'WG' quality which is not suitable for finished work. The various finishes are obtained in any combination on either side of one sheet.

Birch plywood is obtainable in a variety of sizes from 965 by 965mm to 2134 by 1270mm. In many cases the grain of the outer veneers runs the short way of the board. Thicknesses range from 3, 4 and 6mm through 3mm increments to 24mm. The Finnish Plywood Development Association will provide full instructions for its use and finish.

British-made hardwood plywoods
These are made from a variety of South African hardwoods: Khaya, Sapele and Gaboon. They are made in thicknesses from 4 to 50mm and in lengths from 1524 to 3048mm and widths from 600 to 1524mm. They have good faces and are suitable for high-class joinery.

Blockboard
This either has a core of wood strips 25mm wide with outer veneers glued at right-angles to them or there may be a second outer ply as well. The strip core may be glued together or dry-jointed.

Laminboard
Laminboard is similar but has only narrow strips from 1.5 to 7mm wide, usually of hardwood. The core is always glued together and there are usually two outer plies.

Batten board
This is made in the same way as blockboard but the strips are 75mm wide. These boards are made in a variety of sizes and from 12 to 25mm thick.

Blockboards and batten boards are not suitable for French-polished work as the joint lines in the core will, in certain lights, show on the polished surface. This is due to inevitable moisture movement in the core. Any housing parallel to the grain of the cores

should be done with discretion as boards will be weakened and may even fall apart (**Fig. 1.19**).

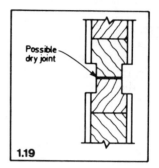

1.19

CHIPBOARD OR PARTICLE BOARD

This is a board made up entirely of wood chips cemented together. There are four qualities or types due to the grading and orientation of the chips in the board. They are:

SINGLE LAYER: Also called homogenous board: all the particles are the same size and tend to give a coarse surface.

LAYER: Also called sandwich board. There are three separate layers of chips, fine on the outside to give a very smooth surface and coarse in the centre. The core is less dense and screws are inclined to have less holding power.

GRADED DENSITY: There are fine chips on the outsides gradually graded to coarse in the centre. Fine surfaces are obtained with a slightly greater density and better holding power for screws.

EXTRUDED BOARD: The mixture of chips and adhesive is extruded as a continuous sheet between heated steel plates. In this method, the chips become orientated at right-angles to the surface of the board. As any shrinkage occurs across the wood chips and not longitudinally to them, these boards shrink or swell in length and width but not in thickness. The stiffness or strength in bending is less but the hardness or resistance to indentation is greater. They are commonly used as core materials for doors.

Fibre board and hardboard
Unlike chipboard, which is cemented together with resin adhesive, the fibres of wood which make up fibre board are broken down into individual fibres and reconstituted using only the natural cementing material which exists in the wood pulp. The board, in its initial state, becomes insulating board but is highly compressed into a comparatively thin but hard material known as hardboard.

Hardboard retains the natural tendency of the original timber to swell and shrink and, if fixed in a building, should be conditioned before use by wetting the back and stacking for 24 hours in back-to-back pairs. As it is a thin material, it should be given several fixings to keep flat. It is better that the board should be too wet than too dry, as it will tend to 'shrink flat' but if it swells it will buckle.

It is commonly obtained in 2400 by 1200mm sheets 2, 3, 4 and 5mm thick but thicknesses up to 12mm are obtainable. Although normally having one matt surface, dual-faced hardboard (smooth both sides) may be obtained.

Normal hardboard is not suitable for external use, but oil-tempered hardboard heated and impregnated with oil may be used in semi-exposed positions. A wide number of decorative surface finishes are available. These include coloured facings of melamine or pvc stove-enamelled in the factory, and wood-veneered facings. Hardboard may also have one side moulded to various patterns.

SAWING SHEET MATERIAL

In normal sawing procedure, there is always a tendency for the underside – whether veneer or chipboard surface – to break away with the downward thrust of the handsaw or circular saw. This may be reduced in handsawing by holding the saw at a flatter angle to the surface of the board. In the case of the circular saw, it can be reduced by raising the table or lowering the saw so that the saw only breaks through about 2cm above the surface. In this way the cut becomes more forward than down.

TYPES OF TIMBER

All commercial timbers are cut from exogenous trees (outward growers) in which, each year, the existing trunk is encircled by a fresh layer of wood substance, thereby increasing its diameter. Speaking in geometrical terms and ignoring natural irregularities, the trunk builds up into an accumulation of concentric cylinders or, to be more accurate, narrowly tapering cones, each of which has a soft layer of springwood and a harder one of summerwood.

They appear as approximate circles at the end of the log, being termed 'annual rings', and may be counted to give the tree's age in years. Timber is divided into two classes known as 'hardwood' and 'softwood'. Although most hardwoods are relatively hard and most softwoods soft, their actual classification is not by density (the softest known timber 'balsa' is actually classified as a hardwood) but by their microscopic structure. In detailing this it must not be forgotten that the components are almost too small to be seen by the naked eye.

Softwood

Softwood has the simpler construction having, mainly, two types of component only. These are 'trachieds': little boxes about 1mm long spliced together at their ends and cemented at their sides. They serve the dual purpose of conducting sap and of giving strength to the timber. These are connected by little plates of a starchy material known as 'medullary rays' which radiate from the centre (the pith or medulla) and serve only to store food. The rays are not usually visible in softwood.

Hardwood

Hardwood also has some trachieds but, in addition, its main components are long stringy members with thick walls, known as 'fibres', which provide the strength and stiffness. There are also hollow barrel shaped units joined into continuous tubes which serve the purpose of conducting the sap and are known as 'pores' or 'vessels'. As well as these, rays are also present but they may vary in thickness from being virtually invisible to a measurable dimension.

Besides its structural framework, as described, timber also contains various oils and resins as well as some volatile substances which give it colour, smell and, in some cases, resistance to decay.

Identifying timber

Although certain timbers have strong superficial characteristics such as combinations of colour, figure, smell, and density which enables them to be recognised with a fair degree of certainty, the only sure way to identify them is by means of a hand lens in the case of hardwoods, or a microscope for softwoods, checking the arrangement of components, trachieds, pores, rays, fibres, etc against prepared schedules as well as looking for more obvious features as given above. A TRADA publication *Examination of Timber* will help with this as well as *Forest Products Research Bulletins 22* and *25*.

DRYING TIMBER

The green log may have more than 100 per cent of its own dry weight in water and this must be removed, to a large extent, before the timber becomes ready for use. It is done today largely by means of kilns in which the drying process is speeded up by the introduction of heating coils.

This is a skilled process involving different drying programmes for the different kinds of timber. In principle, the heat is applied gradually while – to prevent premature drying out of the surface of the timber causing unequal shrinkage and possible splitting – steam is also introduced to increase the humidity to the required amount until the vapour is replaced by that escaping from the (ultimately) heated interior of the plank. The process is continuous, humidity being gradually reduced and temperature increased.

Calculating moisture content

Before the process starts, a sample is cut from near the end of a plank. It is weighed, dried out completely and weighed again. Moisture content is then calculated as

$$\% \text{ MC} = \frac{\text{original weight} - \text{dry weight}}{\text{dry weight}} \times 100$$

This may be repeated at several parts of the kiln and an average taken. Several small planks are now weighed and their dry weight calculated.

Assume the test on sample shows a 35 per cent moisture content and that one of the planks weighs 20kg. Then the calculated dry weight will equal

$$\frac{100}{135} \times 20 = 14.8 \text{kg}$$

This is recorded. After a week the plank is removed and weighed again. It now weighs 18kg, so the present moisture content equals

$$\frac{18 - 14.8}{14.8} \times 100 = 21.6 \text{ per cent}$$

This procedure may be repeated with the same plank whenever necessary. Once the timber is dried to the required amount, it is kept in the kiln to cool with sufficient humidity to prevent the sudden evaporation of moisture from the surface as would happen in dry air outside the kiln.

One effect of bad seasoning is to introduce case-hardening in the plank. It happens when the surface of the timber is allowed to dry out too quickly. The surface wants to shrink but cannot; so it sets, possibly without splitting, in an expanded condition. The drying now continues with the result that the inside of the plank now starts to shrink but is prevented from doing so by the stiffened outer casing. If a short piece is cut from a case-hardened plank and the centre removed it will curl in as in **Fig. 1.20**. The cure consists of

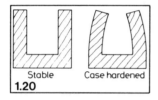

Stable   Case hardened
1.20

returning the timber to the kiln at a high temperature and high humidity; this softens the outer layer and relieves the tension.

Shrinkage

It is generally known that timber is hygroscopic and, even after seasoning, will absorb moisture from a humid atmosphere and swell, or give moisture off in dry air and shrink. Provision must be made for this in situations where humidity changes occur, say from summer to winter.

The greater problem with timber shrinkage is that it occurs unevenly in relation to the annual rings (see **Figs. 1.21, 1.22** and **1.23**). Thus it shrinks about twice as much around the tree as it does radially from the pith or centre to the bark. As the timber is less dense towards the outside of the log there is more shrinkage on the outside of the log than in the centre (see **Fig. 1.21**).

Fig 1.22 shows the position of three timbers in relation to the log from which they have been cut while **Fig. 1.23** gives three exaggerated sketches of the section or shape in which each is likely to finish after drying out from the green state. Thus the plain-sawn timber, having a maximum shrinkage around the tree is going to be narrow. Bastard-sawn timber will shrink to a diamond section while rift-sawn timber will shrink very little in width.

However, there is a third effect of progressively greater shrinkage towards the outside of the tree; this will cause plain-sawn timber to curl or cup on the outside and rift-sawn timber to become thinner away from the heart.

Once the timber has been seasoned and trued-up

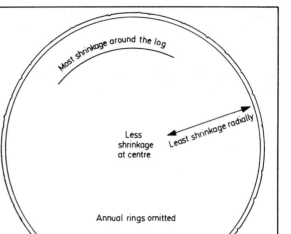

1.21 Shrinkage in log

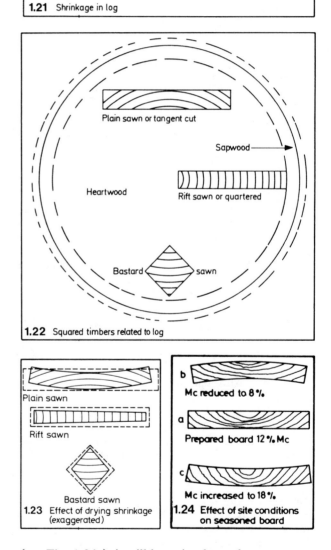

1.22 Squared timbers related to log

1.23 Effect of drying shrinkage (exaggerated)

1.24 Effect of site conditions on seasoned board

(see **Fig. 1.24a**), it will keep its shape, however converted, as long as humidity does not change its moisture content. If, however, it is placed in a very dry situation, it will still tend to cup on the sapwood side as in **Fig. 1.24b**. If placed in a damp situation, a reverse action will take place and it will cup on the heart side (see **Fig. 1.24c**).

This irregularity of moisture movement can be used to an advantage in some situations, an example of which is given in **Fig. 1.25**. This shows a window-

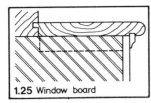

1.25 Window board

board fixed in position with its heart side up. Here unequal drying of the surface exposed to the air, causing the tendency to cup on the face, will be balanced by the natural tendency to cup on the sapwood side as in **Fig. 1.24b**. It is therefore important to ensure that not only the timber is seasoned, but also that it is dried to a degree that, when it is ultimately placed in position, the percentage moisture content will remain unaltered.

There are, of course, situations in which this is impossible, such as the external door of a house facing the prevailing rains or a garden gate exposed to continuous frost and rain in the winter and hot sun in the summer. In such a case, care must be taken to allow for moisture movement which will take place. A solid panel must be able to swell as well as shrink in its groove. Matchboard panels in framed ledged doors must not be too closely jointed. Tenons should be pinned near the shoulders, closer than would be needed for optimum strength, to ensure that the alternating swelling and shrinking do not affect the tightness of the joints.

BS1186, Part 1, 'Quality of Timber' gives a table of maximum and minimum moisture levels for different situations and gives tighter limits for doors than for other joinery. Generally the moisture content should be about 11 per cent for joinery in centrally heated buildings, 15 per cent in other buildings and 18 per cent for external work.

If joints are well made with one of the modern moisture resistant adhesives, this should hold them against a reasonable amount of stress imposed by moisture movement. It must not be forgotten that many adhesives will not achieve their full strength if the moisture content of the glued timber exceeds 18 per cent.

Table 1.2 indicates the percentage moisture movement in a few timbers from equilibrium moisture contents attained in humidities reduced from 90 to 60 per cent.

It will be seen that the timber with the least moisture movement, as well as the least absorption of moisture under similar conditions, is western red cedar. This timber, as well as being one of the most durable, is the most stable, which makes it suitable for such positions as shelves over radiators where the underside may be exposed to considerable heat.

Timber defects

Defects in timber used in joinery are given in BS 1186, Part 1 which cannot be quoted in detail here. In general, it lays down that the timber shall be healthy,

Table 1.2

	Humidity 90% Timber MC %	Humidity 60% Timber MC %	Tangential movement %	Radial movement %
Afromosia	15	11	1.3	0.7
Beech	20	12	3.2	1.7
Douglas fir	19	12.5	1.5	1.2
Iroko	15	11	1	0.5
African mahogany	20	13.5	1.5	0.9
Japanese oak	22	13	2.8	1
Parana pine	21	13	2.5	1.7
Teak	15	10	1.3	0.8
Western red cedar	14	9.5	0.9	0.45

free from insect attack and decay and, in the case of work to be stained or given a natural finish, shall not have any visible or repaired defects or discoloured sapwood. Permitted sizes of knots do not allow them to weaken small timbers. Painted work may have reasonable repairs which must leave a smooth surface.

Shakes (fissures or cracks) in timber are best filled in with wood feathers (strips or tongues of wood fitted into a groove) as in **Fig. 1.26**. A wide chisel is held

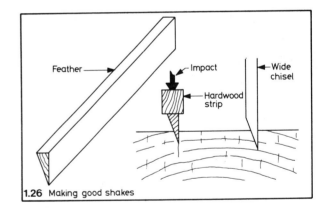

1.26 Making good shakes

upright and driven into the shake the required number of times to give a continuous uniform recess. The feather is then glued and gently tapped in. A strip of wood held over the feather will spread the impact of the hammer and will reduce the risk of splitting it. When dry, the waste should be taken off with a fine panel saw (not chiselled) and finished with a plane.

Other defects met in converted timber are bowing, springing and winding as in **Fig. 1.27**. These are generally due to stresses set up in the growing tree which are released by conversion, so leaving the timber distorted. Further ripping down can produce further distortion, but the timber may sometimes still be used if sawn sizes are kept generous and all the sawing done before any truing-up. The lengths possible will depend upon the degree of distortion.

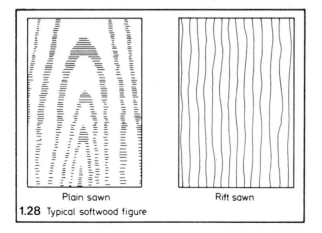

1.27 Faults due to longitudinal stresses

GRAINING

When wood is to be stained and varnished, polished, or given a natural finish, the larger part of the decorative value of the work comes from the figure or grain as it shows on the exposed surface. This is likely to decide the choice of timber used and the way in which the log is converted.

If the work is to have a natural finish, uniformity of colour and a general similarity of figure should be looked for. Stiles of framing, particularly door stiles, should be straight grained. For hardwood joinery, sapwood and knots are generally rejected, particularly when the sapwood is of a different colour and in timbers where the sap is liable to the attack of the lyctus beetle.

Softwoods
In the case of softwoods the figure, if any, is usually given by the contrasting light spring wood and darker summer wood of the annual rings as they break into the surface of the panel. This must be plain-sawn. When the timber is straight grained, the pattern may be roughly as in **Fig. 1.28**. An example of this is pitch

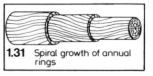

| Plain sawn | Rift sawn |

1.28 Typical softwood figure

pine, not commonly available today. It should be noted that, when rift-sawn, the annual rings, seen on edge, are more or less straight lines. When the rings are more irregular, as in Douglas fir, the figure takes on a more undulating appearance.

Hardwoods
In the case of hardwoods, the composition of the figure becomes more complex. It may be influenced by the way in which the fibres and pores are arranged, thereby giving many subtle graduations of light and shade. The visibility or otherwise of the medullary rays and the ways in which the tree grows, are also influential. Where the rays are thick, they will show up as silvery splashes when the timber is cut radially (rift-sawn) parallel to them.

The commonest example of this is oak which, when cut this way, is known as 'figured' or 'quartered' oak, or 'wainscotting'. Other timbers having this characteristic are Australian silky oak (not a true oak) and to a lesser extent beech (see **Fig. 1.29**). Tangent cut or

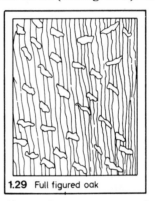

1.29 Full figured oak

plain-sawn oak may have a more or less parabolic grain with the rays showing as little short dashes (**Fig. 1.30**). Figured oak should never be used for flooring as the silver grain is soft and will wear away.

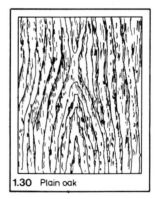

1.30 Plain oak

Sweet chestnut, when plain-sawn, bears a close resemblance to oak in figure, outline, texture and colour but the rays are not large enough to be visible. A characteristic of some timbers of the mahogany type is for successive rings to grow in alternate spirals around the tree, as shown in **Fig. 1.31**. When the log is

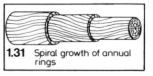

1.31 Spiral growth of annual rings

rift-sawn, these rings appear as alternating light and shade according to whether the grain is towards or away from the eye. They change as the viewpoint alters. This is shown in a simple way in **Fig. 1.32.**

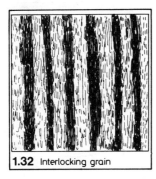

1.32 Interlocking grain

With some timbers, notably sycamore, there is a tendency for the fibres to grow in ripples up the tree, instead of remaining straight. When the log is cut radially, these ripples appear in alternate bands of light and shade (**Fig. 1.33**) and, again, change as the viewpoint alters.

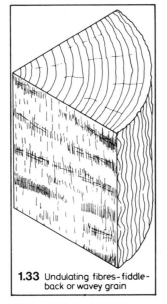

1.33 Undulating fibres – fiddle-back or wavey grain

A characteristic wild grain appearance, known as 'blister grain' but varying between timbers, is given when a veneer is turned off a log (common in preparation of veneers in plywood). The grain more or less repeats itself at every complete turn of the log (**Fig. 1.34**).

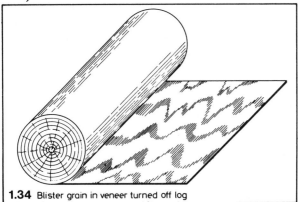

1.34 Blister grain in veneer turned off log

Special patterns

Rich patterns are produced by great irregularities of the grain. They make the timber unstable and only suitable for cutting into veneers. Examples of this are:

BIRD'S EYE: Common to maple but existing in other timbers. It is caused by the massing of small shoots in a part of the tree trunk giving, in effect, a pattern of interlacing bunched knots when cut.

BURR: A beautiful and complex pattern is produced by a cut taken through a growth known as a burr. Formed like a boil on the side of the tree, it is thought to be an effort by the tree to repair damage such as insect attack.

CURL: Exposure of the grain at the intermingling of two branch systems.

BUTT GRAIN: The intermingling of the fibres at the roots.

Sawing for particular grains

For the purpose of stability, where joinery must inevitably be subject to changes in humidity, rift-sawn timber is less likely to give trouble. However, for the purpose of obtaining a particular grain pattern or figure, it may be necessary to produce the maximum amount of either rift- or plain-sawn boards. Thus, figured oak must be rift-sawn, but a bold grain in Douglas fir requires that it should be plain-sawn. When, however, the timber is not likely to be subject to humidity changes, moisture movement becomes less of a problem.

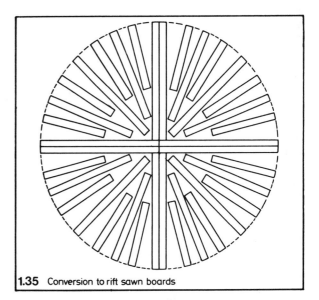

1.35 Conversion to rift sawn boards

Fig. 1.35 shows the section through a log converted entirely to rift-sawn boards. Apart from there being 50 per cent waste of timber, the cost of the work involved in moving the log around for cutting would be exorbitant. **Fig. 1.36** shows a log cut up for plain sawing. Here the log would be turned through 90 degrees each time and, although the wastage would be less, the labour costs would be high. Simpler methods are therefore usually adopted.

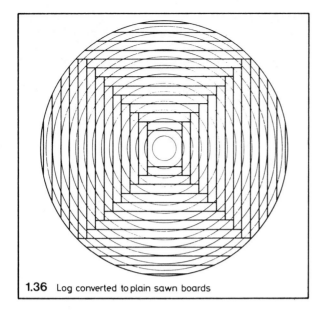

1.36 Log converted to plain sawn boards

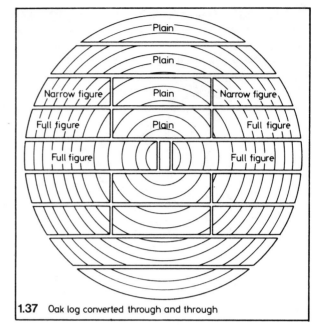

1.37 Oak log converted through and through

Manufacturers concerned with the production of high-class joinery in hardwood, sometimes prefer to keep the timber from individual logs together. This enables them to be reasonably sure of uniformity of colour and general grain structure by taking all the timber for a job from one log. In this case, the log is cut 'through and through' and stacked with stickers between the planks in the actual sequence of cutting, so that the original outline of the log is more or less re-formed. **Fig. 1.37** shows the end of an oak log cut this way. It will be appreciated that both figured and plain oak can be obtained while an appreciable amount of silver grain will also show in surfaces where the angle of the rings is at more than 45 degrees to the cut face.

VARIETIES OF TIMBER

Timber probably has, within the range of softwoods and hardwoods, a greater variety of special qualities and characteristics than any other known material. It is possible to select a timber especially for its density and strength, lightness, uniformity of texture, softness and workability, stability, durability, resistance to wear, colour and grain or figure.

TRADA issue a number of booklets dealing with timbers of the world and their qualities. The subject is also covered by the Princes Risborough Forest Products Research Laboratory and other organisations. BS1186, Part 1 gives a list of recommended timbers and their suitability for certain purposes while BS881 and BS589 (combined) entitled 'Nomenclature of commercial timbers' list most of the timbers available with their botanical and common names, source of origin and density.

The following brief list gives some of the timbers commercially available and the uses for which they are suitable. They are suitable for internal joinery only:

SOFTWOODS: Parana pine, Sitka spruce, European whitewood (white deal).

HARDWOODS: Abura, Guarea, Chilean laurel, yellow meranti, rauli, birch.

The following timbers are suitable for internal and external joinery:

SOFTWOODS: Western red cedar, Douglas fir, long leaf pitch pine, European redwood (red deal).

HARDWOODS: Agba, idigbo, African mahogany, red meranti, red seraya, white seraya, afrormosia, gurjun, iroko, makore, mansonia, European, Japanese and American oak, teak.

Timbers causing ink stains in contact with iron: Western red cedar, oak, afrormosia, sweet chestnut.

Timbers with interlocking grain: Sapele, African walnut, African and Honduran mahogany.

Timbers rift-sawn giving silver grain: All true oaks, beech, Australian silky oak.

Timbers giving bird's-eye figure: Maple, ash.

Timbers giving burr figures: European walnut, elm, ash.

Timbers giving curl and butt grain: European walnut, rosewood.

Extremely durable timbers: Teak, iroko, afrormosia, afzelia, western red cedar.

QUESTIONS FOR CHAPTER 1

Question 1

Name four different types of bit for use in a swing brace. Give the use and limitations of each and state how it should be sharpened and maintained. Answers must be brief.

Note: The information required to answer this question is not given in this article, but it is presented as an invitation for the reader to think for himself.

Assume that 12 minutes are given to answer the question from the time it is first seen. Interested younger readers who are preparing for this type of examination should attempt the question within this time limit.

Question 2

Specify a suitable adhesive for the following purposes and give reasons for your choice together with any safety precautions to be observed:

a. Interior softwood joinery;

b. Stressed skin panel for roofs;

c. Fixing plastic laminate sheeting in workshop with press available;

d. Fixing plastic laminate sheeting on site.

City & Guilds of London Institute, Carpentry and Joinery Advanced Craft, Purpose-Made Joinery, May 1977. No. 5.

Question 3

a. Why is it important that the moisture content of timber is appropriate to the conditions in which it is to be fixed?

b. State a suitable moisture content for:

1. Window frames;
2. Wall panelling in a centrally heated building.

Institute of Carpenters, General Paper, May 1975, No. 4.

CHAPTER 2

Powered Tools

Powered hand tools should not be compared with normal fixed woodworking machinery, to which they are an adjunct and not an alternative. The lightness and comparatively slim construction necessary to their mobility in use becomes a disadvantage when they are fixed to the bench and timbers fed vigorously against them. In addition, the close proximity of the motor to the work point and the subsequent concentration of dust and chippings, when this is fixed, makes it vulnerable and increases the risk of an early breakdown. This is particularly so when the machine has to be inverted in use, allowing the dirt to drop into it.

Considered as portable equipment, however, powered hand tools come into their own, particularly for performing light operations on large pieces such as moulding, cutting, recessing or trimming on countertops or cutting the odd large sheet of plywood. In each case, these require the efforts of two or more operatives to hold them against the fence of the fixed machine. There is also the advantage they become part of the joiner's equipment, rather than the wood-machinist's. Secondary operations can therefore be carried out with their aid without returning the work to the mill. Their usefulness on the site is, of course, indisputable.

SAFETY

Like other woodworking machinery, powered hand tools need to be handled with great care and the safety regulations require that all operatives should be trained in their use. As well as mechnical hazards, involving risk of physical injury, there is also the danger from the source of power (compressed air or electrical) which the worker is holding in his hands.

Accidents from compressed air equipment are mainly attributable to the failure or ejection of an air hose resulting in violent reaction. All hoses should be locked in position, not just a tight push-fit in the socket. The risks from electrical power are more varied and subtle and they need to be fully understood.

Electrical terms

Many people are confused by the various electrical terms used and particularly by the inter-relationship of volts, amperes and watts. These may be considered (to a limited degree) as being analogous to the simple measurement of water flowing through a pipe into a tank. Then the flow rate of water in a unit of time compares to the voltage, the bore of the pipe to the amperage, and the volume of water passing into the tank in that time the wattage. Just as

$$\text{amount of water} = \text{flow rate} \times \text{bore, so}$$

$$\text{watts} = \text{volts} \times \text{amps}$$

$$\text{Therefore} \quad \text{amps} = \frac{\text{watts}}{\text{volts}}$$

$$\text{and} \quad \text{volts} = \frac{\text{watts}}{\text{amps}}$$

The other factor to be considered is the resistance of the conductor measured in ohms. This need not concern us here, other than to say that if the voltage is low, the resistance may be too high and no current will pass.

The greatest danger of electrocution occurs when there is a risk of a large quantity of electricity passing through the body, considered in terms of watts. Thus the accidental contact with a sparking plug of a petrol engine gives an unpleasant shock but the victim generally lives to tell the tale because, although the voltage is very high, amperage is negligible. Inversely a band-saw brazer uses a current sufficient to make the weld red hot, but there is no risk to flesh and blood as the voltage is too low to overcome its resistance.

Mains current

The current from the mains has a high amperage limited only by the capacity of the fuse with a voltage of 240 or more. It will also have sufficient intensity to drive through the human body. The current from the mains, as used in most electrical equipment, fluctuates in the live lead from high positive through zero to high negative. It is in tune with the alternator at the power station, which is turning at 3000 rpm; the neutral lead complements this negative to positive. Any local connection to earth acts in the same way. The main danger from hand-held electrical equipment, apart from the exposed leads, is that the body of the machine can become live through an electrical fault. The person holding it then becomes a conductor to earth with general lethal effects.

Earthing

If, as should be done, the metal body is earthed through a third lead in the cable, the heavy surge of current direct to earth immediately blows a fuse and the circuit is broken. Where there is possible direct contact with the soil, as on building sites, the voltage should be reduced to 110 using a transformer. If the centre of the primary windings is earthed, it will reduce the risk of shock to the user to 55 volts.

An accepted alternative to earthing equipment is to use machines which have been double insulated. These are designed and made so that all exposed casings are of nylon or other non-conducting materials. Additional precautions make a short to the user virtually impossible. Such tools must be stamped with the kite mark and squares symbol as in **Fig. 2.1**.

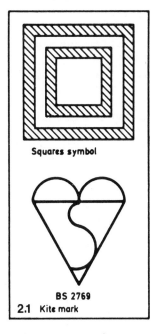

Squares symbol

BS 2769

2.1 Kite mark

Precautions against electrocution

Other necessary precautions are as follows. The supply voltage should be within the narrow range specified on the tool. Plugs, couplers and socket outlets should be separately designed for each type of supply so that wrong connections will become impossible. Cables should be secured to the plug and the machine by cord grips capable of taking any load inadvertently applied (see **Fig. 2.2** which also shows the correct method of wiring plugs).

All extensions should be made with plug and socket connections. Every extension should have a plug at one end and a socket at the other. If two plugs are fitted to the same cable, one will be live when exposed. When long extensions are used, the cable should be heavier to reduce voltage drop.

Electric motors should always be switched on and allowed to run to full power before putting under load. Failure to do this may cause a burnt-out motor. Note that there are always some slight sparks when the brushes rub on the commutator. Electrical tools should therefore not be used where there are inflammable fumes, for example near a spray booth.

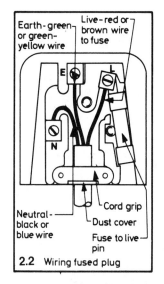

2.2 Wiring fused plug

Precautions for compressed air tools

Precautions in the use of compressed air tools require that, as well as being firmly coupled, hoses should be of the right size for the tool. Leads from the compressor should be as short as possible. Main hoses should be large with shut-off valves to isolate individual machines.

All hoses and couplers should be regularly checked for small leaks which could lead to disproportionate loss of power. All items connected with air supply must be kept clean and dust free. Filters should be cleaned and drained regularly and the tool kept properly oiled. Pneumatic tools in general should be put under load before switching on (the reverse of electrical tools). When it is necessary to check a tool, cut off air supply and release air pressure from the tool before dismantling.

HAND DRILLS

The hand drill is the earliest powered hand tool and still probably the most useful. The chuck may be hand-tightened and final pressure put on with a key operating in a toothed ring from three holes in the body of the chuck. Where possible, the bit should be inserted to its full depth in the chuck and the key should be inserted in all three holes consecutively to tighten.

Morse twist drills are used for drilling metal. These should be of high speed steel. For drilling stone, brick, etc, the bits should be tungsten carbide tipped. The drill should be at least two speed, and the slower speed is used. Tools for drilling timber are similar to the normal brace bits but with a round shank and plain points instead of lead screws. Morse twist drills should not be used for timber, except for small holes, as they may choke with the chips.

A drill may be fixed in a purpose-made stand which has a lever arm giving a feed into the work and thus enabling greater pressure to be used. Fences may be attached to the base plate with length gauges for the positioning of holes without marking out. By using a slightly different stand, a drill may be used for mortising (**Fig. 2.3**). In this case, a hollow chisel is incorpo-

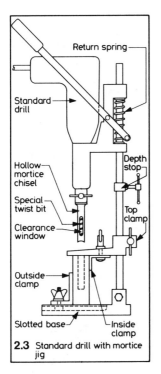

2.3 Standard drill with mortice jig

rated. The special drill bit to remove the core is inserted in the chuck of the drill. The stand also includes a top clamp, plus inside and outside clamps set up to position the timber and hold it down during operations. This is in a sense only makeshift, the method of retaining the timber being somewhat unsatisfactory. The depth stop and return spring and lever are used in the same way in the drill stand.

SAWS

Circular saws
The circular saw (**Fig. 2.4**) is used for general straight cutting. Various saws and cutting discs are available. These include combination rip and cross-cut for timber, cross-cut and planer blades for a finer finish, special nail cutting blades for cutting away old flooring, and a variety of abrasive discs for cutting bricks, tiles, slates, marble and galvanised sheet iron.

The body is hinged to a base plate at the front so that the back may be lifted and locked to give a limited depth of cut. It is also hinged at the near side with a quadrant slot so that it may be canted to cut at an angle of down to 45 degrees. The maximum depth of cut is about 90mm for a 300mm saw.

The top of the saw is guarded as shown in **Fig. 2.4** while the bottom cutting area is protected by a spring guard (not shown) which pushes back to clear the work and instantly returns as the saw is lifted from the cut. The saw cuts on the upward stroke against the timber, (not climbing on to it which would be danger-

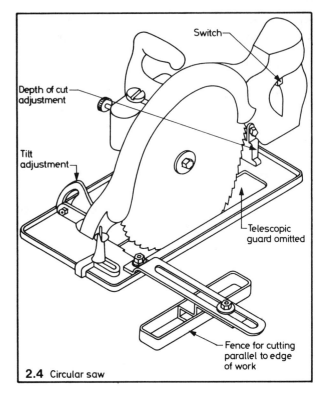

2.4 Circular saw

ous) so that the underside of the cut is the smoother. It may be advisable to cut the work face down.

Reciprocating saws
These are of two types. First, the general purpose saw (**Fig. 2.5**) in which the angle of the blade is controlled by the user to a certain extent. The blade may be up to 300mm long and it can be said to replace the joiner's hand and compass saw. Again the cut is back towards the base plate keeping the work tight to it. It can be used for heavy work in thick timbers.

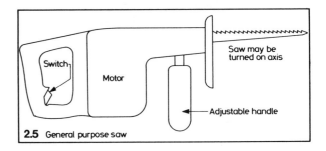

2.5 General purpose saw

The second type is the 'jig' or 'sabre' saw (**Fig. 2.6**), a smaller saw which only cuts to about 75mm deep. It rests on a base plate which must be kept firmly in contact with the work, thus controlling the angle of the cut. The saw body can be tilted in relation to the base plate thus giving a uniform accurate splayed cut.

The powered hand planer
Fig. 2.7 shows a powered hand planer which is held on the work in the same way as a wooden jack plane. It is fitted with a revolving circular cutter block. The back bed is in line with the cutting edge of the block and the front is raised to give the thickness of the cut which may be up to 3mm. Special cutters may be inserted for

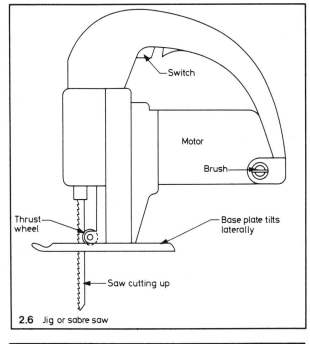

2.6 Jig or sabre saw

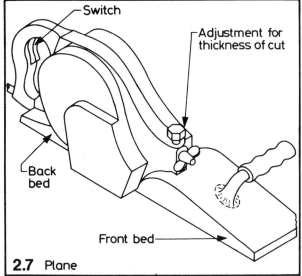

2.7 Plane

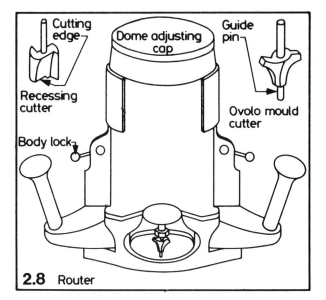

2.8 Router

rebating and moulding. It is available in 50 and 100mm widths and is satisfactory for planing surfaces up to that width, but where cuts have to be made side by side it is difficult to eliminate marks made by the corners of the blades. An adjustable fence is obtainable as a guide when planing narrow surfaces (i.e. as an aid to keeping it square).

ROUTERS

The router (**Fig. 2.8**) is probably the most versatile of all the powered hand tools. It may be used for moulding, recessing, housing, including dovetailing, and shaping to templets. With special equipment it can also be used for carcase dovetailing and for stair string housing. Equipment is also available by means of which it can be inverted in a table and, with the aid of fences, made to act virtually as a miniature spindle moulder. It can also be fitted in a special overhead stand and used as a fixed high-speed router. These latter are, in the writer's opinion, somewhat

makeshift arrangements and will not be discussed further.

It is basically a motor with a vertical spindle to take cutters of a wide variety of different shapes and cutting principles. In some cases, these can be dropped into the surface of the timber and will then cut their way forward. The motor revolves at a speed of around 18,000 rpm. The depth of the cut may be adjusted to a fine degree, usually by turning the domed top of the machine. A fence may be attached for straight work. Firm control of the machine is obtained by grasping two stout handles as shown.

For shaped work, a cutter with a guide pin which rests against the unmoulded edge of the work permits a uniform depth of cut in theory. However its small diameter, together with the wearing effect of the high revolutions, tends to encourage the pin to rub away the surface of the edge with unsatisfactory results. Two sets of equipment provided by manufacturers are lap dovetailing and stair jigs.

Lap dovetailing
The equipment for lap dovetailing (**Fig. 2.9**) consists of two plates at right angles, joined together. One is fixed horizontally on a bench, leaving the other to stand vertically away from the bench. The dovetail part (drawer side) is clamped to the vertical plate and the socket part (drawer front) clamped down on to the horizontal plate. A further plate formed with combs (see **Fig. 2.9** which shows part of the comb) rests on the socket piece under the clamp, the dovetail piece being brought tight up under it.

A guide bush, diameter equal to the dovetail pitch, is contained in a special base plate attached to the machine. This bush runs into the prongs of the comb, first cutting the dovetail openings one at a time and then proceeding forward to cut the recesses in the socket piece. As the cutter leaves each opening, it follows around the semicircular end of the next prong and gives the shape on the inside necessary to fit the conical curved bottom of the socket.

Special jigs are provided to ensure the correct set-up of comb, socket piece and dovetail piece in relation to each other but the three relative positions are:

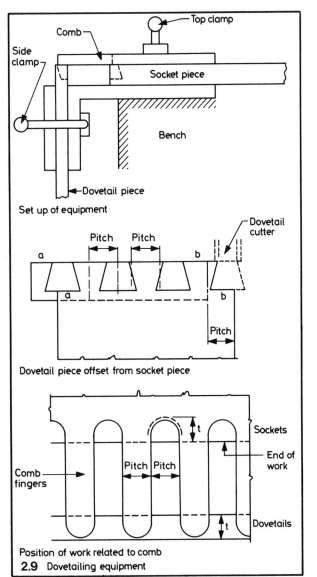

Set up of equipment

Dovetail piece offset from socket piece

Position of work related to comb

2.9 Dovetailing equipment

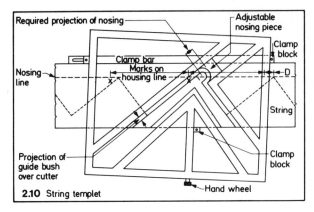

2.10 String templet

room. Given the size of the guide bush, the required width of housing is obtained by selecting the size of cutter giving the desired projection of the guide bush over the cutter diameter.

To set out the string for housing, it is only necessary to put on the nosing line and mark out one step (riser and tread) outline. The templet is then set over this in position for housing as shown in **Fig. 2.10**. The three clamp blocks are positioned as shown, attaching the clamp bar to the rear ones. The distance **D** is then marked along the nosing line and from this a series of lengths equal to the hypotenuse of the pitch board. These can be calculated with an electric calculator and will give the positions for resetting the string templet. To do the other string, the clamp bar is reversed and resecured to the clamp blocks and the procedure repeated.

Trimming laminated plastics
Cutters for trimming laminated plastic (**Fig. 2.11**) can be fitted to the router and work on the principle that the ball-bearing guide rollers position the cut exactly in line with the work edge. Carbide tipped cutters are necessary to avoid the need for frequent resharpening. Two alternatives are shown giving respectively a square and chamfered finish. The former is too risky to use against a laminated edge unless a slight projection is left. Special small routers are also available.

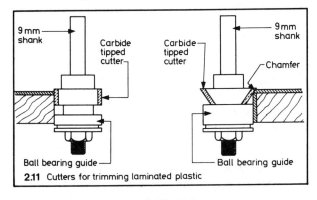

2.11 Cutters for trimming laminated plastic

1. The comb must be set so that the full thickness of the dovetail piece is just left at the top after machining;
2. The socket piece is so oriented that it is offset to the pitch to one side of the dovetail piece;
3. The socket piece is so positioned that the deepest part of the socket is exactly the thickness of the dovetail piece.

Note that when the pieces are fitted together (see **Fig. 2.9**) parts **a** and **a** and **b** and **b** fit together.

If these points are understood, the reasons for the individual setting procedures given by manufacturers should be clearer. If, on trial, the dovetails are too loose they can be tightened by lowering the cutter fractionally and vice versa if too tight. Variations can occur through wear and resharpening of the cutter.

Housing for stair treads
The stair housing jig (**Fig. 2.10**) consists of a flat steel templet. The guide bush moves against its members up and back while the cutter sinks first the tread housing and then the riser housing of each step. The bars of the templet are arranged to allow for wedge

SANDERS

Three types of sander are commonly available: the disc sander, the belt sander and the orbital sander.

Disc sanders
This has a motor body similar to that of the drill. It has a rubber disc fitted to its shaft. An abrasive disc,

secured by a large centre washer, revolves with the rubber back and works with a circular motion on the surface. It tends to leave curved scratches and an uneven surface, and is not suitable for joinery finishes.

Belt sanders

The belt sander (**Fig. 2.12**) has a continuous abrasive paper belt revolving around two rollers, one of which is tensioned. The effective part is that under the base felt-lined pad. Considerable dust is produced and a dust bag becomes a necessity. It has the advantage that it can be used with the grain thus avoiding cross grain scratches. It requires skill to get a good finish and should only be used with a light touch. The work, if loose, needs securing to the bench as the belt tends to throw it back.

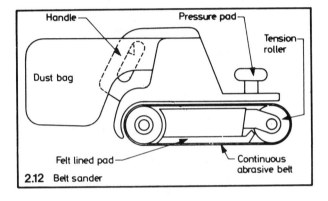

2.12 Belt sander

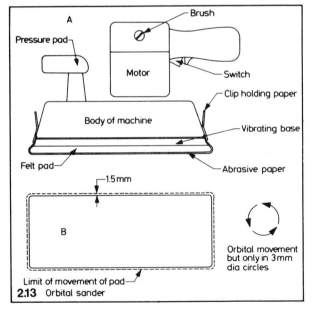

2.13 Orbital sander

Orbital sanders

The orbital sander (**Fig. 2.13**) has a square pad to which is clipped a rectangular sheet of abrasive paper. The pad moves backwards and forwards and sideways in a continuous orbital movement of about 3mm overall. The resulting finish may be very smooth but tends to leave a slightly matt finish on the grain of timber. It is quite satisfactory as a finish to painted work.

A point to note about all hand sanders is that, due to their comparatively small size, they cannot be used

extensively to create or even maintain a truly level surface. Some preparatory work should therefore be done with a smoothing plane to level joints, etc. Indeed it is doubtful if any of them could compete with a skilled craftsman using a smoothing plane, scraper and sandpaper block. However they do save human effort and can be useful where a high finish is not insisted upon.

SAWING MACHINES

Machines for standard production have not varied much in principle over the years. The main developments have been in the ease of set-up and production, and improved finish.

The standard saw for ripping is still the 're-saw' or 'pushbench' which has a fixed saw of 660 to 914mm diameter and a rise and fall table. The fence is adjustable for the width of board to be cut and may be tilted for ripping in section at an angle of up to 45 degrees. It follows that a section to any angle can be cut according to which side of the saw plate the waste is taken.

The groove in the table, to accommodate a cross-cutting fence, has a limited use; the latter is usually too small to suit the heavy work for which the machine is designed.

Further developments include tilting arbour saw benches. The saw itself tilts 45 degrees away from the near side and has a rise and fall movement. The table is fixed, but a groove in the table parallel to the saw enables a sliding fence to be set square or at an angle for cross-cutting or mitring to various angles. It can also be set in combination with the tilt of the saw blade to produce compound angles (**Fig. 2.14**).

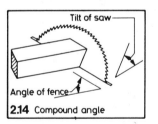

2.14 Compound angle

The maximum saw diameter is usually about 350mm, with spindle speeds adjusted to give a rim speed (diameter $\times \pi \times$ rpm) of 3050 metres per minute.

The modern need to cut large sheets of plywood, blockboard, hardboard, chipboard, etc, has to be catered for. In the simplest method, the right-hand side of the table may be fitted with a demountable extension (with fence), wide enough to take a standard width sheet. Then comes the dimension saw proper, with the cross-cutting table sliding on ball-bearing rollers and with an adjustable fence as well as the tilting arbour and rise and fall saw. To accommodate large sheets, the sliding table may be fitted with an extension, including a telescopic stop-bar to fold away when not in use. Work capacity includes that as previously described, but with greater convenience. Rebating and moulding can also be carried out by replacing the saw with suitable cutter blocks.

Equipment specially made for cutting sheets consists of a vertical frame carrying the sheet, with adjustable vertical and horizontal attached slides supporting a mobile saw-carriage to give predetermined lengths and widths.

Cross-cut saws

The cross-cut saw – originally the pendulum saw and later replaced by the cross-cutting and trenching machine – is used primarily for cutting long sawn timbers into lengths against the cutting list. The saw moves along a horizontal arm over the timber, the cutting action being backwards against a long fence on the horizontal table. A bar is attached to the fence and along this may be set press-back stops. Any one of these may be selected, as required, to suit an item on the cutting list.

The saw is spring-loaded to return to its off position behind the fence. A rise and fall action permits the cut to be made wholly or part way through the timber. The arm may be swung horizontally to give a splay cut across the timber width. It can also be swung in its carriage out of the vertical to give a bevel in the timber thickness.

These two settings may be combined to give compound angles: e.g. for jack rafter cuts in roofing. By replacing the saw with an expanding and grooving head or a half lapping and bevelling head, cross-housings and halving joints may be formed. The particular advantage of this machine is for working long timbers.

Radial saws

A further development is the radial saw. This has a swivelling arm as before, carrying the saw unit, but the saw unit tilts to any angle from the horizontal to the vertical. It can be turned and set through 360 degrees on its vertical axis and then locked in any position along the arm.

Thus, by turning the carriage so that the saw is parallel to the back fence and setting in the required position along the arm, it can be used for ripping. By then tilting it on its horizontal axis, it may be used for bevel ripping. With all these adjustments plus the ability to replace the saw blade with the relevant cutter blocks, rebating, planing or moulding can be carried out to the various angle relationships.

Straight-line edgers

The straight-line edger is essentially a power-feed saw bench in which the feed is by means of a continuous chain, running parallel to the saw. This takes rigid control of the timber, feeding it accurately through the saw to produce a dead straight edge, sufficiently accurate for a glued joint. Alternative versions have the saw spindle above or below the table.

Jig saws

For cutting curved work the machines commonly used are the band saw and jig saw. The jig saw, which carries a vertical blade through a horizontal table with a reciprocating action, is used essentially for internal cuts. The short blade is disconnected and threaded through a hole bored in the timber and then re-attached.

The saws are relatively cheap but soon wear out. The cutting action is comparatively slow and the work needs to be held firmly on the table against uplift.

Band saws

The band saw is used for all other curved work, the sharper curve requiring the narrower saw. The machine and saw must be well maintained and the work fed through gently, particularly when using a narrow blade.

The top wheel of the two carrying the blade puts on the necessary tension by being either weight- or spring-loaded. It is important to keep the correct tension. The saw table may be tilted to give splay cutting. Timber may be free cut, or cut to a pattern or to a circular curve on a jig. This is against a nib on the saw bracket in one case, or off a pin with a radial arm in the other.

OTHER MACHINES

Spindle moulders

Probably the most versatile machine in the small joinery shop is the spindle moulder. It requires a considerable amount of skill in setting up and, in some cases, in operation. Because the use of safety guards tends to restrict movement in some of the operations carried out, it is traditionally regarded as the most dangerous machine.

The early belief that experience was the only teacher and that a missing finger was the necessary trademark of a good spindle hand is, hopefully, no longer held. Indeed it will be found, upon investigation, that nearly all accidents in machine shops can be traced to ignorance or carelessness on the part of the operator.

The main use of the spindle is to work rebates, grooves and mouldings on straight and curved edges of various components of joinery. Other operations possible with special attachments are dovetailing, corner-locking, stair housing, and mortise and tenon joints. Other operations, such as moulding handrail wreaths, can be carried out to a degree dependent upon the ingenuity of the operator.

Planers

The planing machines are primarily the 'surface' planer and the 'thicknesser' or 'panel' planer. The main use of the surfacer is the introductory one of producing a flat face and a straight face-edge square to it on the sawn timber. The timber is then power-fed through the panel planer to give the final thickness and width. The (adjustable) distance of the bed of the table below the cutter block gives the thickness and width respectively. At the same time, it reproduces the accuracy (or inequality) of the initial surface preparation.

The surfacer can, however, be used for wide but shallow rebates, for bevelling edges and for moulded work, particularly on wide flat surfaces. Some standard cutter blocks have secondary caps which are removed so that the cutter can be bolted on.

Tenoning machines

The tenoning machine, in its simpler form, carries two horizontal spindles and two vertical ones to receive cutter blocks. It also has a vertical cut-off saw at the back. When cutting tenons, a rail is clamped against a fence to the front of a sliding table. It is then pushed forward on this, between special cutter blocks on the twin horizontal spindles, to cut the upper and lower cheeks of the tenons. Prepared moulding cutter blocks, bolted to the upper and lower vertical spindles behind the horizontals, then scribe the shoulders out to fit any mouldings on the stiles or mortised members. Finally, the work may be passed through the cut-off saw to bring the tenons to an exact length.

Additional operations may be carried out putting different cutters on the four spindles. For example, wide boards which have gone slightly hollow, may be clamped flat on the sliding table and moulded, end grain, using one of the vertical spindles. The 'joggles' or horns on the stiles of sliding sashes may also be moulded in 'gangs' or banks using the top horizontal spindle with a moulding block.

Mortise machines

Mortise machines may be fitted with two main types of cutter appliances: the chain mortiser and the hollow chisel mortiser. In some cases, both are mounted on the same machine.

The material is clamped against a fence on a horizontal sliding bed. This is traversed by means of a large handwheel as required for the mortise width. The position of the bed may be adjusted and locked vertically to accommodate materials of various widths. A transverse adjustment enables timber to be set under the cutter for the position of the mortise in relation to its thickness.

The hollow chisel contains a special twist-bit to remove the core. It makes a very clean cut when sharp, but is slow in operation and must be used carefully.

The chain mortiser which is, in effect, a bicycle chain with cutting teeth driven at speed around a wheel at the bottom of the guide bar, must be set for the correct degree of play. It must be maintained in good condition to ensure that the mortiser is not ragged or inaccurate.

The advantage of having both chain and chisel fittings on the same machine is that, where there are two different mortise sizes in the same stile – as in a semi-glazed door – by using suitable chain and chisel settings, all the mortises may be cut at one pass.

Sanders

Surfaces, as they come from the planer, are seldom good enough for the final high finish in high-class joinery work. Therefore some type of sander becomes an economic necessity, at least for dealing with wide flat surfaces.

The 'drum' sander is probably the most popular. Using this, the job is power-fed through on a table under large abrasive papered rollers, usually three in a row, with progressively coarse, medium and fine grit. The feed is generally by a continuous belt system. To prevent wear lines forming on the paper, the drums are given rapid transverse oscillation as they revolve. If, in spite of this, the abrasive wears unevenly, wavy lines known as 'snaking' occur on the finished surface.

The alternative to this machine is the 'belt' sander. This consists of a continuous belt of abrasive paper running around two large horizontal pulleys. A uniform tension is kept on the belt, either by introducing a jockey pulley, or by spring-loading the driven one. The work is placed on the table, which is adjustable, so as to bring the surface of the job just clear of the belt when running free. The table can be traversed freely by hand effort. The belt is pressed down on to the work, either by means of a felt-lined hand-held pad, or by a pad attached to an arm sliding smoothly along a stout horizontal steel shaft. The end of the arm is provided with a handle extending well beyond the pad and acting as a cantilever. This gives considerable mechanical advantage to the user.

It should be noted that there is no control over the amount sanded off, other than by the judgement of the operator. A heavy amount of sanding will invariably result in an uneven finish. This machine should always be regarded as a finishing tool, and not as a flattener.

Disc and bobbin sanders

Another useful type of sander is the disc and bobbin, this term being descriptive of the components usually combined in the one machine.

The disc is of accurately machined steel about 900mm in diameter. The paper abrasive is glued or clamped to this disc. The face is vertical with a horizontal table set against it just clear of contact. The table supports the work which is moved backward and forward against the descending face, thus giving an accurate, flat and square face. The table may be tilted for bevelled work.

The bobbin is a vertical cylinder into which the abrasive paper is clamped. It oscillates vertically, as well as turning at speed. It is used for sanding internal narrow surfaces and edges. Tilting the horizontal bed enables conical curves to be sanded.

Lathes

The lathe, used primarily for producing decorative turnings, balusters for stairs, etc, is a specialist machine operated by a turner who may acquire considerable efficiency by regular practice. However, if the lathe is provided with an external face-plate of, say, 900mm diameter with a free-standing tool rest, circular curved rails and mouldings of a diameter not exceeding this may be turned direct. This is instead of making templets and shaping on the spindle.

High-speed routers

The high-speed router comprises a motor unit with vertical cutter, which is cantilevered over a horizontal table. Usually it can be switched to one of two speeds, 18,000 and 24,000 rpm. These high speeds are necessary in order to gain a reasonable periphery speed to the small cutters or cutter blocks invariably used. It has two main operations:

1. Recessing to a specified shaped pattern. The work is attached to a recessed inverted jig moving around a retractable pin centralised in the table under the cutter. So the work done by the cutter follows the outline of the jig recess.

2. Working mouldings, etc, by feeding work along a fence and past a suitable cutter. In effect, using the router as a spindle.

As an alternative to free manually-controlled movement, routers are also provided with compound tables. The work is fixed to this so that it may be wound into the cutters in one of two lines at right-angles to each other.

PRINCIPLES OF MACHINE WOODWORKING

All cutting tools, whether acting in a straight line as in a bandsaw or with a circular movement as a circular saw or planer, have to carry their waste around with them until they emerge from the timber. Then it may fly off with a centrifugal force or drop away. Therefore, a saw deeping, say, 200mm timber, must have room in each gullet for four times as much sawdust as it would if cutting 50mm timber. If the width of the gullet space is doubled, its area will be quadrupled but, as there will only be half as many teeth, each gullet will have to take twice as much sawdust. In theory at least, the capacity of the gullets to contain the sawdust varies in direct proportion to the size of the teeth. In practice, there are a number of factors which tend to modify this theory; but it does explain why fewer teeth cut faster in thick timber.

Saws for thinner cuts

The question of waste is particularly important in relation to timber, because careful cutting may mean that one more item may be obtained from the length or width of a plank. A normal 'plate' saw with the usual amount of set (**Fig. 2.15a**) must produce a lot of waste in sawdust. **Fig. 2.15b, c** and **d** shows saws which can be used in certain circumstances to produce thinner cuts and reduce this waste.

Fig. 2.15b shows a 'ground-off' saw. Only the thin part is allowed to project above the table. It is therefore suitable for multiple cuts in wide boards. **Fig. 2.15c** shows the 'taper' saw. This can be used for splitting thin timber, the thickness of which depends on the maximum increased wedging effect acceptable as the saw stands higher in the table. It can also be

used for deeping a single board into two very thin boards, coming off the saw weak enough to allow the cut to open. The 'swage' saw (**Fig. 2.15d**) is tapered on the inside against the fence only. It can be used for cutting thin boards consecutively off a thick plank.

Cutting sheet materials

Cutting plywood hardboard, chipboard or melamine-faced sheeting – particularly across the grain of exterior plies – presents a risk of splintering or breaking out on the underside. This risk can be reduced by lowering the saw (or raising the table) so that the saw only stands about 12mm above the face. The cutting action then becomes more forward than down (**Fig. 2.16**).

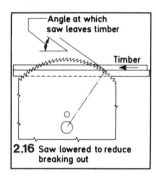

2.16 Saw lowered to reduce breaking out

A modern invention is the incorporation of a scoring saw in the saw bench (**Fig. 2.17**). This cuts in the opposite direction to the main saw, projects just above the table and cuts through the veneer or laminate in front of the main cut. It is made slightly tapered in thickness so that it can be raised to increase the width of cut. This will have been reduced due to wear on the saw.

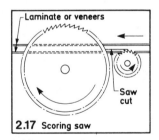

2.17 Scoring saw

Efficient tooth shapes

The separate principles of cutting with, and across, the grain (as described for hand saws) may be applied equally with machine saws. However certain factors can be accentuated due to the power, speed and rigidity of machine equipment.

Thus a rip saw tooth will have a definite lean forward or 'hook' (**Fig. 2.18**), but machine saw teeth are subject to heavy strain. Therefore the point of the tooth must be strengthened by increasing its sharpness angle at the expense of its clearance angle. It is, however, necessary to find accommodation for the sawdust so the back bevel is steepened to give a sufficient open area in the gullet. Cross-cut saws (**Fig. 2.19**) with a negative hook of from 5 to 10 degrees are left with more substance at the point and a simpler tooth shape can be satisfactory.

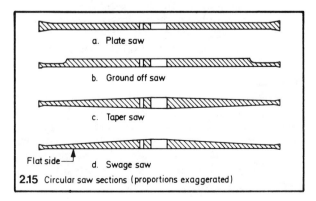

a. Plate saw

b. Ground off saw

c. Taper saw

Flat side —→ d. Swage saw

2.15 Circular saw sections (proportions exaggerated)

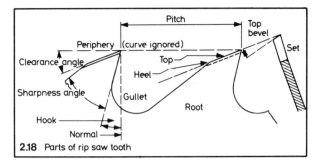

2.18 Parts of rip saw tooth

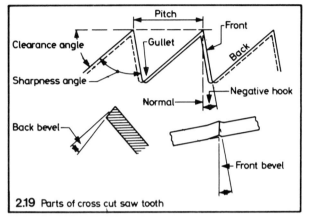

2.19 Parts of cross cut saw tooth

Tears

In the case of planing and moulding cutters common to planers, spindles, tenoners, etc, there is the question of smoothness and freedom from tears as well as efficiency and speed of cutting. Tearing is caused by the shaving being prised up in front of the cutting edge.

It is probable that tearing occurs less with sharp machine tools than with hand tools, because cutting may take place before the inertia of the material is overcome. However the most sure preventative is to reduce the cutting angle. This has the effect, similar to that of the back iron on a hand plane, of pushing back the shaving instead of lifting it.

An extreme example of this is with the French head of the spindle moulder (**Fig. 2.20**) in which the cutting

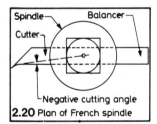

2.20 Plan of French spindle

angle is actually negative. Of course the turned-over edge (as with a hand scraper) has a large cutting angle but is, like the projection of the blade beyond the back iron of the smoothing plane, only minute.

The drawback in reducing the cutting angle in a planer or moulding block is that there is an inverse increase in resistance to cutting, the result of which is a reduced cutting speed and a limit in the amount of work done at one pass. The angle on most cutter blocks is set at around 35 to 40 degrees (**Fig. 2.21a**). This is satisfactory for most work but can be reduced

for difficult timber by putting a front bevel on the cutter (**Fig. 2.21b**) or even reversing it in the block (**Fig. 2.21c**).

Calculating pitch

Due to the circular movement of the cutting edge of the rotary block, the planed surface is never geometrically flat but must consist of a pattern of very shallow hollows. The width of each of these is equal to the distance that the timber feeds forward in the time between when one cutting edge leaves the timber and the next one meets it. The size of this mark is known as the 'pitch' and is obtained by this equation:

Pitch = Feed speed in m/minute × 1000mm
   ÷ number of effective cutters × rpm

Example: Feed speed = 20m per min: RPM = 4500: Number of cutters = 3.

Then pitch $= \dfrac{20 \times 1000}{3 \times 4500} = 1.48$mm

This would be satisfactory, and only a minimum of sanding finish would be required.

Note the use of the word 'effective' in the above equation. If one cutter projects more than the others in, say, a four-cutter block, this negates the effect of the others and the width of the pitch is quadrupled. For this reason the planer blocks on power fed machines are 'jointed': that is to say, the cutters are set as accurately as is humanly possible in the block. Then the machine is started up and, by means of special equipment supplied with the machine, an abrasive block is wound along the periphery, parallel to the axis and just touching the knife edges. The cutting circle of each knife then becomes identical. The 'flat' formed, varying slightly with degrees of inaccuracy, should not exceed $\frac{1}{2}$ to 1mm. Otherwise any knife on the cut surface feeding forward will come into heavy contact with the rising heel, creating friction and vibration.

Cutting or moulding timber across grain

When the cut is made on the end grain, the main problem is the risk of splintering out at the end of the cut. This may be reduced by clamping or nailing or otherwise positioning a backing piece. When the cross grain cut is made on the side, the extreme fibres need to be severed before they can be removed. This is achieved by a spur attached to the end of the block, or by some other means, which projects about $\frac{1}{2}$mm beyond the periphery of the cutters (**Fig. 2.22**).

The importance of safety in woodworking machinery cannot be over-stressed. Its observance, or otherwise, can be a matter of life and death. Every operator should be fully aware of the dangers involved.

A common error is the reluctance of the operator to fix the necessary guards when making preliminary tests before the final set-up. All guards should be in place before starting a machine and feeding it at all times. All guards should be such that the minimum of cutter is exposed. Hands should be kept as far away as possible by using spikes or push sticks for feeding. Small or short pieces of timber always constitute a

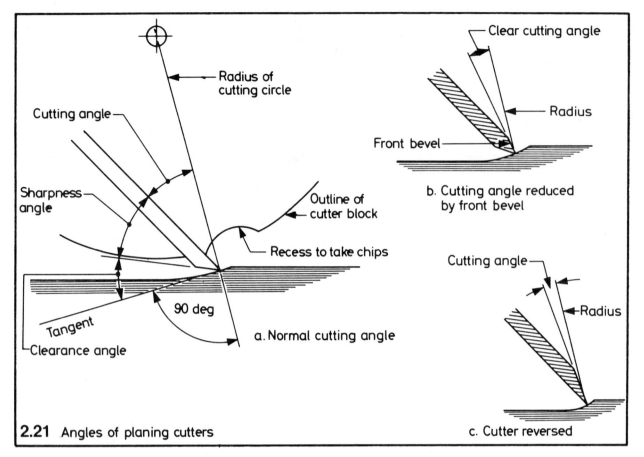

Radius of cutting circle

Cutting angle

Sharpness angle

Outline of cutter block

Recess to take chips

90 deg

Tangent

Clearance angle

a. Normal cutting angle

Clear cutting angle

Radius

Front bevel

b. Cutting angle reduced by front bevel

Cutting angle

Radius

c. Cutter reversed

2.21 Angles of planing cutters

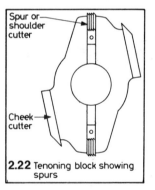

Spur or shoulder cutter

Cheek cutter

2.22 Tenoning block showing spurs

risk while being machined. They should be held in jigs with clamps or screws; and the jigs should have handles, which can be gripped by the hands, not merely finger-holds.

Another fault is the tightening of nuts and bolts far too much by extending the leverage of a spanner with a length of tube, or hammering it tight. If the right spanner is used for the job, it will have been designed to give the right degree of tightness at normal hand pressure.

Three safety rules, where the setting and adjusting of cutter blocks are involved, are:

1. Go over all the nuts on fences, guards and cutter block with the spanner in a methodical sequence as a final exercise;
2. Spin the cutter block by hand to see that it is not fouled by guards or fences;
3. Remove any spanners and any loose material from the table before finally starting up.

When switched on and running free at full speed, the block should hum sweetly. If there is undue noise or vibration, switch off and check cutters for balance, etc.

The Factories Act, the Woodworking Machinery Regulations, 1974, and the Health and Safety at Work, etc, Act, 1972, must be understood by all persons who have responsibility for the use of woodworking machinery. The reader is also recommended to study *Health and Safety at Work, No. 41: Safety in the Use of Woodworking Machinery* published by the Department of Employment and Productivity.

QUESTIONS FOR CHAPTER 2

Question 4

A number of closed stair strings are to be cut out to house the steps. Describe how this operation can be carried out, using the portable powered router.

City & Guilds of London Institute Examination, Carpentry and Joinery Advanced Craft, Purpose-Made Joinery, May 1977. No. 9.

Question 5

A number of short rails 600 by 60 by 30mm have to have stop rebates run on one edge as shown in **Fig. 2.23**. Sketch a safe method of performing this operation at the vertical spindle.

City & Guilds of London Institute Examination, Purpose-Made Joinery, May 1977. No. 7.

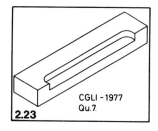

CGLI – 1977
Qu.7

2.23

CHAPTER 3

Doors

The simplest type of external door is the ledged and braced one made up from standard widths of match-boarding in softwood, assembled with wrought, or even oval wire, nails clenched at the back. **Fig. 3.1** is a back view of the door. The diagonal braces really act as struts or props and should always be inclined down to the hanging edge. The bottom of the drawing shows how the brace is set out on paper, although this is no problem dealing with the timber itself.

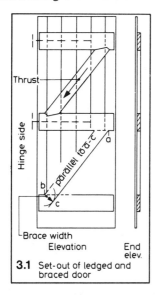

3.1 Set-out of ledged and braced door

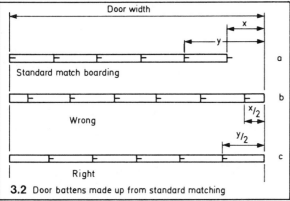

3.2 Door battens made up from standard matching

It is seldom likely that the door width will be an exact multiple of the individual batten sizes, so the outside boards must be reduced (see **Fig. 3.2a**). If the make-up width is merely halved to form the outside boards two very narrow strips result as in **Fig. 3.2b**. The correct method is to take the make-up width back over the next board and divide by 2, always giving more than half a batten width as in **Fig. 3.2c**. It will be noticed that the same number of boards are used in each case.

This principle can be applied universally to all setting out involving making-up to accumulated widths: e.g. in floorboards, floor tiles, matchboarded wall linings, etc. Narrow strips can always be avoided. Very little machine work is involved in ledged door construction, and this is confined to squaring-off and ripping the prepared timbers.

Decorative ledged doors
Figs. 3.3 and **3.4** illustrate a modification to a ledged and braced door specified for alteration to an old building of half timber construction. A high standard of general neatness was asked for. The top half of **Fig. 3.3** shows the method of setting out the curved brace. Starting with a middle ogee curve, the diagonal line **a–b** was bisected twice (into four). A point **d** in the second bisector to come in the curve was selected and the bisector of **b–d** continued to cut the previous one and give a common centre at C_1, C_2 being diametrically opposite.

Suitably increased and reduced radii were used from these centres to give the brace outline as shown in **Fig. 3.3**. Handmade wrought iron rose-headed nails were used for assembly. The holes were pre-drilled and small recesses were chopped out; then the protruding nail ends were turned carefully over with a punch to finish flush (see **Fig. 3.3**). **Fig. 3.4** is a partly filled elevation with a section through the battens.

The major machining operations, apart from initial preparation and squaring-off, was in the moulding of the boards or battens, the cutting out and shaping of the braces, and the chamfering of braces and ledges. Assuming a number of doors had to be done, the

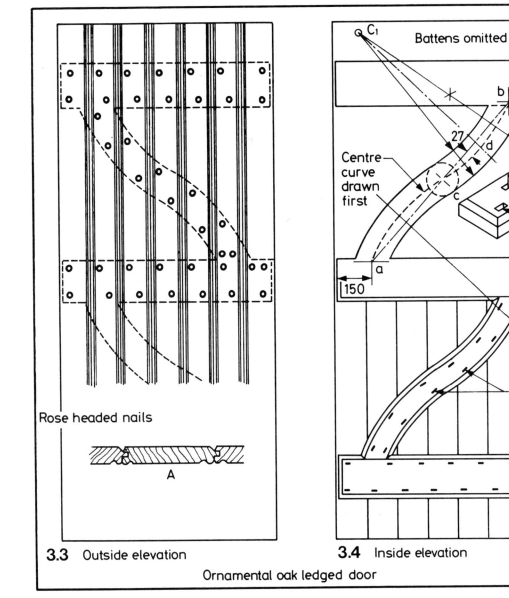

Rose headed nails

A

3.3 Outside elevation

3.4 Inside elevation

Ornamental oak ledged door

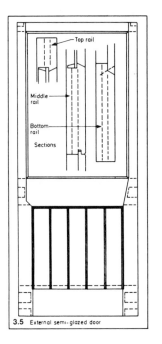

3.5 External semi-glazed door

braces would be band-sawn and shaped off a prepared templet on the spindle moulder, against a circular planer block running the templet against a ball-bearing collar. The tongueing, grooving, and face-moulding of the battens would be done on the spindle using a straight fence. The chamfering of the ledges and the braces would also be done on the spindle using a ring fence.

Semi-glazed doors

A typical semi-glazed door with matchboarding below the lock rail is shown in **Fig. 3.5**. The construction is familiar to most joiners, but it is introduced here for the purpose of discussing alternative treatments.

The lower part is similar, in principle, to the framed, ledged, and braced construction. The boards are tongued and grooved together, and tongued into the stiles and into the rail at the top. They could be taken through past a reduced-in-thickness bottom rail to the bottom of the door but, in my opinion, this would leave the exposed and once-only painted end grain of the boards continuously exposed to accumulated, as well as splashed-up, rain. It is better to finish on the bottom rail as shown.

The boards are nailed into a rebate which is splayed to drain off the water. To accommodate the reduced top part of the stile, alternative mitred and gunstock shoulder joints are shown on the middle rail.

The set-out of gunstock joints seems to be a problem to some joiners. The easy way to do this with even the most complex arrangement of moulds, rebates, etc, is to draw the elevation of that part of the door around the joint. Ignore the actual shoulder, but put in outlines and intersections of all mouldings and rebates worked on the solid. Joining the outermost points of these intersections will always give the shoulder. This needs to be done for both front and back. The rails should be tenoned face-down on the tenoner table so that, for the gunstock joint, the bevels will have to be alternatively acute and obtuse in relation to the fence of the table. The method of doing this, using a tapered pack will be described later.

It is a basic principle in all machine set-ups to do the set-up as accurately as possible when the machine is still. With the mortise and tenon joint, if the marking gauge is set accurately to the hollow chisel, and the chisel in the machine set accurately to the gauge mark on the stile; then if the tenon cutters are set with equal accuracy to the gauge marks on the rail, the joint is bound to be right. The end grain of the marked-out rail should be smooth (planed if necessary) and brought into light contact with the end of each cutter block. The 'scribing' or shoulder cutters should just touch the gauge marks at the tops of their peripheries (see **Fig. 3.6**).

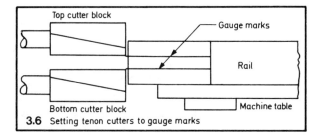

3.6 Setting tenon cutters to gauge marks

EXTERIOR DOORS

Ordinary panelled doors may be used for external openings, provided that they are kept painted to seal the panel intersections. With hardwood unpainted doors, the rain may run down the face of the panel into the groove; this trapped water may then keep the panel edge continuously wet. The edges of plywood or end-grain solid timber are vulnerable in such conditions.

Period panelled doors
Fig. 3.7 shows a period-type solid panelled door which would be traditionally made in oak. The panels are grooved the full thickness into the sides and tops of the openings but, as seen in **Fig. 3.8**, are tongued at the bottom with the shoulder cut down over the weathered edge of the rail. Another feature of this

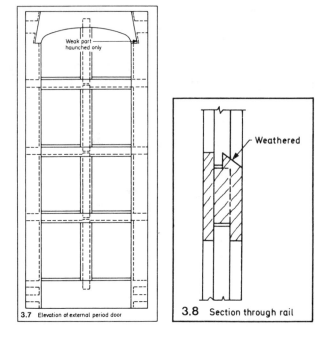

3.7 Elevation of external period door

3.8 Section through rail

door is the semi-elliptical inner shape to the top rail. The shoulders are cut in to avoid a feather edge against the stile, a weakness accentuated by the direction of the grain. This part still remains vulnerable and it is recommended that the tenon is kept above the weak part, which would be likely to shear off under the stress of assembly.

Where double tenons are formed in wide rails, as shown in the bottom rail in **Fig. 3.7**, the space between the tenons should be as wide as possible without unduly weakening other parts of the joint. This is to avoid shear, due to possible unbalanced wedging up. A general rule for wide middle rails is that the tenons should each be one quarter of the available width leaving a half width between them, but common sense and discretion are better than rigid rules. It should not be forgotten, in the case of the various strong weather-resisting adhesives, that a wide glued joint surface with a well-fitting joint tends to add to the overall strength.

Horizontally boarded doors
Figs. 3.9, 3.10 and **3.11** relate to an external door with horizontal boarding on the outside. The boards are tongued into the undersides of the rails and into the stiles, and are rebated one over the other and over the rails on the bottom edges. Reduced vertical muntins halve the span of the boards between the stiles. The whole of the structure is covered with plywood on the inside with rebated cover moulds as shown in **Fig. 3.10**. **Fig. 3.11** shows sectional details.

In order to look right, all the boards should be of the same width, adding up to the vertical height they have to cover. The position of the lock rail will be given by the combined widths of the four bottom boards. The information concerning net widths is most accurately and conveniently obtained by the calculation which follows.

Assuming that the door height is 1980mm and the widths **a, b** and **c** (**Fig. 3.11**) are 50mm, 182mm and

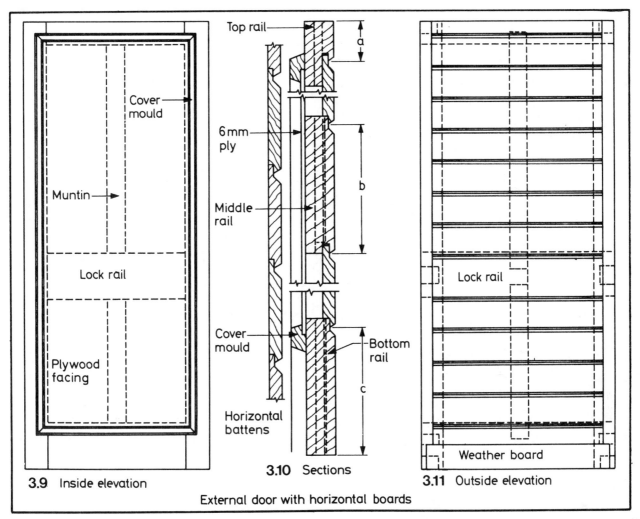

3.9 Inside elevation

3.10 Sections

3.11 Outside elevation

External door with horizontal boards

182mm, then the face width of each batten (bottom edge to bottom edge)

$$= \frac{1980 - (50 + 182 + 182)}{11} = 142.2mm$$

Add about 12mm for the rebate,
then each board = 154mm.
The bottom edge of the lock rail will be

$$182 + 4 \times 142.4 =$$

751.6mm from the bottom edge of the door.

Note that the outer face of the tenon must be in line with the back of the boarding and its maximum thickness must be half of that left. There are not many machining problems; the top rail and stiles can be rebated first and then grooved, using a square-cutter block with the cutters standing free of the top. The muntins, which are barefaced tenoned, can be worked to the same setting clamped on to one board.

Diagonally boarded doors

In **Fig. 3.12**, an ornamental pattern is created with diagonal boards moulded on the face. Only the top and bottom rail and stiles are the full thickness of the door; the other members are reduced to come behind the pattern boarding. The pattern boards are interleaved with half-round beads, all rebated together, to add interest to the design.

The intermediate rails are bareface tenoned to the stiles for maximum strength but the muntins, which support the centre joints in the boards, are tenoned centrally into them. The back of the framing is grooved all round to take 4mm plywood panels which cover up the board joints and make the door draught-proof (see **Fig. 3.13**).

The cheapest way of making up the patterned front would be to nail into the rebates in the stiles and rails. Then they can be butted together and nailed in the middle to the muntins. A better method is to tongue the boards into the stiles and top rails as shown in **Fig. 3.14**. The centre-joints are halved together, glued with a resin adhesive, and screwed together from the back (see **Fig. 3.15**); the beads would be treated in the same way.

In order to present a proper appearance, all the boarding must be of equal face width. The half length at the top and bottom must be equally spaced, cutting half way on to the top and bottom rails respectively. The overall panel height is divided into as many equal spaces as there are boards (see **Fig. 3.12**). Then, from the second division up, one of the beads is drawn as shown in **XY**. This will give the splay to which all the beads may be set out. No other angle will do. The individual measurement may be calculated and then the bottom part of the panel set out full size to give all the necessary information.

The construction and machining is straightforward. The moulding of the pattern boarding can be carried out on the surfacer using moulding cutters bolted to

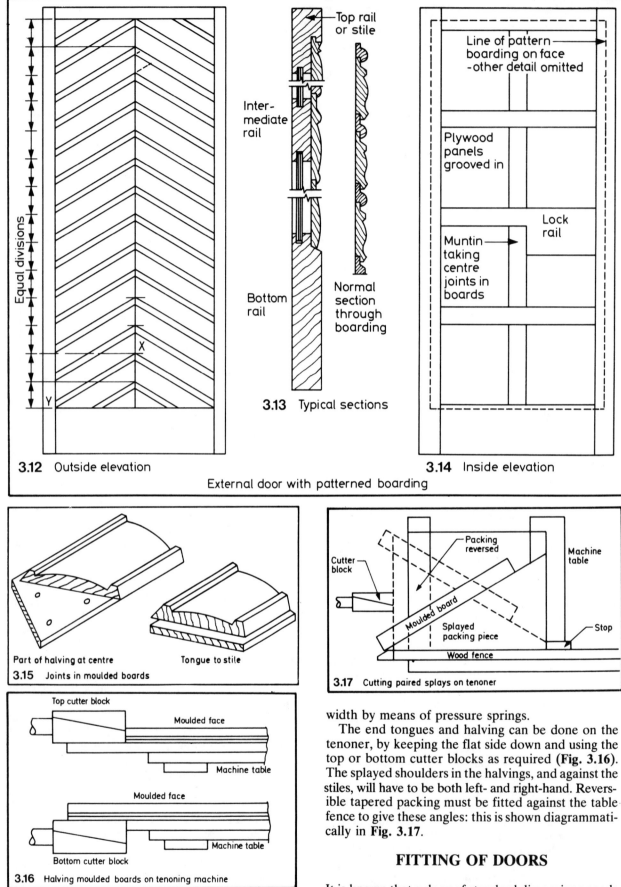

3.13 Typical sections

Top rail or stile

Inter-mediate rail

Bottom rail

Normal section through boarding

Line of pattern boarding on face -other detail omitted

Plywood panels grooved in

Lock rail

Muntin taking centre joints in boards

3.12 Outside elevation

3.14 Inside elevation

External door with patterned boarding

Part of halving at centre

Tongue to stile

3.15 Joints in moulded boards

Top cutter block

Moulded face

Machine table

Moulded face

Machine table

Bottom cutter block

3.16 Halving moulded boards on tenoning machine

Cutter block

Packing reversed

Machine table

Moulded board

Splayed packing piece

Stop

Wood fence

3.17 Cutting paired splays on tenoner

width by means of pressure springs.

The end tongues and halving can be done on the tenoner, by keeping the flat side down and using the top or bottom cutter blocks as required (**Fig. 3.16**). The splayed shoulders in the halvings, and against the stiles, will have to be both left- and right-hand. Reversible tapered packing must be fitted against the table fence to give these angles: this is shown diagrammatically in **Fig. 3.17**.

FITTING OF DOORS

It is known that a door of standard dimensions needs to have its closing edge eased so that it may be shut without rubbing. This is sometimes overdone, result-

the circular block. However the timber will have to be kept in firm contact with the planer bed over its whole

ing in badly flushed face-plates to locks and other fittings. Where doors are of heavy construction, this adjustment is accentuated. It is advisable to know exactly how much the edge must be bevelled, in this case, and make one job of it; rather than overdo it or indulge in a strenuous exercise of trial and error.

Fig. 3.18 shows how the bevel may be obtained precisely. It is given here, as it contains the basic

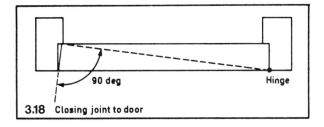

3.18 Closing joint to door

principle which may be applied to any kind of closing joint in any kind of fitting. It may be explained thus. Take a line from the centre of the hinge, wherever the hinge may be, to the furthest inner point of the closing edge. A line taken square to this, back to the opposite edge will give the minimum bevel required.

External door frames are usually made to open inwards, and range in section from 100 by 50mm upwards. The size depends upon the size and weight of the door, the fixing available and, where cost is not the first objective, upon appearance.

The standard frame (**Fig. 3.19**) is put together with mortise and tenon joints. The maximum thickness of the tenon equals half the thickness of the timber left to the side of the rebate. The inside of the frame may be checked to receive the finishing plaster. For ease in construction, the finishing mould is made the same depth as the rebate. When the construction is heavier, the influence of the worked section on the joints becomes less critical and the tenon may be made central (**Fig. 3.19**).

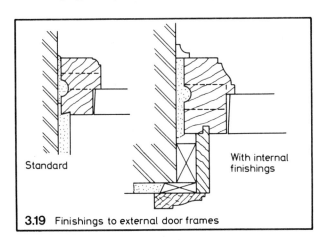

Standard   With internal finishings

3.19 Finishings to external door frames

It is important to note that any moulding which comes within the thickness of the tenon cannot be machine scribed. Thus the small square against the rebate in **Fig. 3.20** has to be cut back by hand – a simple job in this case. In the section, the brick jamb is shown lined and finished on the inner wall face with an architrave, nailed or secret slot screwed.

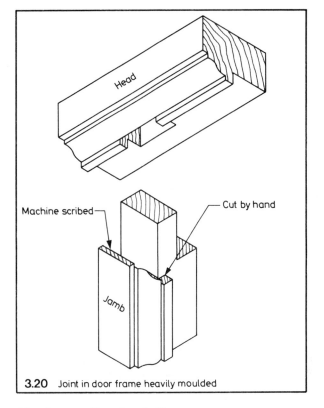

Head

Machine scribed   Cut by hand

Jamb

3.20 Joint in door frame heavily moulded

Weatherproofing thresholds

One problem with external doors, particularly in exposed positions, is that of rendering the threshold watertight. Two methods are shown here.

In **Fig. 3.21**, a weather bar is grouted into the concrete threshold and the bottom edge of the door is rebated over it. Water running down the door is

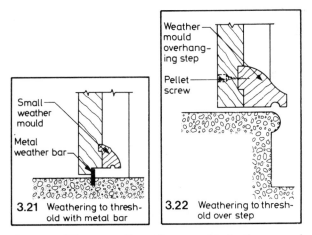

Weather mould overhanging step

Pellet screw

Small weather mould

Metal weather bar

3.21 Weathering to threshold with metal bar

3.22 Weathering to threshold over step

thrown off by a small weather mould. In the second method, shown in **Fig. 3.22**, the threshold is a step and the water is thrown clear of the step by a large weather mould extending over its edge. Being large enough to get stepped on, this mould should be securely fixed.

PANELLED DOORS

Panelled framing was originally introduced so that the overall moisture movement (swelling and shrinkage) could be confined to that in the narrow perimeter of the framing. The frames were unaffected by the movement in the panels, which were free to adjust within their grooves.

The introduction of plywood, in which consecutive veneers impose mutual restraint across the grain, each to the other, presented the joiner with large sheets, 99.9 per cent stable, from which panels could be cut with a virtual guarantee of no moisture movement under normal fluctuations of ambient air humidity. There is no logical reason why plywood panels should not be glued into their grooves, thus giving a complete rigidity in the direction parallel to the panel surface, independent of any strength existing in the frame joints. Practical problems which would need to be overcome would be getting the glue cleanly into the grooves, jointing the narrow framing to maintain strength against twisting and finding accommodation for locks and catches. Ignoring proportions imposed by traditional aesthetics, it would seem that a strong door could be designed by reducing the face width and increasing the thickness of the stiles and rails. Remember that thickness becomes the depth when the stresses of usage are compared with loads on a beam: the deflection formula for this relates the stiffness directly to the breadth (stile width) and to the cube of the depth (frame thickness).

Panelled doors are designed mainly with horizontal rails as in **Fig. 3.23** and with rails and muntins as in **Fig. 3.24**, or a wide variety of combinations of these

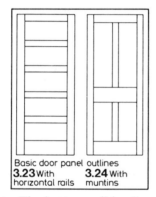

Basic door panel outlines
3.23 With horizontal rails   **3.24** With muntins

arrangements. The bottom rail in all cases is at least twice the width of the stiles. Doors of the type shown in **Fig. 3.23** would need upright locks with lever handles and of **Fig. 3.24** type would need horizontal locks and knob furniture.

Door furniture

It is important to be able to order hinges, locks and furniture at an early date and of the correct hand (i.e. opening the right way). A number of complicated rules have been devised for this and the ISO, in which the BSI is now interested, is in the throes of producing a standard specification on this. They use the terms 'clockwise' and 'anticlockwise' as against 'left' and 'right' hand.

If in doubt, it is better to provide a sketch plan of the door with the position of the hinges and fittings when ordering. The simplest way of obtaining the correct hand, in my opinion, is as follows:

1. Hinges and mortise locks: stand on the side of the door opening away from you. If the hinge (say a

rising butt which is 'handed') is on the left, it is a left-hand hinge and vice versa. If the lock is on the left, it is a left-hand lock, and vice versa.

2. If the fittings (say a rim lock or a night latch) is on the face of the door; stand on the opposite side to that carrying the fitting. The hand is given by that edge of the door to which it is attached: left-hand if on the left, and right-hand if on the right.

3. When its action is affected by the way in which the door closes (e.g. a rim lock), if the door opens away from the viewer it is a straightforward left- or right-hand, according to position as before.

4. On the other hand, if it opens towards the viewer, the hand is still given by the position of the fitting on the door, but it is described as having a 'reverse' bolt or 'reverse' action.

Designing panelled doors

The design of panelled doors may be enriched in many ways, the commonest being by the way in which the edges of the panel and framing are moulded. Sections of mould treatment to framing are given in **Fig. 3.25**. When the mould is worked on the framing

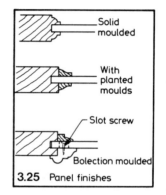

Solid moulded

With planted moulds

Slot screw

Bolection moulded

3.25 Panel finishes

itself, it is described as 'stuck on the solid' or 'solid moulded'. A separate mould fitted into the panel recess is known as a 'planted mould'. However, when this is rebated over the framing giving a bold appearance, it is called a 'bolection mould'.

Common mistakes among students in drawing the elevation is to show the shoulder lines wrongly in relation to the mouldings. This results in subsequent errors in setting out and in writing cutting lists. As shown in **Fig. 3.26**, the shoulder for solid moulded

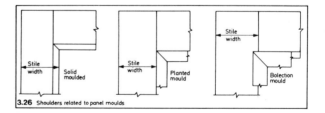

Stile width   Solid moulded   Stile width   Planted mould   Stile width   Bolection mould

3.26 Shoulders related to panel moulds

work has to be extended to the mould line. The moulding is separate from it and is drawn inside the framing for planted moulds; while the bolection mould overlaps the shoulder line.

Fixing mouldings

Planted moulds are pinned in position: use either panel pins, punched in and stopped for softwood, or needle points for polished hardwoods. The latter are brittle steel needles driven in with a pin hammer to the required depth, after which the surplus is snapped off. The break occurs just below the surface and the small hole is virtually invisible. A litte glue should preferably be used against the rail as the needles have a limited holding power.

Where solid timber panels are used in doors, any fixing of mouldings, etc, should only be to the framing, unless some other provision is made for the panel to swell or shrink. Bolection mouldings fixed against a panel can be slot-screwed through the panel (**Fig. 3.25**), if the slots can be covered on the back by, say, a planted mould. The slots should be across the grain with the screw in the centre of the slot. The two screws at the centre of the panel at the grain end need not be slotted but can be driven tight; this will ensure that shrinkage out of the side grooves will occur equally towards the centre.

It must be appreciated that, where a French polish finish is specified on joinery, the process will require the continuous smooth application of a moist rubber which must not be pushed into corners. Thus, on high-class work, panels must be polished before setting into framing and mouldings polished before they are mitred into position.

Raised finishes

Enrichment of panels commonly involves some sort of raised surface. This may be done by moulding all the four edges of a solid panel; or by tongueing suitable moulded margins around the edges of a central rectangle of laminboard or blockboard – the surfaces are then veneered over the joints. It is essential that the timber used should be at the required percentage of moisture content to reduce the risk of subsequent opening of the mitres.

The different types of raised finishes are shown in **Fig. 3.27**. Their relevant appearances in elevation are shown in **Fig. 3.28**. It should be noted that, when a panel is finished with a planted or bolection mould, it must start with a flat margin to accommodate the moulding.

The raised panels will have to be moulded on the spindle moulder. They can be moulded held upright with the face against the fence. This has the advantage that there is the minimum projection of the cutter; but the disadvantage is that any variation in the panel thickness will show in the bad fit of the panel into the groove.

The alternative is to mould the panel with its back on the table. This will ensure that the edges fitting into the grooves will be automatically gauged to thickness, but the operation will require the maximum projection of the cutter. This can be reduced using a 'whitehill' type cutter block. The cutter block should be well guarded and it is essential the panel should be under pressure to keep it firmly on the table as the slightest amount of lift will ruin the work.

The difficulty will be increased if the panel has gone hollow or round on the face. Probably, the first way is the best way to make sure that the timber has been worked to an accurate thickness.

FLUSH DOORS

Flush doors are probably the commonest type of door used today. Design must be limited to surface decoration in the form of veneer patterns or paintwork. Their success is due to the availability of modern adhesives which enable the outer skins of plywood or hardboard to be positively cemented overall to a solid or skeleton core. This produces a rigid, stable, flat unit, parallelling in stiffness the stressed skin panel used in modern roof construction.

Design considerations

Flush doors used in modern domestic buildings are usually of skeleton construction with thin plywood or hardboard outer skins. The essentials are that the core should be so assembled so that the skins are supported, at intervals of not more than 75 to 100mm, with continuous glued contacts; that the perimeter framing should be stout enough to take the extra stresses imposed on the edges; and that the door should be lipped at least on the vertical edges to protect the vulnerable edges of the plywood or hardboard. The face width of the lipping should be sufficient to allow for the normal reductions common to fitting.

The only satisfactory way to assemble these doors is in a press. The use of nails cannot give the necessary contact between glued surfaces while local depressions can occur where the nails are driven in. All pockets formed within the core should be ventilated. This is not so much to reduce condensation and damp as to prevent the formation of airtight cavities, pressures or partial vacuums within. These vacuums cause 'ghosting' – the appearance of the skeleton pattern on the board faces. Provision must be made within the skeleton frames for the accommodation or support of hinges, lock furniture, kicker plates, postal plates, etc. The presence of these supports should be known, or indicated on the surface.

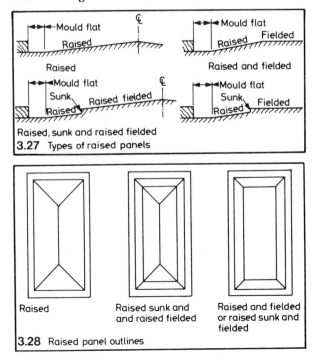

3.27 Types of raised panels

Raised | Raised sunk and and raised fielded | Raised and fielded or raised sunk and fielded

3.28 Raised panel outlines

Mass-produced flush doors generally require the introduction of sophisticated systems and elaborate jigs which it would not be worthwhile to set up for the limited productions in purpose-made joinery. It is therefore simpler to form the skeleton with a relatively stout outer frame plus narrow horizontals suitably spaced to take the surface boards used: the thicker the facings, the fewer horizontals can be used. When a glazed opening has to be formed, this is simply a matter of inserting horizontals with verticals between after the manner of trimming a floor opening.

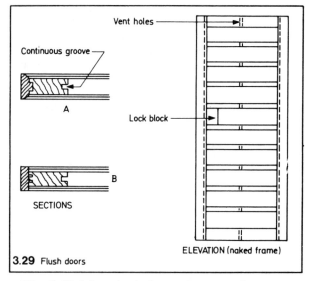

3.29 Flush doors

Fig. 3.29 (elevation) shows the normal construction. The horizontals are tongued into continuous grooves in the stiles as shown also in sections **A** and **B**. If the door is to be veneered, the veneer is best applied before assembly. Section **A** shows the plywood mitred against the lipping, which is left with a narrow flat showing to allow for fitting without exposing the plywood edge. In situations like this, tolerances in making and fitting the frame must come within this margin given to the door edges.

Fig. 3.30 (elevation and section detail) shows a flush door suitable for construction when no press is available. The door must be mortised and tenoned together for full strength in standard construction,

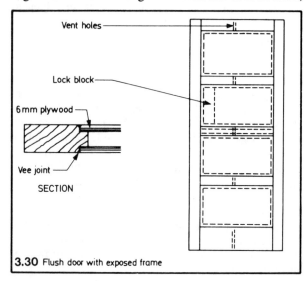

3.30 Flush door with exposed frame

but with rebates on both sides to take plywood panels. The door is assembled and cleaned off. Then the panels are fitted and glued in with a liberal application of contact adhesive to the bearing surfaces, but keeping exposed joint lines clean. The panels do not, in this case, add to the structural strength as the contact adhesive has a low shear value. When the panels are on both sides, however, there is no way in which they can be forced off. No attempt should be made to conceal the joints: the intersections should be finished with a very small neat 'vee' by putting a slight chamfer on the panel and the edge of frame.

Sound insulation

When flush doors have to be sound-resisting to a high degree, they must be made solid and heavy throughout their thickness. The core may then be either a glued assembly of vertical laminae or it may be framed up with stiles and rails with cores of composite materials. A cheaper, but less effective, alternative is the semi-solid core with laminae, either 'hit and miss' or suitably spaced apart and tongued into horizontal rails.

Fire resistance

Fig. 3.31 gives details of a one hour fire resisting door constructed according to BS459. This standard has now been withdrawn and as it has not been replaced

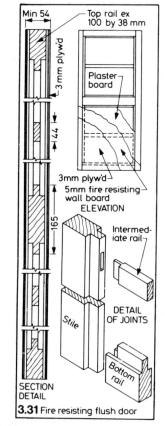

3.31 Fire resisting flush door

by any other standard dealing with the same matter, the onus is on the contractor to prove by tests that the door is fire resistant to the extent required according to the 1985 Building Regulations 1985 Approved Document B/2/3/4 appendix A table A1 section 9.

In the writer's opinion the requirement of a fire resisting door are as follows:

(1) the bulk of the door requires to be of fire resisting and insulating materials. Plasterboard would seem to be ideal for this, Gypsum of which plasterboard is constructed, contains 21 per cent waters of crystallisation which have to be driven off at high temperature before calcination takes place. Plasterboard is also a good insulator.

(2) the door must be structurally sound and not likely to fail in its construction.

(3) there must be no weak spots through which fire may penetrate. The door shown in **Fig. 3.31** does seem to have many of these qualities. There is a lap of 25mm on all construction joints. The timber framing when deprived of air carbonises after losing water and forms a protective insulating barrier and it is protected by a fire resisting insulating wall board. In the writer's opinion the door could be improved in two ways.

(a) by the use of a thermosetting resin adhesive and (b) by filling the hollow centre core with 19mm thick plasterboard. Fire resisting doors should be fitted into frames with 25mm rebates. Hinges should be steel, not plastic. No nails should be used where they be early exposed to the heat.

Some timbers, notably Guriun, Jarrah, Burmah Padauk, and Teak have a high resistance to fire, compared with other timber, doors, 50 to 75mm thick with solid centre tongued panels of the same thickness, particularly if metal faced are suitable for fire doors.

FRAMES

Internal doors may be hung in any of a wide variety of walls from 50mm partitions to walls $1\frac{1}{2}$ bricks or more in thickness. The latter situation is only likely to be met in the conversion of old brick buildings.

Thin partition walls
In the case of thin partition walls, these are only of sufficient strength when of unbroken construction between wall, floor and ceiling. Any frames in wall openings of less strength must be sufficiently strong to carry the door and reinforce the weakened wall. This strength can only be provided by the introduction of

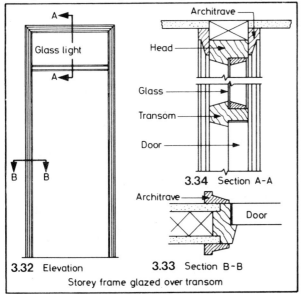

3.32 Elevation   3.33 Section B-B
Storey frame glazed over transom

storey frames firmly secured at floor and ceiling level.

Fig. 3.32 shows the door frame itself carried to the full height with a glass or plywood panel between the transom and head. Section **B–B** (**Fig. 3.33**) is a horizontal section showing the frame rebated to take the plaster with covering architraves. Section **A–A** (**Fig. 3.34**) is a vertical section. It must be noted that the head has been packed down sufficiently to accommodate the architrave in agreement with that in section **B–B**.

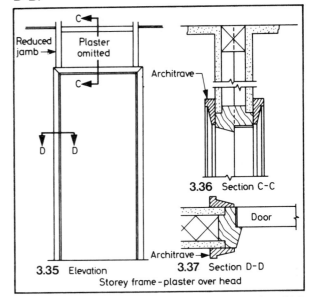

3.36 Section C-C
3.35 Elevation   3.37 Section D-D
Storey frame - plaster over head

Fig. 3.35 shows the elevation of a frame in which the full height jambs are reduced above the door head. This allows the wall surface to carry over, supported either by partition blocks or expanded metal. **Figs. 3.36** and **3.37** are sections giving relevant

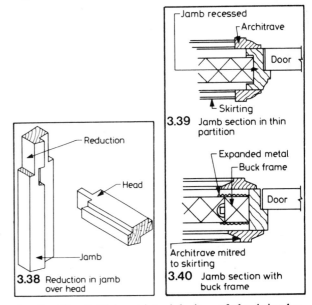

3.38 Reduction in jamb over head
3.39 Jamb section in thin partition
3.40 Jamb section with buck frame

details. **Fig. 3.38** is a pictorial view of the joint between head and jamb showing the reduction of the jamb to take the plaster overlay. **Fig. 3.39** is a section showing a jamb recessed to take, and contain, the partition. Where additional stiffness is required, a separate frame of storey height known as a 'buck frame' is fixed first to form the door opening and to support the wall. This is shown in section in **Fig. 3.40**.

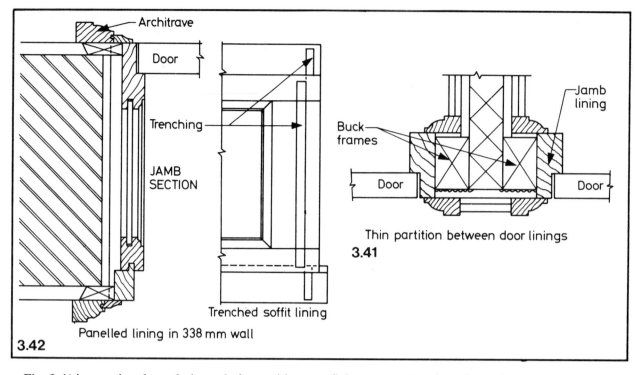

Thin partition between door linings

3.41

JAMB SECTION

Trenched soffit lining

Panelled lining in 338 mm wall

3.42

Fig. 3.41 is a section through the end of a partition wall with doors on either side. In this case, support to the wall can only come from the door framing. The use of buck frames in this case is especially desirable. Note that the flat on the architrave is sufficiently wide to form a stop to the return skirting.

Linings for half brick walls

As the thickness of the partition wall is increased to half a brick, or more, its stability ceases to become suspect. The soffit to the opening can be formed with a concrete lintel and thinner linings. These obtain their support from the walls and lintel used within the opening. The thickness of the lining is governed by the need for stiffness between fixings at spacings of from 450 to 600mm, and for sufficient depth on the face to take the hinge recesses, screws and lock fittings.

In cheaper constructions, 22mm linings are built up with stops nailed on to form the door rebate. These may be nailed on after the door is hung and may cover the stout nails used for the initial fixings. In better class work, the thickness of the lining is increased to leave a face thickness of 22mm or more after being rebated for the door in the solid. It should be noted that there should be a clearance of about $1\frac{1}{2}$ to 2mm between the back of the rebate and the door in painted work to take the accumulation of six coats of paint (three on each face) and avoid the rubbing which would otherwise take place.

Linings are usually taken to the face of the plaster on each side of the wall. On cheap domestic work, they form the screed for the plasterer; but in better class work, rough grounds are accurately fixed to the wall prior to plastering. These form a stop and screed to the plaster as well as a firm fixing and level bed for the linings. These only need to be inserted after the plasterwork has been completed (an essential when linings are varnished, cellulosed or polished before

fixing, as usually takes place with hardwood linings).

Traditionally, when plaster work was three coat – render, float and set with an ultimate thickness of 19 to 22mm – rough grounds were fixed on each face of the brickwork. In the case of stout walls, cross-bearers were dovetail notched between as shown in Fig. 3.42. With modern practice, and plaster thickness limited to about 12mm, this is no longer

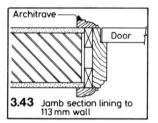

3.43 Jamb section lining to 113 mm wall

possible. The rough grounds, when fixed, are now nailed to the face of the jambs, projecting the required amount beyond the brickwork either side as in Fig. 3.43.

Lining for thicker walls

When the wall exceeds a half brick in thickness, single board linings are no longer practical and they have to be framed up with horizontal rails, either exposed or concealed. If the plain appearance is to be maintained, the widths can be filled in between stiles with a plywood panel. It this is 6mm or more in thickness, it can be set in with a tongued joint as in Fig. 3.44. This section shows the alternative to architraves with the plaster taken into a groove in the lining, and the intersection being finished with a cover mould.

As an alternative to the provision of framed linings, a single lining of fairly stout proportions could be used. This is set to one face of the opening leaving a plaster reveal finished to a skirting to the opposite face, as shown in Fig. 3.45. It could relate to a doorway leading out to a room of secondary importance.

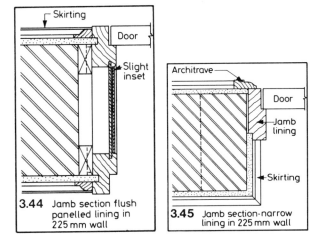

3.44 Jamb section flush panelled lining in 225 mm wall

3.45 Jamb section·narrow lining in 225 mm wall

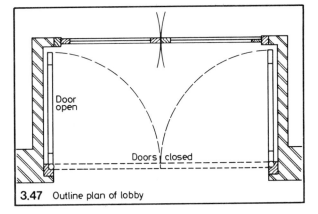

3.47 Outline plan of lobby

The use of framed linings in a thick wall is shown in **Fig. 3.42**. In that section, one stile is shown rebated to take the door; the other is grooved to take a make-up member forming the balancing rebate. This enables some allowance to be made for variation in the wall thickness. The trenched soffit lining shows the way in which the stopped grooves in the head-lining are set back to take the bareface tongues of the parts forming the jamb rebates.

Metal casings

As an alternative to wood fixing grounds, metal casings can be fixed to the wall, as in **Fig. 3.46**. These are commonly used as a preliminary to fixing 'door sets'; these are doors completed and ready hinged to linings with their furniture attached. Considerable accuracy is needed in this method. The joint between the lining and plastered wall is covered by a small mould.

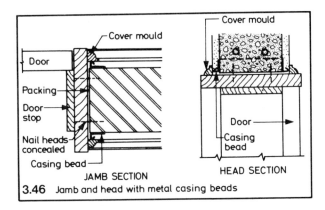

JAMB SECTION   HEAD SECTION

3.46 Jamb and head with metal casing beads

A DOOR DESIGN FOR AN ENTRANCE HALL

Fig. 3.47 is the outline plan of a lobby or vestibule. The walls may be of brick, as shown, or wood framing panelled out. It is intended to be used in public buildings or offices and the doors are kept open back during the day to give the appearance of panelled linings. They are only closed when the premises are locked up. The front elevation of the door is, therefore, enriched with bolection moulds and raised panels, while the back (not seen when the building is occupied) is plain, with a bead and butt finish.

Sectional details, including the hinging joint, are shown in **Fig. 3.48**. The joint presents a very neat appearance both open and closed. The set-out of the joint is done from different centres for the door edge and for the jamb, the idea being to give a working clearance with a neat fit where showing. Details of the swing door at the back of the lobby are shown in **Fig. 3.49**.

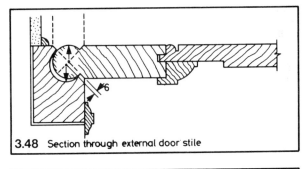

3.48 Section through external door stile

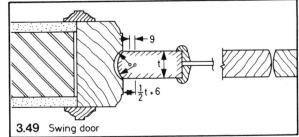

3.49 Swing door

The doors would be set in floor springs with top pivots, the centre being so set that the door shows a working clearance of 6mm away from the jamb when open. The recess in the jamb is worked to a radius 9mm less than that of the door edge so as to give a clearance in the unexposed recess. Other parts of the section (**Fig. 3.49**) show a glass panel retained by rebated beads and a slight round on the meeting stile.

SPECIAL AND SHAPED DOORS

The doors described in this section are those requiring some special technique or the application of some geometrical principles in design and construction.

A door with a central circular panel
Fig. 3.50 shows the elevation of a door with a central circular panel. This was chosen because of the prob-

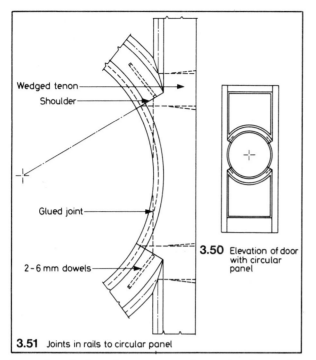

Wedged tenon

Shoulder

Glued joint

2–6 mm dowels

3.50 Elevation of door with circular panel

3.51 Joints in rails to circular panel

ness of the angle of the grain, the stile has to be widened at the intersection. This is most economically done by jointing pieces on as shown in **Fig. 3.51**. It will be seen that there is still an area of cross grain, which maintains the risk that the rail may shear along the line of the tenon. This risk can be greatly reduced by drilling into the shoulder tight against the tenon on each side and inserting dowels. Assuming that the door is 44mm thick and the tenon 15mm thick, this leaves 14mm of shoulder each side to take 6mm dowels.

The rest of the construction is straightforward but, if the grain is to remain exposed, care should be taken to ensure that the panel is inserted with this exactly vertical.

Double margin doors

Where the opening is of an unusual proportion, so that one door would look too wide but a single one of a pair would be too narrow to admit a person comfortably, two doors can be permanently wedged together so that they become as one (**Figs. 3.52** and **3.53**). The meeting stiles are rigidly held together by putting in matching through mortises into the double width of stile. Then folding wedges are driven home.

If the framing is solid moulded, the thickness of the wedges must come within the panel groove but, if the edges of the frame are concealed by planted or bolection moulds, the wedges may be thicker. It is impor-

lem of reducing the amount of cross grain at the joints. As there are no other intermediate rails, these curved ones must be expected to take a certain amount of strain.

In order to shorten the rail and so reduce the acute-

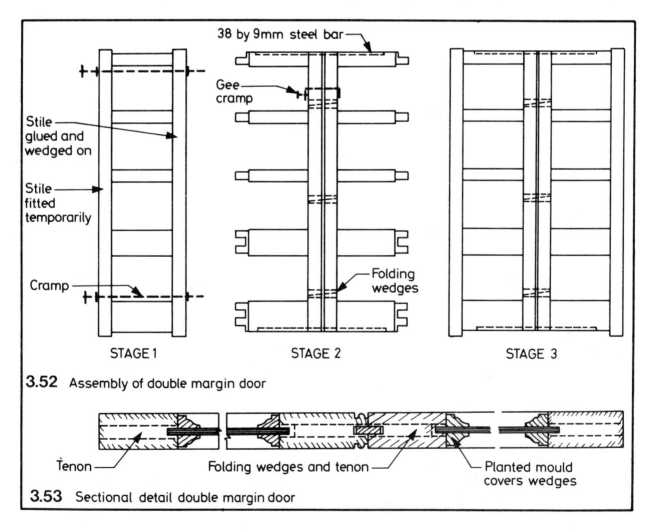

38 by 9mm steel bar

Gee cramp

Stile glued and wedged on

Stile fitted temporarily

Cramp

Folding wedges

STAGE 1   STAGE 2   STAGE 3

3.52 Assembly of double margin door

Tenon   Folding wedges and tenon   Planted mould covers wedges

3.53 Sectional detail double margin door

tant to ensure that they are ultimately chopped back below the grooves or any subsequent shrinkage of stiles may cause trouble. The wedges serve the dual purpose of holding the stiles together and also of stiffening the door generally against lateral flexing of the joints. The wedges should therefore be made of strong hardwood and each pair should be 50 to 75mm wide. Additional stiffness is given by a 9mm thick steel bar housed into the top and bottom edges to nearly the full double door width.

The two individual doors are fitted together and the inner tenons only glued and wedged, **Fig. 3.52** (stage 1). The meeting stiles are then shot, tongued and rebated together as designed. The horns are cut off, the housings carried through from the rails, and the stiles are glued, cramped and wedged together. The steel bars are then inserted, see **Fig. 3.52** (stage 2). Finally, the panels are inserted from either side, the outer stiles fitted and the door cramped up, see **Fig. 3.52** (stage 3). In the sectional detail (**Fig. 3.53**), it will be seen that the meeting stiles are tongued together. A bead is worked on one stile only to emphasise the joint. This stile must be the width of the bead wider than its mate.

Communicating doors with different designs on each side

In important public buildings, stately residences, etc, adjoining rooms may be panelled in different kinds of timber. The communicating door must then form an integral part of the design to each room. In effect, two thin doors must be made, 28 to 32mm thick, which are then joined together by dovetail keys through the framing.

The doors are made up, fitted together dry, levelled off on the back if necessary, then taken apart. The dovetail keys are housed into the backs of the framing of one door (**Fig. 3.54**), driven tight, cut off exactly in line with the members, and levelled off. Each stile or rail is then placed back to back with its paired member and the key positions are marked. Each key is then removed from the first door and screwed on to the marked position on the other member. All the individual pairs are then put together by tapping home the keys (**Fig. 3.55**).

Fig. 3.56 shows the method of finishing the edges with mitred and double tongued lippings, a small square being left on to allow for fitting. The lipping of the closing stile should match the room it opens into, the lipping of the hanging stile matching the other. The jamb is also made of two different timbers, the joints being strengthened with dowels at about 225mm centres. The section in **Fig. 3.56** illustrates different finishes with plywood panels and solid moulds on one side and raised solid panels and bolection moulds on the other.

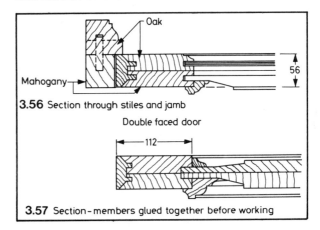

3.56 Section through stiles and jamb

Double faced door

3.57 Section – members glued together before working

In my opinion the process of making up two different doors is completely unnecessary. With the proven reliability of modern adhesives and the careful selection of the right one for the job, it is only necessary to make up all the framing members and panels into two thicknesses of the desired different timbers and glue these together in the square. If necessary, gap-filling glues can be used as none of these joints will eventually show; **Fig. 3.57** shows the simplified construction. A necessary precaution would be to ensure that all the timber was of the correct moisture content to avoid possible unequal shrinkage movements.

A semi-circular headed door

The construction of doors and frames with semi-circular and other types of curved shaped heads usually present problems of avoiding weaknesses caused by cross grain. **Fig. 3.58** is the elevation of a semi-

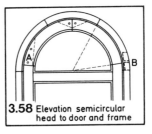

3.58 Elevation semicircular head to door and frame

circular headed door and frame. The frame in this case is formed with three segments in solid timber. This gives a minimum of wastage and avoids too much

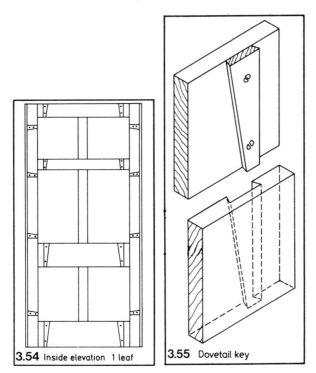

3.54 Inside elevation 1 leaf

3.55 Dovetail key

cross grain. **Fig. 3.59** shows a hammer-headed tenon joint used at the springing of the frame. The other joint is formed with hammer-headed keys, as in **Fig. 3.60**, which is as **Fig. 3.59** but double-ended.

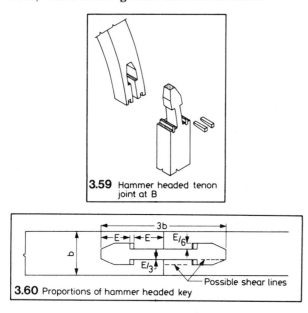

3.59 Hammer headed tenon joint at B

3.60 Proportions of hammer headed key

This drawing illustrates a logical proportion in the design of the joint, assuming that its length is three times the timber width. As it may fail by shear, either in the key or in the head, the values of **E** must be all the same. The tension in the neck and the compression on the shoulders will then be the same. The safe fibre stress in tension and compression parallel to the grain is about six times the sheer value. To make the neck of the key **E/6** would be practically too slender, so this has been made **E/3** and the two shoulders each **E/6**.

The door head is formed with only two segments. This is satisfactory as the greater face width of each curved segment, together with its reduced radius, means that the area of cross grain is less. The joint at the head is formed with a loose key and that at the

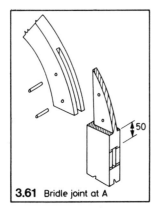

3.61 Bridle joint at A

springing with a bridle joint (**Fig. 3.61**). The advantage of the bridle joint and the loose tongue is that they reinforce the cross grain in the segments. The joints should be assembled with G-cramps to hold the cheeks tight against the tongue.

As the transom rail comes on the springing (**Fig. 3.58**), the mortise to receive its tenon would cut off

the springing's tongue if its shoulder were on the springing also. By keeping the shoulder 50mm above the springing, this is avoided. The curve of the head will, however, follow a little way into the stile. To accommodate this, a small piece can be glued on the stile. Alternatively it can be made a little wider and passed over the surface planing machine, stopping just short of the shoulder to leave the curve required.

A templet should be prepared for each of the different shaped segments to be cut, which should be marked 'one-in-the-other' on a suitable plank, as shown in **Fig. 3.62**. While economy is necessary, this should not be achieved at the expense of any unbalanced cross grain. If only one or two items have to be prepared, the work can be cleaned up by hand, perhaps finishing with the disc and bobbin sander for convex and concave curves. However, if a fair number have to be done, they can be shaped on the spindle moulder with a templet tacked to the segment bearing against the ring fence and the cutter block underneath it. The timber is then either planed to shape, or shaped and moulded in one action (**Fig. 3.63**).

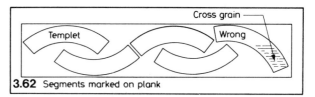

3.62 Segments marked on plank

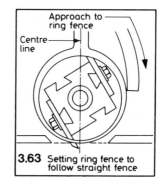

3.63 Setting ring fence to follow straight fence

Semi-elliptical door heads

An alternative method of forming curved heads is by building them up in two or more layers to break joint as shown in **Fig. 3.64**. In this example, the jambs are continued above the springing and halved at the back to fit in with the built-up construction. It becomes

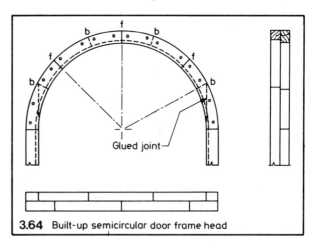

3.64 Built-up semicircular door frame head

necessary to joint a piece above the springing on to the jamb to continue the curve. The segments are butt-jointed; the layers are screwed together and pelleted to cover the screws.

If the frame fits into a recess where one face of the frame is largely covered, the screws should be inserted from this side.

Where curved work is circular or segmental in outline, all the ribs can be identical to give the same amount of cross grain. However, when it is elliptical in outline as in **Fig. 3.65**, there is the problem of avoiding excess cross grain at the ends. The end ribs should therefore be kept as short as reasonably possible. In this case, the joints in one layer will not come in the centre of the other.

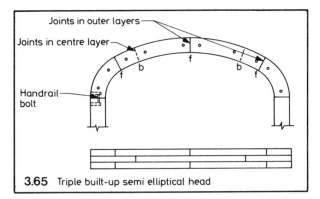

3.65   Triple built-up semi elliptical head

JOINTING CURVED MEMBERS WITH BOLTS

An alternative method of jointing curved members in frames and in doors is by the use of handrail bolts as in **Fig. 3.66**. Holes drilled normally to the joint face in each piece take the bolt, while mortises are cut into the sides to take the nuts. One nut is square and the

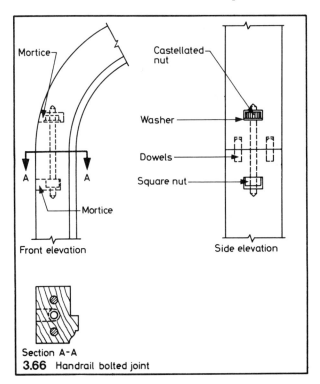

3.66   Handrail bolted joint

bolt first threaded into this; the other nut is castellated (circular, with notches around).

To assemble the joint, the castellated nut, bearing against a washer to reduce friction, is driven round with a handrail punch or old screwdriver to tighten the joint. Two short dowels are positioned, as in section **A–A**, to keep the joint rigid. It is essential that the holes be drilled accurately.

To mark them out, they can be squared over and gauged or marked by pricking through a zinc templet. However the simplest way is to drive two 12mm panel pins into one joint surface, behead them 2mm high and then press the two pieces of wood together to mark the centre on the other piece.

Drill bits tend to wander initially into wood. To stop this from happening, give the hole a start with an engineer's centre punch making a conical depression.

Door with fanlight
Fig. 3.67 is the elevation of a door with a fixed fanlight over. This is an integral part of the frame, bars being tenoned directly into the head and transom. The joints between the transom and the jamb and between the jamb and the head coincide: they must be

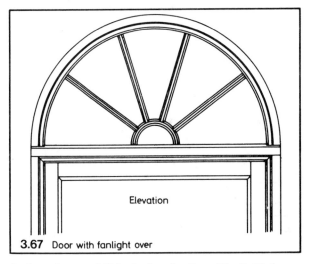

3.67   Door with fanlight over

designed not to fall foul of each other. **Fig. 3.68** shows how the problem is solved by using a hammer-headed tenon joint between the head and the jamb, and by fitting the transom with twin tenons on either side of the hammer neck.

The transom is recessed into the jamb on the outer face as a weather protection and the head fitted on to it (**Fig. 3.69**). It will be seen also that the heavily moulded edge to the frame continues under the weathering of the transom with a scribed mitre to the jamb.

The moulded bars butt against the flat of the head and the weathering of the jamb. The semi-circular bar from which the others radiate is fragile and cross grained, being cut from one piece. The grain should be vertical so that the ends carry tenons. Being so small it must, in the interests of safety, be formed with a jig. Even if the frame is of softwood this should be cut from a dense hardwood. **Fig. 3.70**, plan and section **A–A** illustrates a jig which can be used for both bandsawing and moulding. **Fig. 3.71** shows a fitting to the bandsaw for guiding the timber against the saw;

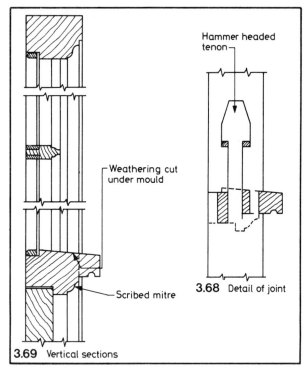

3.68 Detail of joint

Hammer headed tenon

3.69 Vertical sections

Weathering cut under mould

Scribed mitre

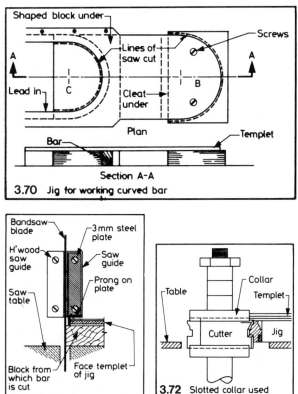

Shaped block under

Screws

Lines of saw cut

A   A

Lead in   C

Cleat under

B

Plan

Bar

Templet

Section A-A

3.70 Jig for working curved bar

Bandsaw blade

3 mm steel plate

H'wood saw guide

Saw guide

Prong on plate

Saw table

Block from which bar is cut

Face templet of jig

3.71 Guide plate on bandsaw

Table

Collar

Templet

Cutter

Jig

3.72 Slotted collar used with jig

and **Fig. 3.72** shows the method of moulding on the spindle moulder.

The jig starts with a 9mm plywood templet cut to a convex semicircle at one end to the outer radius of the bar, and a concave semicircle at the other end to the inner radius of the bar. A cleat under the convex end positions the square block from which the bar is to be cut. A block of equal thickness, with a semicircular cut-out, is fixed to the templet at the concave end (the radius of the cut being that of the outside of the

bar). The sides continue to support the lead-in on the templet. A steel face-plate with a dropped prong is screwed to the saw guide of the narrow bandsaw to form a guide for cutting the curved bar to follow the templet (**Fig. 3.71**). Procedure is as follows:

The block from which the bar is to be formed is screwed in the jig (through the waste timber) as at **B**, **Fig. 3.70**, and sawn on the bandsaw, keeping the templet against the prong.

It is then taken to the spindle moulder to be planed and moulded in one operation against the templet with the slotted collar cutter block (**Fig. 3.72**). This should be suitably guarded.

The moulded block is then placed and pinned at **C** (**Fig. 3.70**) and the concave edge first cut and then moulded as before.

Glued laminate curved heads
Another method of forming curved heads or other similar curved work is by glued laminated construction as shown in **Fig. 3.73**. This is very strong but is also the most expensive method and not suitable where the natural grain is a feature of the design. The thickness of the laminate needs to be from 1/100 to 1/150 of the radius of curvature. They must be pressed together in a shaped former.

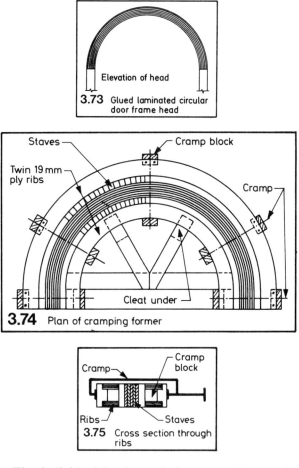

Elevation of head

3.73 Glued laminated circular door frame head

Staves

Cramp block

Twin 19 mm ply ribs

Cramp

Cleat under

3.74 Plan of cramping former

Cramp

Cramp block

Ribs

Staves

3.75 Cross section through ribs

The individual laminate, being very thin, needs continuous support during the setting time of the adhesive. **Fig. 3.74** is the plan of the cramping former and **Fig. 3.75** shows the cross-section through the ribs. Semicircular convex and concave formers are built up with twin plywood ribs tied together with staves on the contact surfaces and notched cramping blocks on the backs. The inner convex one is rigidly braced and serves to maintain the true shape. The staves should be lined with paper to avoid the risk of sticking.

BUILDING LININGS TO A CONICAL HEAD

Fig. 3.76 to **3.80** deal with the method of building linings to a conical head over splayed jambs to a semicircular headed doorway. The work appears to be complex but is simplified when we realise that the edges of all curved members lie in vertical planes. In order to draw the elevation (see 'half elevation' **Fig. 3.76**), the vertical section must be drawn to obtain the desired radii. If the cross-sections of the rails are enclosed in boxes (**Fig. 3.77**), the widths are projected across the elevation; this will give the radii to draw the templets for marking out (**Fig. 3.76**).

The curved ribs start as rectangular sections: the thicknesses are given in **Fig. 3.77**. To obtain the ultimate shape, continuous lines are gauged around the ribs as **a**, **b**, and **c** in the outer rib, and **d**, **e**, **f**, and **g** for the inner rib (**Fig. 3.78**). The ribs are then worked back to these lines.

The cuts giving the rail thicknesses can be made on the bandsaw with the table tilted. The grooves for the panels can be cut on the high-speed router against a short curved and bevelled (conical) fence. The router head and cutter is tilted to the required amount (**Fig. 3.79**).

The plywood panels
To obtain the flat outline of the panels (thin plywood afterwards bent to shape), the end section line (**Fig. 3.77**) is continued down to the springing. The intersection is the apex of the geometrical cone coinciding with the curved face. Using this intersection as a centre, draw the stretch-out of the curved face, the measurement **1–2–3** being transferred from the half elevation. Adding 12mm to the sight line all round will give the flat shape of the panel. Note that the true position of the muntins, as well as their slightly tapered shape, are given. To be absolutely correct, the panel should have been drawn from a slightly

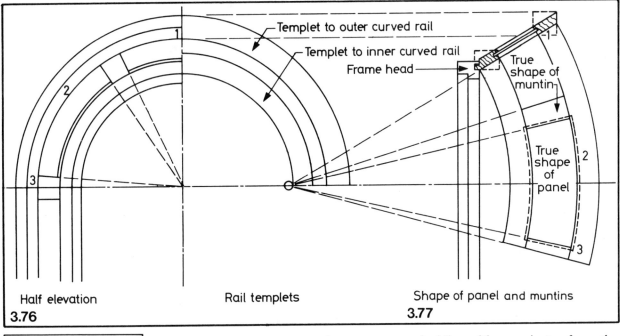

Templet to outer curved rail
Templet to inner curved rail
Frame head
True shape of muntin
True shape of panel

Half elevation   Rail templets   Shape of panel and muntins
3.76   **3.77**

longer centre coinciding with a projector from the panel face, but there is little practical difference.

The plywood panel, while easily bent directly across the fibres of the face grain, will tend to resist taking up the conical form. This resistance may be countered by using very thin plywood and gluing radial strips to the back before bending (**Fig. 3.80**).

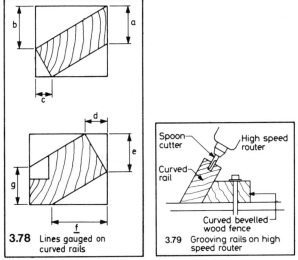

3.78 Lines gauged on curved rails

Spoon cutter
High speed router
Curved rail
Curved bevelled wood fence

3.79 Grooving rails on high speed router

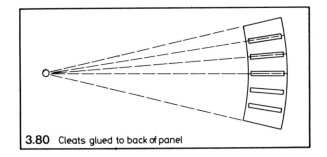

3.80 Cleats glued to back of panel

CALCULATIONS FOR PANELLING TO SPLAYED JAMBS

Panelling to splayed jambs and head involves the use of some geometrical principles in order to obtain the correct shapes and bevels. The vertical section must be drawn first, and from this the widths of rails in elevation obtained for the head. As the head and jamb splay are, in this case, both equal, these widths can be projected to the intersection mitre and from this the jamb stiles drawn.

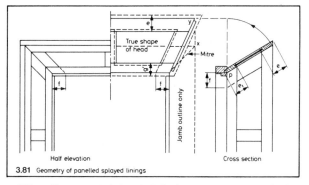

3.81 Geometry of panelled splayed linings

The distance **f** (**Fig. 3.81**), however, can only be drawn by obtaining the true outline in order to obtain this dimension; the diagrams are self explanatory. To obtain the true face of the head, the face width in section is swung up and projected across to intersect a vertical from the mitre to give the points **y**. The widths **e** and **e₁** transferred from the section give the extra widths to allow for bevelling and tongueing.

The bevel necessary to the formation of the angle joint between head and jambs may be found by first planning the face edge to the section necessary to bring it into line with the wall surface. Square across this and mark down on the inner and outer faces to the developed bevel already found. If the cutting is to be done on the dimension saw, the dihedral angle will have to be given to the machinist. **Fig. 3.82** shows how this is obtained.

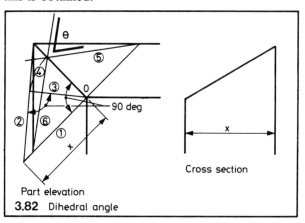

Part elevation

3.82 Dihedral angle

Having the outline elevation and section of the corner of the lining (i.e. its geometrical form), draw line (**1**) making the length equal to **X** in cross-section. Draw line (**2**) and then (**3**) square to line (**2**). From centre **O** swing line (**3**), making curve (**4**), down to the mitre line and draw lines (**5**) and (**6**). These, produced as shown, give the angle to which the dimension saw should be tilted for the joints between jambs and head. The fence on the sliding table sets, at the same time, the bevel giving the true shape of the head.

QUESTIONS FOR CHAPTER 3

Question 6
The outline of the top corner of a glazed panel with a shaped top rail is shown in **Fig. 3.83**. Sketch details of the joint between the top rail and stile.

City & Guilds of London Institute Examination, Purpose-Made Joinery, 1977. No. 8.

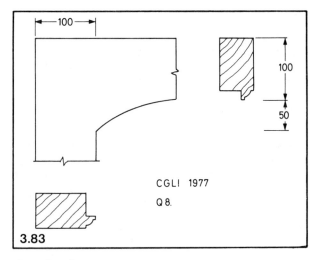

CGLI 1977
Q 8.

3.83

Question 7
A fire report on a public building calls for both half hour and one hour fire check flush doors and frames, constructed to BS459, Part 3. Sketch horizontal sections to show the construction of both types of doors and frames.

Institute of Carpenter Associate Examinations, General paper, May 1977. No. 1.
Time allowed: 10 minutes.

Question 8
A segmental headed door to a bank is 1200mm wide and ex50mm thick with a height of 1900mm at the springing line and 250mm rise. The framing has solid stuck mouldings and is arranged to take five horizontal raised and fielded panels.

   a. To a scale of 1:10, draw an elevation of the door and indicate the joints;
   b. Specify a suitable timber;
   c. Draw, to a scale 1:1, a section through the jamb, stile and part of the panel.

Institute of Carpenters, Associate, Joinery/Shopfitting, Written and Drawing Test, May 1976. Question J/S5.
Time allowed: 30 minutes.

CHAPTER 4

Windows

Of all the timber construction in a house, windows have always been the most vulnerable to the weather. Although traditional designs have, in the past, proven satisfactory – provided normal maintenance, regular painting, etc, were carried out – modern methods of construction have accentuated old problems and presented new ones. The increase in efficiency of heating systems, resulting in higher internal temperatures, has intensified the degree of humidity within a building. Thus creating considerable condensation on windows. The situation has been further aggravated by the absence of ventilation previously provided by the suction from hot gases rising from the open coal fire up the 23cm (9in) square flue. Furthermore the discarding of glazing bars, while favouring the maximum of light and the minimum effort in window-cleaning, has permitted the virtually uninterrupted flow of water to concentrate in pools on sills or window-boards. This can be to the extent that, failing daily attention in the winter, they may never be dry.

Windows in a building are also a significant source of heat-loss, not only by conduction through the glass, but also by draughts created by wind or temperature variation through ill-fitting sashes and casements. Finally, they may form a minimum barrier to unwelcome sounds from a busy street, airfield or other noise source.

Definition of terms
BS565, 'Glossary of terms applicable to timber, plywood and joinery', only defines the components of cased-frame and casement windows. In so far as the latter are relevant to this chapter, they are used throughout. Although most of the terms are commonly adopted, the definitions of the framed units may not be popularly known, see **Fig. 4.1**.

A light hinged at the side is a 'casement'.
A light hinged at the top above eye-level is a 'ventlight'.
A light at the bottom of the window, generally below a casement, is a 'sublight'.

In the absence of other definitions, and following accepted practice, all other types of opening lights will here be referred to as 'sashes'.

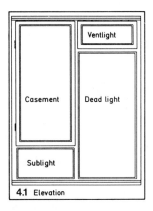

4.1 Elevation

Durability of timbers
The problems identified above have highlighted the need for sound and scientific construction, while the durability of timber, particularly softwoods, needs some fresh investigation. The increase in the amount of sapwood being supplied, particularly of pine or European redwood, due to economic pressures and difficulties of supply, is a cause for some anxiety. Tests carried out by the Princes Risborough Laboratory indicate that this sapwood is less durable than that of spruce or European whitewood. The latter's sapwood is not easily identified. Some preservative treatment would seem to be indicated.

Tests carried out at the laboratory with a solution known as 'pentachlorophenol' in which was incorporated some water-repellent waxes, have brought good results in the treatment of both pines and spruces, although impregnation of the latter is more difficult. To avoid excessive absorption of water with the resultant swelling, distortion and failure of surface finishes, the following precautions are advisable:

1. The initial moisture content of the timber should be about 16 per cent and the finished joinery should be protected in storage and on the site so that this is not exceeded.

2. All joints should be well fitting with no voids. Joint surfaces should be well glued with a suitable water-resisting resin adhesive so that the contact surfaces (particularly end grain) are sealed and the joints themselves are impervious.

3. All near horizontal flat surfaces exposed either to rain or condensation should, where practical, be weathered at least 9 degrees to the horizontal.

4. The closing joints between casements or sashes and frames should be close-fitting on surface contacts as a check to wind-driven rain. They should have sufficient clearance within the rebates to accommodate unavoidable moisture swelling and eliminate capillary action; the latter being assisted by suitable capillary grooves.

CASEMENT WINDOWS

Traditional windows comprised square-edged casements fitted straight into rebates. They had their joints directly exposed to the weather, but modern window construction does take care of all the above structural requirements.

Fig. 4.2 and **4.3** are horizontal and vertical sections through a typical 'stormproof' window. It will be seen that the cover provided at **a**, where surfaces are in reasonable contact, forms a check to the wind; while the clearance in the rebate at **b** is wide enough to allow for some swelling and to form a check to capillary action. The grooves in the casement and frame further assist in this.

The 9 degree splay, which is a feature of all edges, provides a weathered surface on all horizontal members. The vertical section in **Fig. 4.3** illustrates constructional details at head transom and sill. The top rails of casements and ventlights must be protected from the weather at all times by a suitable drip-mould.

A section of a glazing bar where needed is shown in **Fig. 4.3**. This is stub-tenoned into the rail or stile of the casement in the usual way. Fixed or dead lights are normally formed by glazing directly into the frame rebates as shown. If, however, the design includes glazing bars, a normal casement light is provided to take them; this is then nailed direct into the frame rebate.

Where a light comes under a transom, unless the transom itself is weathered and projecting beyond the top rail, coverage must be given by a drip-mould tongued to the bottom rail of the ventlight over (see **Fig. 4.4**). The weathering to the sills (**Fig. 4.3**) is shown either with a narrow drip-mould or a wider sub-sill. The purpose of these is to throw the water clear of the wall under. The width is therefore governed by the position of the window in the wall. By the nature of their function, drip-moulds, weather-moulds and sub-sills are greatly exposed to the weather and can with advantage be formed in a durable hardwood.

Lights are hinged to frames by means of cranked butts set into the rebate with the knuckle on the face. The closing joint on narrow lights, such as ventlights, must have an appreciable splay to give the necessary

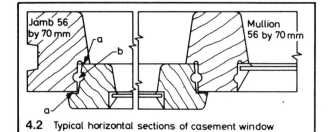

4.2 Typical horizontal sections of casement window

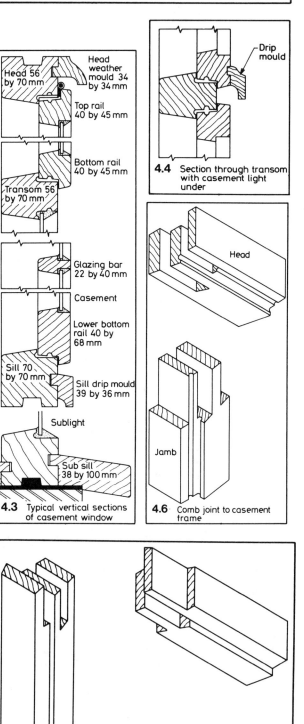

4.4 Section through transom with casement light under

4.3 Typical vertical sections of casement window

4.6 Comb joint to casement frame

4.5 Comb joint to casement light

clearance. The splay in the standard rebate section is sufficient to accommodate this.

Casements are framed up by means of a comb joint (**Fig. 4.5**). This may be carried out on the tenoning machine using a special set of cutters in place of the scribing block, or it can be done using a special jig on the spindle moulder. The joint is specially designed for glued assembly, because there are twice as many glued surfaces as with a single mortise and tenon. The joint is cramped up and then pinned with a wood or metal star dowel.

The frame may be constructed in the same way (**Fig. 4.6**) but, if it must be left with horns for building into the wall, the normal mortise and tenon joint becomes necessary. The transom must also be fitted in this way, as shown in **Fig. 4.7**.

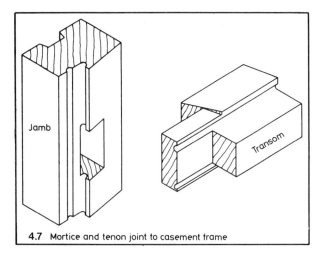

4.7 Mortice and tenon joint to casement frame

Double glazing

When it is necessary either to combat excessive condensation, reduce heat loss, or cut out noisy street sounds, insulation in the form of double-glazing or double windows become necessary. **Fig. 4.8** shows the method where the window is double glazed *in situ*. The outer glass is puttied in in the usual way, but the inner pane is beaded in with removable beads incorporating a tape sealant. Breather holes are drilled in the bottom rail or sill at the rate of one 6mm hole per 0.5m² of glass area.

Some explanation would not be out of place here. The capacity of the air to carry water vapour depends upon its temperature. Its humidity, which is a measure of this capacity, is the percentage of water vapour which it will carry at the time. If the volume of air is 100 per cent humid, it cannot carry any more vapour but if, without any other changes, the temperature is raised 'X' degrees (values are not important), the humidity will drop to 80 per cent. This is because it is now capable of carrying more water vapour. If, however, the temperature is lowered 'X' degrees, there will be an excess of water vapour. This will be expelled on to the cold surface which is causing the temperature drop, in the form of condensation.

With double glazing, the air between the two panes insulates the inner one and reduces this temperature drop. It also reduces, or eliminates, the condensation taking place. However, as timber is a porous material, it cannot be separately glazed to form a permanently

sealed pocket. Air and water vapour will tend to seep in, encouraged by the suction created by the cooling of the air in the cavity.

However, in the winter when condensation is most likely to occur, the temperature of the outer air will be lower than that of either pane of glass or of the air-pocket enclosed. If this air pocket is sealed off as well as is possible from the inner air, but given access by means of breather holes to the outer air, its humidity will tend to level up with that of the outer air. However, as the air pocket will be warmer, condensation cannot take place.

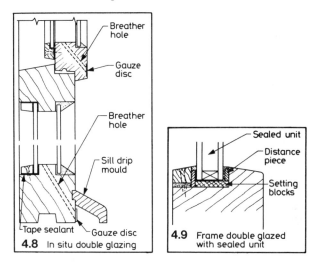

4.8 In situ double glazing

4.9 Frame double glazed with sealed unit

To ensure against the accident of special climatic variations, the beads to the inner pane should be removable. To prevent the entry of dust, insects, etc, the breather holes should be covered on the outside with gauze or protected in some other way.

Fig. 4.9 is the section through a sill of a window with sealed units. The cavity between the panes is filled with dehydrated air, which is sealed all round the edges of the panes with continuous spacers plus an overlapping foil tape. The unit should be treated with the utmost care prior to glazing to protect the seal. It should rest in a special wide rebate on plastic setting blocks one quarter of its length from each end. The thickness of the putty or setting compound should be maintained by other plastic distance pieces, one pair opposite each fixing screw in the bead, as shown.

For maximum efficiency in insulation, the spacing of the panes of glass is critical to the following limits:

THERMAL INSULATION: Efficiency increases up to a spacing of 20mm, beyond which there is no improvement. This is because above this width a circulating current of air is set up by the differing temperatures of the inner and outer glazing, which cancels out the reduction in straight conduction.

SOUND INSULATION: The ideal spacing of panes is about 250mm. Under the impact of sound, a pane of glass tends to act as a vibrating diaphragm with a definite resonance or wave length. A second pane of the same overall dimensions and thickness will have the same resonance and will vibrate in sympathy. Varying the thicknesses of the two panes in the window will eliminate this.

In order to get the wide spacing between the panes, it is generally more convenient to have double windows: say an outer casement window opening outward and an inner one opening inward. The alternative is to have sliding sashes on the inside. For maximum efficiency, the windows should also be isolated from each other, and from the structure, by interposing soft materials such as insulating boards.

Inward opening casements

In situations exposed to high winds, casements can be made to open inwards. These also have the advantage that they can be cleaned from the inside. The disadvantages are that they are difficult to make watertight at sill level and may foul curtains when opening.

Fig. 4.10 shows the elevation and **Fig. 4.11** the plan in simple outline of an inward opening window with two casements. These are hinged to close together in lieu of providing a centre mullion. The principles used in this construction can be applied to French casement doors. **Fig. 4.12** is the vertical and **Fig. 4.13** the horizontal section through the framing.

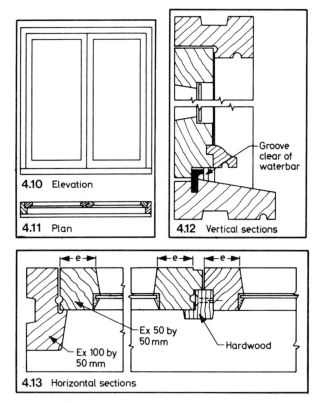

4.10   Elevation

4.11   Plan

4.12   Vertical sections

Groove clear of waterbar

Ex 50 by 50 mm

Ex 100 by 50 mm

Hardwood

4.13   Horizontal sections

From **Fig. 4.12** it will be seen that the rebates protect the head of the window against the weather, but special treatment is needed at the sill. A metal weather-bar is shown grooved into the sill and the bottom rail is rebated to close over it. Additional protection is given by a throated weather-mould tongued into the rail. It is important that the throating in the jamb should come in front of the weather-bar, otherwise it will carry the water down behind the bar.

The rebate between the meeting stiles of the casements needs some additional protection against the weather to which it is likely to be very much exposed. The simplest method is to nail a cover mould over the joint. In my opinion, this is not sufficiently robust: the

modification given in **Fig. 4.13** provides solid construction capable of withstanding physical misuse as well as stresses imposed by the weather.

PIVOTING SASHES

Pivot-hung sashes

An alternative method of providing opening lights is by means of pivot-hung sashes. These are balanced horizontally about centre pivots, are easy to operate and are suitable for large sashes or for high windows which have to be operated by cords or rod opening gear.

Fig. 4.14 shows the elevation, **Fig. 4.15** the plan, and **Fig. 4.16** the vertical section with basic details of construction. The top of the sash opens inward. The pivot should be about 25mm above centre in height so that the window tends to close by gravity. The window is weather-proofed at the head and jambs by means of beads, separated near the pivots. The beads above the pivot are nailed to the sash on the inside and the frame on the outside; those below are nailed to the sash on the outside and the frame on the inside.

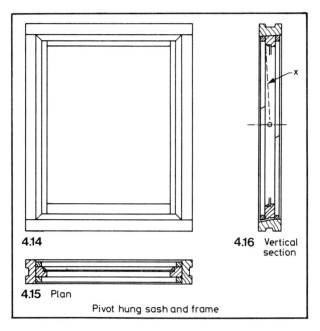

4.14

4.16   Vertical section

4.15   Plan

Pivot hung sash and frame

The cuts or joints in the beads must be arranged so that the beads nailed to the sash swing clear of the cut ends of those nailed to the frame. The top rail and the head to receive it must be given a splay for opening clearance (see **Figs. 4.16** and **4.17**). This splay is pronounced, being accentuated by the short radius of the swing. The normal weathering to the sill will, itself, provide sufficient opening clearance at the bottom. Note that there is no outer bead to the bottom of the window, because this tends to form a rain trap.

The usual type of fitting for pivoting the sash is sketched in **Fig. 4.18**. The plate with the pivot is fixed to the frame and the socket plate to the sash. Note that there is a shoulder to the pin which keeps the sash clear in the opening when both plates are housed in flush.

If it is required to be able to move the sash from the frame (see **Fig. 4.19**), then the cuts in the beads must

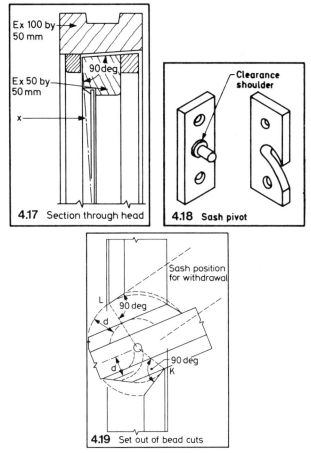

4.17 Section through head

4.18 Sash pivot

4.19 Set out of bead cuts

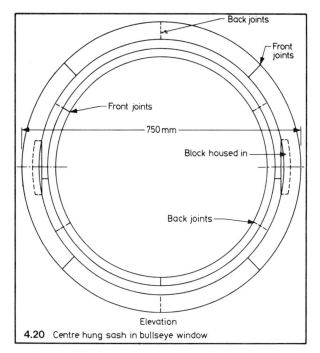

4.20 Centre hung sash in bullseye window

be arranged so that the sash may be lifted back and up a distance square to its face, which is equal to half the thickness of the sash plus half the diameter of the pin.

The complete set-out of the joint is as follows:

1. Mark the centre of the pin on the jamb width and draw a circle of diameter equal to the width of the sash over the beads.
2. Tangent to this circle draw a line at the angle to which the sash is required to open.
3. From the point **K**, where this cuts the bead, join back to the centre. Then the joint in the inner bead will be square to this.
4. Increase this radius by the distance **d** and draw a curve cutting the top bead at **L**.
5. Join back to the centre and draw the cut in the outer bead square to this.

If the sash is lifted at an angle square to and meeting this cut, it may be withdrawn. The space between the upper and lower beads on the frame does show a clear way through the joint with the risk of entry of rain in exposed positions.

Bulls-eye windows

Figs. 4.20 to **4.23** illustrate the construction of a circular or bulls-eye window with a pivot-hung sash. The frame and sash can be built up in one of several different ways. In the example given, each is assembled from two thicknesses of ribs to break joint midway. They are put together with screws, which are sunk below the surface and pelleted. The inner width of the frame must be flattened around the pivot area to permit free movement, as shown in **Fig. 4.20**.

This is best achieved by housing a block into the curved surface, as shown in **Fig. 4.21**, with curved rebates on the outsides. These fit the frame so that they come level with and continue the outer bead surfaces.

The opening clearance level at the upper and lower extremities of the sash, indicated in the section **Fig. 4.22** is reduced to nil at the sides. The outline for this is obtained geometrically by taking the original radius of the sash but lowering the centre by the distance **W** on the outside and drawing another curve for the easing on the top of the sash. Raise the centre by the same amount for the easing at the bottom of the sash on the inside (see **Fig. 4.23**). The cuts into the beads are similar to those on the previous example, but no provision can be made for lifting. If the same type of pivot is used, the outer top bead will have to be removed to enable the sash to be withdrawn.

Alternatively, another type of pivot is available consisting of a hollow socket with an outer thread.

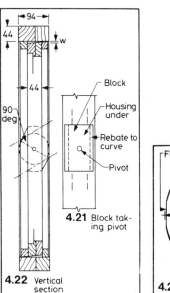

4.21 Block taking pivot

4.22 Vertical section

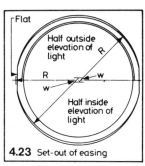

4.23 Set-out of easing

This enables it to be screwed into a hole prepared in the frame, the pivot being screwed through a similar socket in the sash to engage its centre-hole. The pivot is inserted or withdrawn from the inside sight-line of the sash.

A double-glazed pivot-hung sash

Another type of pivot-hung sash window, incorporating double glazing, is illustrated in **Figs. 4.24** to **4.31**. It is made with varied modifications under different

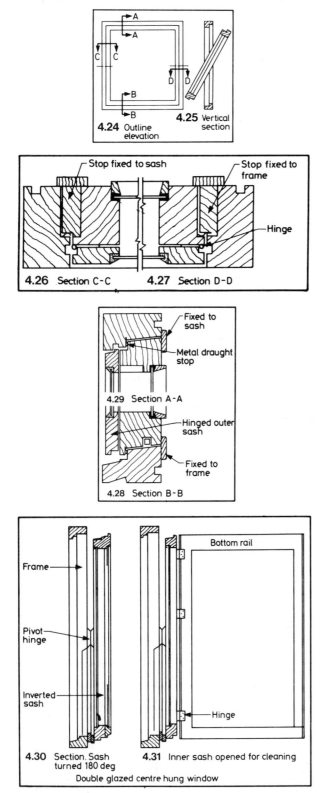

4.24 Outline elevation

4.25 Vertical section

Stop fixed to sash   Stop fixed to frame

Hinge

4.26 Section C-C   **4.27** Section D-D

Fixed to sash

Metal draught stop

4.29 Section A-A

Hinged outer sash

Fixed to frame

4.28 Section B-B

Frame

Pivot hinge

Inverted sash

Bottom rail

Hinge

4.30 Section. Sash turned 180 deg   **4.31** Inner sash opened for cleaning

Double glazed centre hung window

patents. A thin glazed frame is hinged to the side or top of the main sash to provide the insulating cavity. The movement, on a compound action pivot hinge, causes the sash and its satellite to travel downwards and inwards through an angle of 180 degrees to finish upside down and clear of the frame on the inside. Then the outer (now inner) sash can be hinged open for the purpose of cleaning (see **Figs. 4.30** and **4.31**). Reference to **Fig. 4.24** will show where the sections in **Figs. 4.26** to **4.29** are taken from.

It will be seen that the glazing of the sash is fully sealed from the room atmosphere. However the joint between the two sashes allows some ventilation from the outside air. From a general study of all the sections, it will be seen that, instead of beads as before, stops are fitted in rebates which coincide in the sash and frame. The stops are fitted to the sash above the pivot and to the frame below the pivot; thus the lower part of the sash, being free from projection stops, is able to move through the top of the opening in the frame (which is also free from stops) to complete the reversing movement.

The same principle is used, but with a swing of under 90 degrees, for single-glazed windows. The hinge in this case is a simple back flap at the inside pivot level.

BAY WINDOWS

The construction of bay windows is similar to that of the normal casement. The only additional work is in

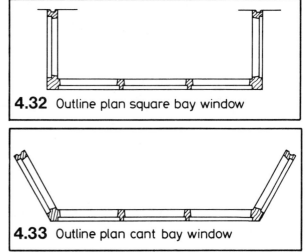

4.32 Outline plan square bay window

4.33 Outline plan cant bay window

the construction and assembly at the corner posts. Basically bay windows are of two types: either square bays (**Fig. 4.32**) or cant bays (**Fig. 4.33**). Elaborations of these types differ more in outline than in the principle of construction.

The corner posts may be formed from two jambs, which are mitred together as shown in section in **Figs. 4.34** and **4.35**. In this case, there is no problem in jointing, as the jambs may be simply tenoned or comb-jointed into the heads. The mitred frames are fitted together after assembly.

Some economy may be achieved by cutting these from planks as shown in **Fig. 4.36**. When corner posts are each in one solid piece, comb joints cannot be used. Then assembly is usually by means of L-section tenons into the head and sills as shown in **Fig. 4.37**. If the sills are narrow, with sub-sills or drip-moulds, jointing is no problem. If they project 75mm or more where the window is set back, they must be separately jointed.

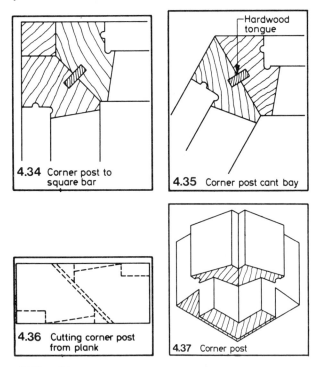

4.34 Corner post to square bar

4.35 Corner post cant bay

4.36 Cutting corner post from plank

4.37 Corner post

Wide sills

The problem with wide sills is that they are exposed to the extremes of seasonal changes. During the summer they will shrink and the mitre joints will close tight; but during the winter they swell which causes the mitres to open and let in the wet. Filling the mitres when open only makes the siutation worse in the next dry spell.

However, timber, being composed of cells which

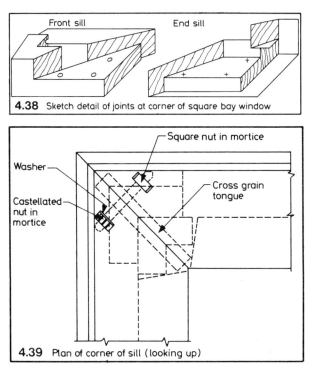

4.38 Sketch detail of joints at corner of square bay window

4.39 Plan of corner of sill (looking up)

Square nut in mortice

Washer

Cross grain tongue

Castellated nut in mortice

can be crushed under pressure, can have its movement controlled if the restraint is sufficiently rigid. **Fig. 4.38**, drawn in oblique projection, illustrates a halved mitre joint to a sill. If this is put together with a powerful gap-filling adhesive (say resorcinal formaldehyde), this should restrain it against any moisture movement.

Fig. 4.39 shows the sill assembled with a handrail bolt; a cross-grain hardwood tongue has been inserted at a convenient level to maintain the alignment. Its position should be far enough out to have the maximum control over the mitre, but it should also be long enough to ensure that the timber does not shear.

DOUBLE-HUNG SASH WINDOWS

Double-hung sash windows are those in which the lights, termed 'sashes', slide vertically (one behind the other) to open and provide ventilation. Although they have been largely replaced in domestic work by hinged or pivoted casement windows, they are (when properly made) draughtproof, offer complete resistance to wind, open or closed, and may be adjusted to provide closely controlled ventilation at both top and bottom levels. When properly maintained, they are easily operated even in strong winds. They are therefore eminently suitable for large windows in offices and public buildings in exposed positions.

Fig. 4.40 is an elevation of a typical sash window. In the interests of weather protection, the outer sash must be at the top in the closed position. In order that each sash may be left in any vertical position, and for ease of operation, the weight of the sash must be exactly counterbalanced by either a system of springs acting upwards, or by weights hanging from cords or

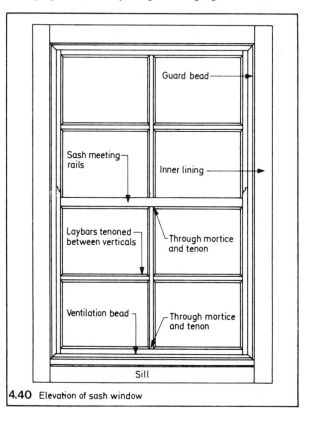

Guard bead

Sash meeting rails

Inner lining

Laybars tenoned between verticals

Through mortice and tenon

Ventilation bead

Through mortice and tenon

Sill

4.40 Elevation of sash window

chains. These pass over pulleys and are attached to the sash stiles. As the method of suspension or support governs the design of the enclosing frame, these systems will be dealt with separately.

Spring balance double-hung sashes

Fig. 4.41 shows a 'unique' spiral balance, the top end being attached to the window frame and the bottom to the sliding sash. As the sash is lowered, the spiral rod is withdrawn from its casing under tension. The spiral rod is threaded through a nylon bush attached to a torsion spring. The tension on the spring is increased by the rotation of the bush around the spiral as the sash is lowered. The effect of this is to create a lifting force on the spiral.

To prevent the unwanted progressive extra tension, which would be produced by this lift, the spiral is made with a uniformly increasing pitch, thus giving an unvarying lift throughout the full height of travel.

When ordering the balances, it is necessary to state the height of each sash and its weight when glazed. Three types of balance are available, to take weights up to 13kg, 20kg and 45kg respectively. The heavier types have a different appearance; the spiral rod is enclosed within the torsion springs.

Fig. 4.42 shows a typical section through one jamb of a window designed to take spiral balances. In this case, the jambs, formed from ex 50mm thick timber, are recessed to take the balances. In the closed position, only one sash could be seen in any horizontal section. The sashes are separated by a 9mm parting bead. The channels in which the sashes slide, are formed by an outer lining, extending beyond the face of the pulley 'stile' (or jamb) to the outer sash and by a guard bead for the inner one. In order to gain access to the sashes and balances at any time, the parting bead is made a dry, hand-tight fit into its groove. The guard bead is secured with small pins or cup screws.

The guard bead is shown fitted into a shallow rebate. Although this is not always done, it does have the advantage of positive repositioning when the beads have to be removed at any time. Also, as the bead is a little thicker, it will need fewer fixings.

Fig. 4.43 shows an alternative arrangement in which the balances fit into recesses in the sash stiles.

This has the effect of shortening the effective length of the tenons in the sashes, although this can be countered by increasing stile widths. It also helps to avoid unwanted water traps.

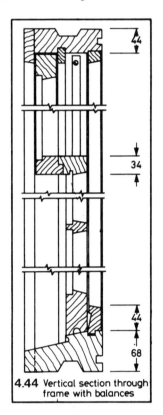

4.44 Vertical section through frame with balances

Fig. 4.44 is a vertical section through the window. The meeting rails between upper and lower sashes are in alignment and should be midway in the sight height of the window if both panes are to be the same size. The rails meet with a slightly splayed rebated joint. This joint must be made correctly to allow for sash movement.

The purpose of the rebate, apart from providing a draught stop, is to prevent a knife being slipped up from the outside to open the sash fastener. The meeting rails are as thin as stability will allow, to permit the maximum of glassed area.

It will be noticed that the glass fits into a groove in the meeting rail of the lower sash. The greatest strain likely to be put on the meeting rails is when force is applied either to lower the outer sash or to raise the inner one. Where any vertical glazing bars are used, these should be taken through to the full height of the sash and the lay bars should be stub-tenoned between them. The vertical bars should then be through-tenoned to the rails and wedged. In this way, they will provide extra support to the meeting rails.

The grooves or recesses in the pulley stiles or sash stiles (as the case may be) should be 16 by 18mm, 19 by 21mm and 26 by 27mm respectively for the three different types of balance. In order that they should not unduly weaken the stile, it may be advisable to increase the section.

Leaflets giving detailed instructions for fixing the spiral balances are given by the manufacturers, but briefly they are as follows:

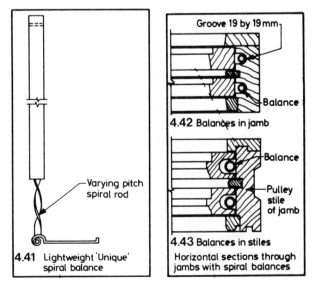

Groove 19 by 19 mm

— Balance

4.42 Balances in jamb

— Balance

— Pulley stile of jamb

4.43 Balances in stiles

Horizontal sections through jambs with spiral balances

— Varying pitch spiral rod

4.41 Lightweight 'Unique' spiral balance

1. Place the sash in position resting on the sill. Insert the balance in the groove fixing the top to the pulley stile with the drive screw provided. Do this on both sides of course.

2. Lift the sash to the top and prop it up.

3. For the lightweight balance (**Fig. 4.41**), twist the spiral by means of the bracket about five times anti-clockwise. Then attach it lightly to the bottom rail or meeting rail as the case may be. Do this to both balances and check that they do hold the sash up; if so fix securely. The balances should not be over tensioned.

4. The heavier types of balance are inserted into the grooves as before but the brackets are fixed right away. The sash is then lowered clear of the end of the spiral rod and the tension is put on against a ratchet by means of a screwdriver in the empty slot (**Fig. 4.45**).

Where the top sash has horns standing below the meeting rail, a steel channel is screwed to the sash stile and the bracket is inserted into this (**Figs. 4.46 and 4.47**).

It is necessary to fit stops to limit the travel of the sashes at the top and bottom of each jamb. Otherwise damage may occur to the mechanism. In **Fig. 4.45**, a 38mm stop is shown screwed to the jamb to limit the travel of the inner sash at the top. A 108mm stop is screwed to the jamb at the bottom to limit the downward travel of the outer sash. To get the maximum amount of ventilation, it is therefore necessary to lift the inner sash 108mm off the sill.

An alternative type of suspension for vertically sliding sashes is the 'Beclawat' steel tape spring sash balance (**Fig. 4.48**). It consists of a coiled rustless steel tape wound on a spring-loaded steel drum in a square box. This is fixed flush to the jamb with a clip attached to the sash stile.

It is ordered to the correct loading required, but some adjustment is possible with a key fitted into a square recess in the spindle (**Fig. 4.48**). It is probably more suited to such items as serving hatches which need to be either fully opened or fully closed.

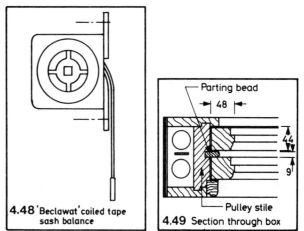

4.48 'Beclawat' coiled tape sash balance

4.49 Section through box

Parting bead · 48 · 44 · 9 · Pulley stile

WEIGHT AND PULLEY VERTICAL SASHES

The traditional method of counterbalancing sashes is by use of weights and pulleys. This is still considered to be the best method for windows with sashes of an area of 1.85 sq. m or over; but it involves the providing of hollow jambs, or 'casings', to receive the weights (**Fig. 4.49**). These consist of pulley stiles, 28mm minimum thickness, between which the sashes slide. They are boxed out by inner and outer linings to form the hollow casings within which the weights are suspended. The vertical section is shown in **Fig. 4.50**.

The casings are closed by back linings, usually of exterior grade plywood nailed in position. The inner and outer linings may be straight nailed to the pulley stiles but, in better jobs, a tongued and grooved joint is formed.

The sashes are separated by parting beads which are dry grooved into the pulley stiles. The weights are separated by a parting slip which is slotted through the extended pulley head with a dowel or nail driven through the end to rest over the slot. The slip then hangs free.

The pulley stiles are housed into, and nailed through, the pulley head, and then housed and wedged into the sill (**Fig. 4.51**).

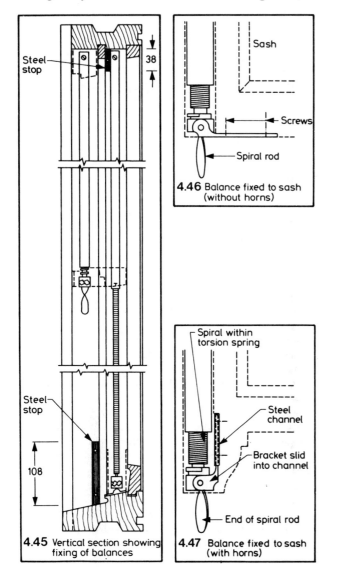

Steel stop — 38

Sash

Screws

Spiral rod

4.46 Balance fixed to sash (without horns)

Steel stop — 108

Spiral within torsion spring

Steel channel

Bracket slid into channel

End of spiral rod

4.45 Vertical section showing fixing of balances

4.47 Balance fixed to sash (with horns)

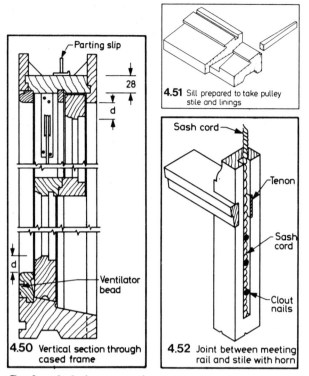

4.51 Sill prepared to take pulley stile and linings

4.50 Vertical section through cased frame

4.52 Joint between meeting rail and stile with horn

Cord and chain suspension

The cords or chains from which the sash weights are suspended, pass over sash pulleys in the stiles and are fixed to the sash stiles. **Fig. 4.52** shows the simpler method of attaching cords using clout nails, while **Fig. 4.53** shows the method using knots. A figure-of-eight knot, tied as shown in **Fig. 4.54**, gives the necessary bulk to prevent it slipping through the eye. The same knot is used to fix the cord to the cast-iron weights.

When chains are used, these may be attached to the weights and sashes in various ways. **Fig. 4.55** shows one way. The chain is attached to the weight by means of a split pin behind a washer. It is then attached to the sash stile by means of a metal bar slotted across the recess and secured with staples.

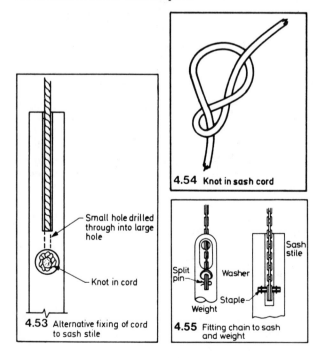

4.54 Knot in sash cord

4.53 Alternative fixing of cord to sash stile

4.55 Fitting chain to sash and weight

Access to the pulley boxes

In order to gain access to the boxes to hang the weights, and for future repair work, a pocket piece is cut out in the pulley stile as shown in **Fig. 4.56**. The cuts across the grain are made as far as possible with a dovetail saw and completed with a broad very thin 'pocket chisel' which is sharpened both sides. If the wood is damped, it will tend to recover from the slight crushing received and close up the joint.

Alternatively, holes of about 9mm diameter may be drilled from the back of the pulley stile in as far as the housing for the parting bead to provide clearance for the toe of the dovetail saw. The longitudinal cut down the centre of the parting bead groove may be done on the circular saw, with a hand-reciprocating saw or with a simple pad saw. A tap with a hammer will then split the fibres between the cuts and release the pocket piece.

If two oval wire nails are inserted in the cut as shown in **Fig. 4.57**, this will lift the splayed end and close the thin gap made by the dovetail saw; the slight projection is planed off. The pocket piece only then needs to be fixed at the bottom with one screw.

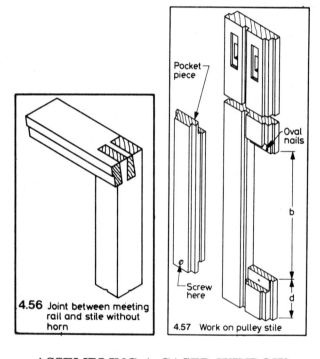

4.56 Joint between meeting rail and stile without horn

4.57 Work on pulley stile

ASSEMBLING A CASED WINDOW FRAME

The procedure for assembling a cased window-frame is as follows.

The pulley stiles are inserted and wedged (with waterproof glue) into the sills. They are aligned with the sill and sighted through 'out-of-wind' with each other. A slight twist in the sill would provide cause for some adjustment here.

The pulley head, which is housed for the pulley stiles, should then be nailed and glued. The frame is laid inner face down, on two out-of-wind bearers fixed to the bench. It is squared up with a squaring rod and kept in that condition by blocks nailed to the bearers. The outer linings are then nailed in position.

The joints between head and jamb lining should be made with tongued or rebated joints. The frame is then turned over, checked again for square, and the inner linings are attached. If tongues are formed on the pulley stiles, they should be cut off the pocket pieces. Care must be taken that these are not nailed through the linings. Blocks cut between the linings over the pulley stiles will support the joints in the linings and provide a means of wedging the window frame down when fixing.

Calculating weights for sashes

Sash weights may be either lead or cast-iron. Although the latter is much cheaper, it may be necessary to use lead for heavy sashes, particularly when the sash width is greater than its height and the convenient length permissible in the weight is thus limited. The formula for calculating the length of cast-iron weights is:

$$L = \frac{145,857\,Z}{WB}$$

For lead weights, it is:

$$L = \frac{92,494\,Z}{WB}$$

Z = known weight of sashweight in kg
W = sectional width of weight in mm
B = sectional breadth of weight in mm

Where round weights are used, substitute 0.7854 d^2 (d = diameter) for WB which is really the cross-sectional area of the weight.

To obtain the minimum sectional dimensions of casings and pulley sizes for large windows, starting with the minimum sizes for robust construction – thicknesses of, say, 22mm or more for linings; 38 to 50mm for pulley stiles; and 60 by 70mm for sash stiles – it is first of all necessary to obtain the dimensions of the weights being used. The cross-sectional area must be such that the length is not excessive.

Calculating glass thicknesses

Thickness of glass in relation to its surface area and degree of exposure to wind is dealt with, in detail, in the British Standard CP152. For example, take a sash window measuring 1.5 by 1.7m overall. The thickness of glass is 4.5mm, weighing 11kg/m²; and it has wood sashes with 70 by 60mm stiles, weighing 570kg/m³. This calculation is to approximate values; it is safer to weigh the glazed sash when actually ordering weights.

Area of glass = 1.38 × 1.58 × weight =

1.38 × 1.58 × 11kg = 24kg

Volume of timber (averaging thin meeting rail and stout bottom rail) =

2(1.7 + 1.36) 0.06 × 0.07 = 0.0257m³.

Therefore weight = 0.0257 × 570 = 14.6 9kg = about 15kg.

Therefore total weight of sash = 24 + 15 = 39kg. Each weight must therefore be 19.5kg.

As the sashes and the spaces in the box behind them are only 60mm wide or thick, the weight cross-

section is practically limited to 50 by 50mm. If cast-iron weights are used, their individual length =

$$\frac{145,857 \times 19.5}{50 \times 50} = 1138\text{mm}$$

This length would be awkward to get into the sash pocket unless this was made very long. Therefore it would be better either to increase the thickness of the sashes giving more room in the box for larger weights or to use lead weights. Length of lead weight =

$$\frac{92,492 \times 19.5}{50 \times 50} = 722\text{mm}$$

which should be satisfactory.

Referring to **Fig. 4.58**, it will now be seen that the minimum safe diameter of the pulley will be 70mm and the inside width of the jamb casing will have to be about 70mm to allow for the insertion and free running of the weights. The inner lining must be at least 70 + 38 = 108mm and the outer ones about 124mm wide. The precise length of each weight will only be known when the sashes are weighed after glazing. The weights of the lower sash should be 0.5kg lighter than the sash so that its own weight tends to keep it closed. Those of the upper sash should be 0.5kg heavier so that the pulley weights keep it closed.

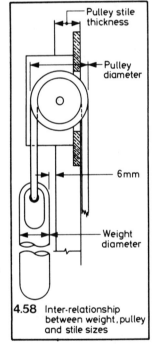

4.58 Inter-relationship between weight, pulley and stile sizes

The construction of the sashes requires some consideration. The top and bottom rails are tenoned to the stiles with frankings, instead of haunchings; but the joint between the meeting rail and the stile depends upon whether it finishes flush with the stile or whether the stile is left with a joggle or horn. The extension of the stile as a horn enables a stronger joint to be made (**Fig. 4.52**). Note that where the rebated rail extends over the stile, it is housed into the face, thus making a stronger job and avoiding a feather edge. Where no horn is left on, a dovetail joint should be used as in **Fig. 4.57**. The cord groove is omitted to enable the joint to be shown more plainly. Without the horns the windows can be opened to their fullest extent, both up and down.

THREE-LIGHT WINDOWS

Where there is a three-light window with only the central area opening, the boxed mullions necessary to contain the sashes do obstruct some light and tend to look clumsy. This can be avoided by taking the sash cords or chains over the tops of the fixed side lights into casings at the jambs leaving the width of the mullions the thickness of the pulley stiles plus the cover of the linings on either side.

There are two methods of doing this. One is to take the cords through holes in the pulley heads over inverted pulleys fixed to the heads and down to weights in the jamb casing as in **Fig. 4.59**. In this case, the inner head lining must be removable in order to give access to the pulleys when replacing cords.

In the second method the pulleys are fixed to the pulley stile in the normal way but are kept as high as possible. The cords are taken over them to the jamb casings as before (**Fig. 4.60**). Grooves are formed in the top rails of the fixed top sashes to take the outer cords and a cover mould, mitring up with the guard beads, is used to conceal the inner cord (**Fig. 4.61**). Both the fixed sash and the cover board must be removable to give access for replacing cords.

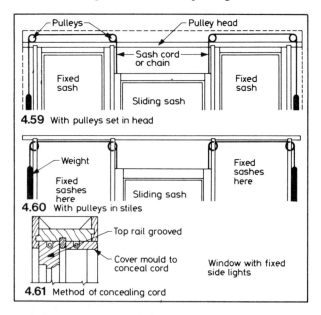

4.59 With pulleys set in head

4.60 With pulleys in stiles

4.61 Method of concealing cord

Window with fixed side lights

Double-cased mullions

Where a window is formed with two or more sets of sliding sashes, the mullions will normally be double cased as shown in section in **Fig. 4.62**. To reduce the width of this box, where sashes on either side are of the same weight, a single sash weight may be used with a pulley attached so that it acts for both sashes (**Fig. 4.63**). Its weight will have to be doubled so that it will almost certainly be of lead.

If the section of the weight must be increased still more to provide the necessary load, this will mean an increase in the thickness of both the sash stiles and the linings to the boxed mullion. The pulley on the sash weight should be of a size to allow the cords to hang straight or tension on them will be increased at the top of the weight lift.

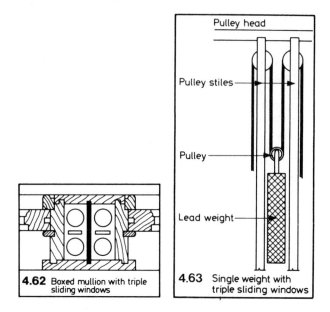

4.62 Boxed mullion with triple sliding windows

4.63 Single weight with triple sliding windows

SHAPED WINDOW HEADS

When the construction of shaped window heads has to be considered, this may be carried out in a number of different ways. **Figs. 4.64** to **4.68** relate to a semi-circular headed sash window. The left-hand side of **Fig. 4.64** shows half of the head with the inner lining removed. **Fig. 4.65** is a vertical section on the centre-line, while **Fig. 4.67** shows a sketch in oblique projection giving details of construction.

These drawings show one method of forming the curved pulley head. It is built up in three layers, the centre layer being the parting bead, which is permanent down to the springing. The ribs are butt-jointed to break joint, providing good laps with each other and with the parting bead. The curved linings are tongued to each other, glued and nailed to the head and glue blocked as shown, using moisture resistant glue.

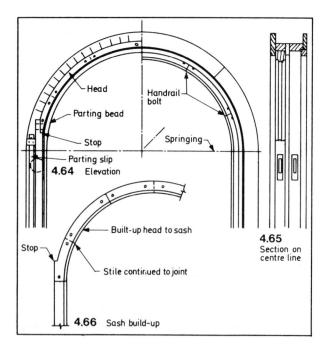

4.64 Elevation

4.65 Section on centre line

4.66 Sash build-up

The pulley stile is continued beyond the springing and the curved soffit is cut sufficiently short to form a solid stop to the sash. The stile of the sash is continued beyond the springing (**Fig. 4.66**); this avoids any impact on the curved head of the sash, which risks breaking the glass. It will be seen that the pulley stile is recessed to take the head which is screwed and glued to it. A slotted block, screwed to the pulley stile carries the parting slip.

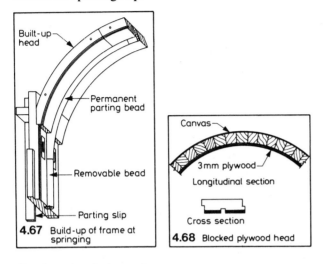

4.67 Build-up of frame at springing

4.68 Blocked plywood head

Head made of plywood

An alternative method of forming the head is by means of thin plywood bent around a former and backed by staves fitted and glued to the plywood and to each other. The former must be wide enough to allow screws to be driven through the staves into it, above and below the plywood band, in order to secure them while the glue sets (**Fig. 4.68**).

The timber for the staves should be machined to the correct section in one or two long lengths, cut off to the necessary extended short sections and drilled for the screws. Little fitting should then be needed. Canvas should be glued to the back of the finished member to seal the surface and limit distortion from unequal shrinkage.

The head should be fixed as soon as possible after construction. As the inner and outer linings will have to be fitted against the end grain of the staves, the head should be tongued to the linings. The tongues can easily be formed on the spindle, but the grooves in the linings will have to be done with a router. Use either the fixed machine or the powered hand tool using the standard cylindrical cutter which cuts on its end and side. The parting bead will be grooved into the head, not built in as before.

Head made of laminated veneers

A third method of constructing the head is by laminating with veneers built up to the required thickness. The maximum thickness of each laminate is dependent upon the type of timber used, but generally is not more than radius ÷ 100. It will have to be clamped around a former.

The head of the top sash may be built up in two layers. The joint in thickness may conveniently go on the rebate line, but the fixing screws must be sunk and pelleted. In this case, the timber in the stile continues

to the first joint: i.e. a halving is formed to fit into the built-up head. See **Fig. 4.68**.

Alternatively, the ribs forming the head may be of the full thickness butt-jointed and handrail-bolted together with two dowels in each joint to give rigidity. The timber in the stiles should again be continued above the springing.

INSTALLING WINDOWS ON SITE

Work on site comprises the fixing of the windows in the brick opening. The jambs should be recessed deep enough to contain most of the width of the casing. The frame is secured by wedging it against the sill with folding wedges and down against the pulley stiles.

Attaching sash cords or chains

The sash cords or chains also have to be attached to the weights, taken over the pulleys and fixed to the sashes. The procedure is to take one continuous length or hank of cord plus a length of thin twine with a strip of lead (called a 'mouse'), or short chain. Knot the mouse to the twine which, in turn, is tied to the cord. The mouse is dropped into the casing over each pulley in turn and pulled out through the pocket, the cord following. The routine is:

1. Over inside left pulley out through pocket.
2. Over inside right pulley, out through pocket.
3. Over outside left pulley, out through pocket.
4. Over outside right pulley, out through pocket.

A weight is then attached to the end of the cord, inserted in the relative (outside right) recess through the pocket and pulled up to the pulley. The cord is temporarily nailed to the pulley stile and cut to length. Another weight is then attached to the cut end and the procedure repeated in the reverse order of threading.

The guard bead and parting bead are removed and the sashes are secured to the ends of the cords, outer sash first. Then the parting bead and guard bead are inserted in the necessary order, to keep the sashes in position. The sliding clearance on sashes should be about 3mm each way to allow for three coats of paint on all contact surfaces. However, if the pulley stiles are of a durable hardwood such as teak, they should not need painting.

Sash cords are obtainable in diameters of up to 9mm, requiring 75mm pulleys, to take loads of up to 25kg. Chains, with their relevant pulleys, may be obtained to carry loads of up to 90kg.

There are various proprietary makes of sash fasteners but all are attached to the meeting rails and, in effect, lock them together. Heavy sashes will require sash lifts fixed to the bottom rail of the lower sash. These are sometimes also attached to the underside of the meeting rail of the upper sash.

ROOFLIGHTS

Lights fitted to either flat or pitched roofs need special consideration beyond that given to windows built into walls of buildings for four main reasons. These are:

1. They are generally fully exposed to the weather, wind and rain, not being protected by any adjoining buildings.

2. When pitched (as they usually are), they have to resist the penetration of water flowing over them, whether wind-driven or in a steady downpour.

3. Their high position leaves them exposed to the cold air on the outside and warm air of maximum humidity on the inside. As the insulating properties of the glass are low, excessive condensation on the underside of the glass is unavoidable and must be dealt with.

4. Special provisions must be made to ensure water-proof joints between the broken roof covering and the light by setting it above the roof plane and by providing suitable gutters and flashing.

Skylights

The simplest type of roof light with which the joiner is concerned is the skylight. A skylight basically consists of a glazed light or sash fitted to a curb which keeps it above the roof. It is usually associated with pitched roofs but may also be fixed to a flat roof.

Fig. 4.69 shows a vertical section parallel to the rafters, while **Fig. 4.71** is the cross-section normal to the roof pitch. An opening is formed with trimming, trimmer and trimmed rafters. The first two usually are 75mm thick, to take the resulting concentration of loads. A 38 to 50mm thick curb is then fitted into the opening. Lead, zinc or Nuralite gutters are formed at the back and to the sides of the curb, and flashings are taken out over the tiles at the lower end.

The width of the curb must be such that the sash is at least 100mm above the general roof surface and should extend down to the face of any plaster or boarding ceiling which lines the rafters. The width can be increased where the skylight is in an exposed position or is at the lower edge of a large roof with a build-up of water flowing down.

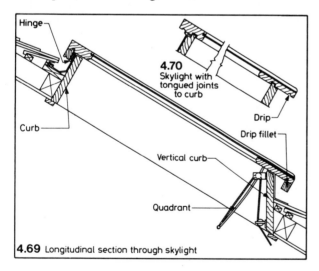

4.69 Longitudinal section through skylight

To give the maximum amount of light, the lower plane of the curb may be vertical, as in **Fig. 4.69**; although it is often left square to the pitch, as in **Fig. 4.70**. A drip is necessary to protect the joint between the curb and the sash. This is most effectively done with tongued timber fillets as shown in **Figs. 4.69** and

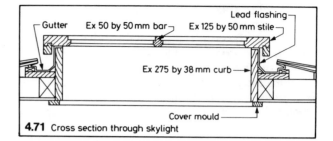

4.71 Cross section through skylight

4.71. The alternative of tongueing the curb into the sash, and checking the water with a drip-groove is shown in **Fig. 4.70**. The sash may be fixed or hinged to open as shown in **Figs. 4.69** and **4.70**.

Hinges and screws should be of brass or some other non-rusting material. Where there is a drip fillet, the hinges must be positioned as shown in **Fig. 4.69** to allow the sash to open.

The curb is jointed at the corners with either dovetail or tongue and groove joints. When making the dovetail joint, if a narrow whole pin, kept a little way in, is used, instead of the usual half-pin at the ends, this will help to hold the wide boards against possible cupping. Intermediate dovetails and pins can be the same size. These details are shown in **Fig. 4.72**. Note that the pitch of a dovetail should be related to the grain direction and not necessarily to the edge of the timber. This is emphasised in **Fig. 4.73**.

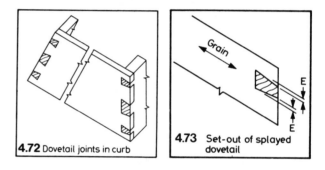

4.72 Dovetail joints in curb

4.73 Set-out of splayed dovetail

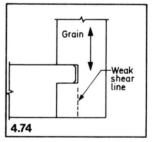

4.74

When the alternative tongued joint is used, a very weak shear plane will occur against the bottom of each groove because the groove will cut across the grain. The tongue should, therefore, be less than half the timber thickness, say one third (see **Fig. 4.74**).

Fig. 4.75 shows a sketch of the sash or light carried by the curb. It will be seen that the stiles and bars have good sized rebates to carry the glass which fits up into a groove in the top rail. To avoid a water trap, the glass must be taken out over the bottom rail or 'apron'; its thickness is accordingly reduced.

To dispose of the condensation already discussed, which forms on the underside of the glass, by leading it out on to the roof, there are two methods available.

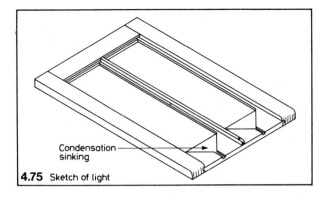

4.75 Sketch of light

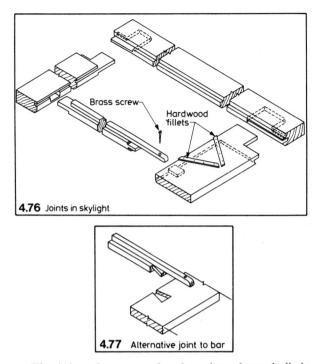

4.76 Joints in skylight

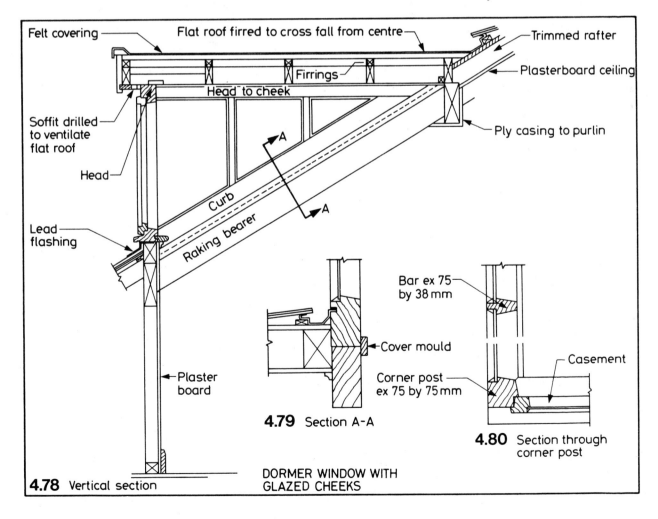

4.77 Alternative joint to bar

Either a Y-shaped recess is sunk in each bay, as in **Fig. 4.75**, or the thickness of the bottom rail is further reduced, thus leaving a narrow space under the glass. The glass is then given further intermediate support by narrow hardwood fillets secured by small brass pins or screws (see **Fig. 4.76**). The Y outline in each case enables the water to be channelled away while forming a check to the wind.

Fig. 4.76 also gives details of joints between various members. On small skylights, as shown, the bars are stub-tenoned to the top rails; but with very large ones with a number of bars, alternative tenons should be taken through and wedged. The bars may be stub-tenoned to the bottom rails (**Fig. 4.76**), or dovetailed as in **Fig. 4.77**. The top rail is tenoned to the stiles and the bottom rail is bareface tenoned.

The joints do not need to be taken through (it is perhaps better to protect the end grain of the tenons) but should be pinned with dowels. When assembling bareface tenon joints, they should not be cramped tight or the stiles will pull hollow on the top where there is no shoulder. The joint between the curb and

4.78 Vertical section

4.79 Section A-A

4.80 Section through corner post

DORMER WINDOW WITH GLAZED CHEEKS

plaster lining should be covered with a suitable band mould or fillet.

When skylights are fitted to a flat roof the sash should be given an additional fall to a minimum of about 20 degrees. The roof covering is turned up the curb and protected by flashing carried in under the sash. The curb may be very deep at the top and it may be advisable to frame it up with corner posts and rails covered with WBP plywood.

Dormer windows

When there is an attic or room in the roof with side walls formed to the room with timber studding or ashlering, the lighting and ventilation can be from a vertical window (known as a 'dormer') standing above the roof with triangular cheeks framed back to the sloping roof surface. When the cheeks are boarded and covered with felt, lead or tiles, the whole job becomes a piece of carpentry work built *in situ*. Then a suitable casement or sash window frame is inserted. If the cheeks also are glazed, then they are formed up with the dormer front into one and covered with a flat or pitched roof. Selected details of this construction are shown in **Figs. 4.78**, **4.79** and **4.80**.

The corner posts between the cheeks and the front window can be ex 75 by 75mm to 100 by 100mm according to the size of the dormer. A raking bearer stub-tenoned into the purlin and corner post, takes the weight of the cheek. This is formed with a head and raking bottom rail (or curb) deep enough to take the glass line well above the roof slope. These are tenoned together at the back end and also tenoned into the corner post.

In effect, the cheeks and front framing are assembled with the posts in the same way as for a bay window. One or more casements, with mullions as necessary, may be fitted into the front frame according to dormer length. The whole is covered with a flat or pitched roof taken back and weather-proofed to the main roof.

In **Fig. 4.78** a flat roof is shown. The joists are firred to give a cross-fall both ways from the centre. Short noggings resting on the front head, carry the outer joist. Battens are cut between these, that give a nailing to the plasterboard ceiling. **Fig. 4.79** is section A–A on **Fig. 4.78** indicating the method of finishing and weather-proofing the joint between the cheeks and roof. **Fig. 4.80** shows the junction between the cheeks and the front frame at the corner post. The glass to the cheeks is fitted direct to the framing because the mullions are strong enough to take the weight of the dormer roof.

It is advisable to ventilate the roof space over the dormer. Holes covered inside with gauze are drilled in the soffit at the overhang. Further holes can be drilled through the centre of each joist.

LANTERN LIGHTS

These are complete framed-up systems which can, in effect, be compared with the top half of a greenhouse. They are usually placed on a flat roof to give light and ventilation over a stairwell, the table in a billiard room, or anywhere in a large building where side lights are not available. **Fig. 4.81** shows the general appearance. There are four main constituents as follows:

1. A curb to lift the structure a safe distance above the main roof surface and clear of the water flow.
2. A low, vertical, glazed frame containing opening lights and of similar construction to a bay window.
3. The glazed roof to the light which may have either hipped or gable ends.
4. The internal finishings.

When the roof is of timber construction, with timber or steel binders (if large), the opening will be trimmed between the binders and the curb built directly off these binders and trimmers. The firring to the fall of the roof will have to be provided for. This may mean off-setting as in **Fig. 4.82**. The curb will have to be deep enough to lift the sill of the lantern at least 125mm above the roof surface. The roof covering will have to be dressed up the side of the curb and its edge covered by a flashing taken under the sill.

If the roof is of concrete (see **Fig. 4.83**), the curb is also likely to be of concrete which is cast with it. The

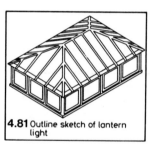

4.81 Outline sketch of lantern light

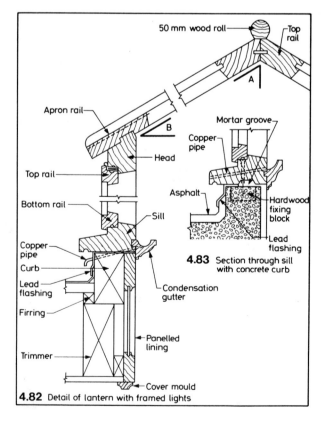

4.82 Detail of lantern with framed lights

4.83 Section through sill with concrete curb

asphalt covering must be taken up the side of the curb. The flashing may be taken under the sill as before, but the sill may be bedded in mortar. Some fixing to the concrete must be provided for before casting.

The vertical framing (**Fig. 4.82**) uses a typical bay window construction with casements. These may be either top-hung, as shown, or pivot-hung and are operated by rod or cord opening gear.

Excessive condensation, as previously described, is likely to occur with all side lights. All horizontal surfaces from the glass outwards should be weathered down to a condensation gutter tongued to the inside of the sill. The water collected is taken by means of a copper pipe into the outer air through the curb. According to the class of work specified, the inside of the well may be panelled, as in **Fig. 4.82**, or merely finished with plywood, chipboard or plasterboard lining. A concrete curb is likely to be plastered, as in **Fig. 4.83**.

The glazed roof of the lantern may be hipped or may have gable ends. A hipped roof construction has been taken as an example because it is more interesting geometrically. One method of construction is to provide two end and two side sashes similar in principle to the skylight in **Fig. 4.75** with the stiles splayed to the developed roof surface. Thus the end sashes will be triangular and the side sashes trapezoidal (see **Fig. 4.81**). Glazing bars are introduced as necessary.

Fig. 4.82 gives sections of the top rail, bottom rail (or apron) and frame head. The top rail is grooved to take the glass and the meeting top rails and hip stiles are mitred together as shown in **Figs. 4.82** and **4.84**.

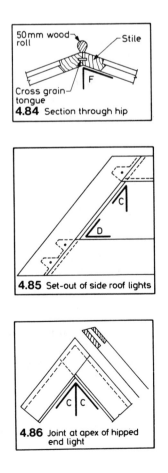

4.84 Section through hip

4.85 Set-out of side roof lights

4.86 Joint at apex of hipped end light

The apron rail (**Fig. 4.82**), which must have provisions for disposal of condensation as in **Figs. 4.75** or **4.76**, is grooved to take the tongue on the head. **Fig. 4.85** shows how the side hip stile is mortised to the top and bottom rails. **Fig. 4.86** gives the apex joint to the hipped end stiles. It is not possible to assemble this with a haunched mortise and tenon joint. Either a bridle joint or halving must be used.

Setting out a lantern roof

In order to set out the work, some geometrical development becomes necessary. **Fig. 4.87** shows how the lengths and bevels are obtained. Taking

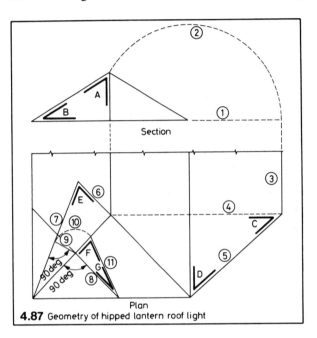

4.87 Geometry of hipped lantern roof light

bevels as lettered, **A** and **B** are self-evident and are used to obtain the edge bevels of the top rail (**Fig. 4.82**) and the splay of the head.

Bevels for setting out the side lights are obtained as follows. Extend the eaves line (1). Pivot the rafter length about the eaves (2) and project down (3). Take a horizontal from the apex plan (4), project to cut (3), and join up as shown.

Next the bevels **C** and **D** and the length (5) are used for marking out the stiles and the shoulders of the rails (**Figs. 4.85** and **4.86**).

The bevels to the hip stile edges (**Fig. 4.84**) are half the dihedral angle on a plane square to the hip line. To obtain this; set off rise (6) square to hip plan and draw true length of hip (7). At any convenient point, draw line (8) square to hip plan and from the intersection draw line (9) square to line (7). Swing line (9) down on to hip plan (10) and draw line (11). Then **F** is the half dihedrangle required.

The grooves for the loose tongues on the stiles and top rails should be made before assembly, using a jig off the spindle table. This is set to bevel **B** for the top rails and bevel **G** for the hip stiles. To provide a means of holding the lead flashing over the mitred joints, lead rolls are fixed as in **Figs. 4.82** and **4.84**.

Alternative method of construction

An alternative to building the glazed roof with sashes

as just described, may be to build it up entirely from stout, uniform-thickness, rebated bars jointed together at the ridge and to the lower frame head at the eaves. This is shown in plan in **Fig. 4.88** and section **Fig. 4.89**.

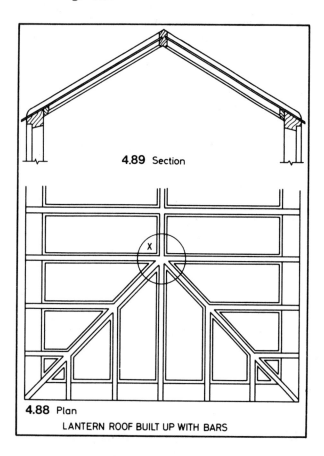

4.89 Section

4.88 Plan

LANTERN ROOF BUILT UP WITH BARS

In order to have a satisfactory intersection at all the joints, the bars need to be of different sections. The method of obtaining these is shown in **Fig. 4.91** in conjunction with bevels obtained from **Fig. 4.87** already described. The roof pitch is first drawn and the accepted common bar section put in square to this. The widths **W**, covering overall bar thickness and rebate widths, is to remain constant throughout.

To obtain the ridge section, take lines (shown dotted) through the section to cut the centre line of ridge and return towards the opposite pitch. These are cut by vertical projectors to widths **W**, which give the required ridge section.

To obtain the hip bar section, two stages are necessary as follows:

1. Take the centre line of the ridge cut by rakers from the common bar as before (shown in **Fig. 4.92**) and from these intersections draw line bevel **E** (**Fig. 4.87**) to the vertical.
2. Cut these by another line square to them in any convenient place and then from the intersections made, draw lines both ways at angle **F** (**Fig. 4.87**) and again cut off widths **W** as before and join up.

In building up the glazed roof, the head of the vertical frame is integral with the bar construction. The lower part of each bar is tenoned into the head

and the part left by the rebates is continued over the head with provision for condensation disposal as before.

The intersection between the ridge and common bar may be a simple mortise and tenon joint, but where all other members are bunched at the ridge ends, it will probably make a stronger job if a finial is introduced as in **Figs. 4.90** and **4.93**. The finial needs to be octagonal in section and of such a size that the width of each flat is equivalent to the bar thickness.

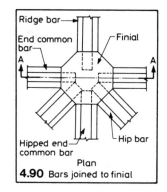

4.90 Bars joined to finial

The bars are tenoned to the finial, the thickness of each tenon is that of the reduced part of the bar and its depth is the maximum possible (**Fig. 4.93**). Note that the rib shoulders are square in plan: the only bevels needed are the rafter plumb cut **A** for the common bars and the hip plumb cut **E** (**Fig. 4.92**) for the hip bars. Intermediate bars cut on to the hip bars will require hip rafter bevels **C** and **A**.

If, however, a finial is not used, the members will all have to be mitred together at the ridge ends. This involves some interesting geometrical and constructional problems. Marking-out procedure will be as follows. Draw the plan of intersections full size (**Fig. 4.94**), also construct a long mitre box into which a bar will fit snugly and deep enough for the widest bar (the hip) (**Fig. 4.95**). Then the geometry of the mitre bevels is based on the fact that, if a plumb cut is placed on any roof timber, any measurement taken square off the plumb cut is a plan measurement. The bevels obtained will be those to be placed on the mitre box: i.e. as it was on the unbacked timbers.

Fig. 4.96 is the set-out of the common bar. Projectors are drawn square to the centre line on plan, representing verticals. The bevel **A** (**Fig. 4.91**) set off the projector lines and the side of the bar drawn. The mitre intersections are then projected from the plan, as shown, and squared over the width **W** representing the top edge and joined back to the centre line to give the cutting bevels.

The same procedure is used for the hip bar using bevel **E** (**Fig. 4.91**). The bevels for the end common bar or longest jack are the same as the longer one on the common bar already obtained.

The bunching of the bars at the ridge end makes their assembly difficult. This will be simplified, and the job strengthened, if a 19mm hardwood key is introduced, see **Fig. 4.94**. The job should be assembled with waterproof glue.

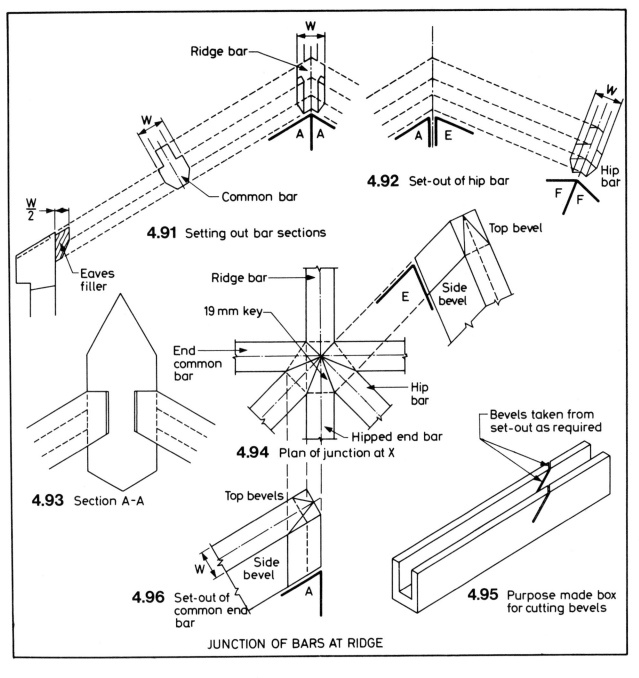

4.91 Setting out bar sections

4.92 Set-out of hip bar

4.93 Section A-A

4.94 Plan of junction at X

4.95 Purpose made box for cutting bevels

4.96 Set-out of common end bar

JUNCTION OF BARS AT RIDGE

QUESTIONS FOR CHAPTER 4

Question 9

A works office adjacent to an airport has a casement window of 100 by 75mm rebated frame and 44mm moulded sash as shown in **Fig. 4.97**. Draw a horizontal section through the jamb to show any recommended modifications to reduce the passage of sound when:

    a. The existing window is retained;
    b. A new window is inserted.
    (Scale half full-size.)

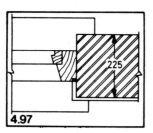

4.97

Institute of Carpenters Associate Examination, March 1969. No. 6.

Question 10

During alterations to a large country house, it is discovered that, although the hardwood sills are sound, the lower part of the pully stile and outer linings of a number of boxed frames are decayed. State the repairs necessary.

Institute of Carpenters Associate Examination, May 1973, General Paper. No. 11.
Time allowed: under 10 minutes.

Question 11

Describe the problems associated with the fitting of lights in the roofs of buildings and, with the aid of simple sketches, state how they may be dealt with.

(A suitable question related to the article was not available from a past examination paper.)
Time allowed: 20 minutes.

CHAPTER 5

Partitions and Panelling

The terms 'screen' and 'partition' seem to be used indiscriminately in many cases; although dwarf screens, vestibule screens and the various types of screens used in churches are never referred to as partitions. The specialised construction of the latter will not be included here and, with the exception of the dwarf screens, the others will be referred to as partitions.

In both cases the terms are used to describe framed wooden structures not integrally part of the building but erected to give varying degrees of privacy to the rooms partitioned off. Thus, when the sole purpose is to give visible separation such as between office staff and the general public, a dwarf screen about 1m high is satisfactory. Where a greater measure of privacy and protection is needed, but where the business done is not especially confidential, the partition may be of a full door height, say, 2m. If, however, complete separation by sight and sound is required, the partition should be taken to the full room height. A partition may be panelled in hardwood, to a high degree of finish; or in softwood; or it may be glazed; or flush with plywood, hardboard or some other form of modern board facing.

DWARF SCREENS

Fig. 5.1 shows the elevation of a dwarf screen 1m high, panelled, and with a wide surmounting capping. This capping is necessary to all screens and partitions, other than those of full height, in order to provide some lateral stability. The example shown has a central door.

The screen must be stiffened on either side of the

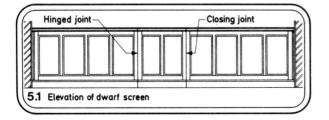

5.1 Elevation of dwarf screen

door and this may be done with metal brackets (**Fig. 5.2**) screwed to the frame stiles and to the floor on the private side of the screen. They may be concealed behind a pilaster if it is desired. Alternatively, if preparation is made before laying the floor, the stiles may be taken through it (loose boards being left as necessary) and fixed to bearers cut between the joists.

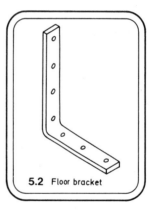

5.2 Floor bracket

A cover mould should be used over the joints against the walls and scribed to the plaster if necessary. A skirting may be fixed, of the same section as the room skirtings. A good finish is ensured if the cover mould is identical with, and is mitred or scribed to the top member of the skirting and the bed mould under the capping (see **Figs. 5.3, 5.4** and **5.5**). The capping is fixed flat to the top rails of the screen and not housed as this would complicate the arrangements for the hinged joint. The capping should be recessed into the wall each end. This will help to stiffen it. It will be noted that the top member of the skirting is mitred with the cover mould, but the top member of the room skirting is butted against the cover mould and the lower member mitred with the screen skirting. In setting out joinery framing it will not look right unless the actual show widths are the same. Thus, in **Fig. 5.3**, E–E–E are identical although the actual stile and rail widths may vary.

The joint in the capping over the hinge must be a rule joint, as shown in **Fig. 5.6**, unless parliament hinges are used. These could constitute a nuisance as they would have to project beyond the capping to be effective. **Figs. 5.5** and **5.6** show the method of setting out the rule joint. The position of the hinge centre should be drawn on the plan and from this the inner and outer lines of the capping drawn in their position with the door open to the required angle. **Fig. 5.6** shows this clearly.

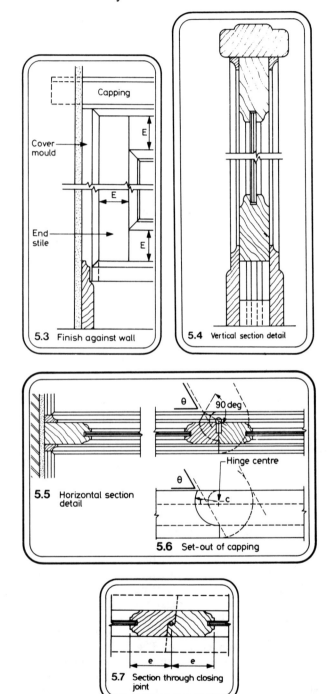

5.3 Finish against wall

5.4 Vertical section detail

5.5 Horizontal section detail

5.6 Set-out of capping

5.7 Section through closing joint

The arc radius **T–C** is the smallest to which the rule joint can be set out. The doors will have to close with a rebated joint as in **Fig. 5.7**. This will have to be splayed with its angle square to a radius from the hinge centre to the innermost point of the joint in the capping (**Fig. 5.8**). The bed moulding will have to follow the same lines. The capping and skirting will

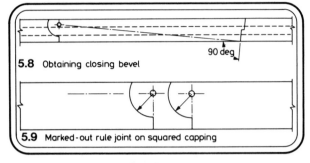

5.8 Obtaining closing bevel

5.9 Marked-out rule joint on squared capping

have to be splayed in the same way to permit the necessary clearance in opening. The principle in finding the splay is the same (**Fig. 5.5**). However, as the bed mould and skirting on the door will have to swing in under the fixed capping, the stiles will have to be recessed to a circular outline (cylindrically) to permit the passage of these members inwards.

Fig. 5.9 shows the procedure. The line of hinge centre should be marked and squared around twice, checking first that the timber itself is square in section. Then the compass points are gauged from the edge under and over and the hinge centres are emphasised with a fine pricker. The rule joint curve can then be marked under and over (four times) with a pair of finely sharpened joiner's compasses for the curve and a striking knife for the shoulder.

The male and female cuts are made to within about 2mm, using a fine band saw or jig saw. They are finished off with a scribing gouge and paring chisel half way from each side. The two parts may then be fitted together straight and cleated on the back into one effective length. Then they are moulded to the required section on the spindle moulder.

DOOR-HEIGHT PARTITIONS

Fig. 5.10 shows a simplified elevation of a partition about 2m high in a wide room. It will be appreciated that, unless an occasional post can be taken up to and fixed to the ceiling, the stiffness of the whole partition from wall to wall must depend upon the longitudinal members. When a door causes a break in the continuity of these members, the ultimate strength of the partition must lie in the uninterrupted capping.

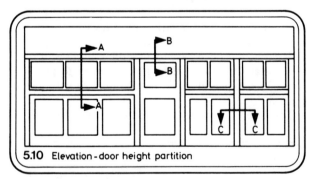

5.10 Elevation - door height partition

The deflection formula for a simply supported uniformly loaded beam is:

$$D = \frac{3}{384} \quad \frac{wL^3}{EI}$$

The formulae for other types of loading only vary in the coefficient. For a rectangular wooden beam:

$$I = \frac{bd^3}{12}$$

so by substitution the equation becomes:

$$D = \frac{3}{384} \quad \frac{12WL^3}{Ebd^3}$$

As the only thing that can vary is the capping size, all other symbols except D can be given the value of X so we get:

$$D = \frac{X}{bd^3}$$

As D stands for deflection, the lower the value of D the greater the stiffness. Note also that, as the load is horizontal, the width becomes d and the depth becomes b.

Compare the stiffness of a 100 by 75mm capping on a cross-section area 7500mm² with a 150 by 38mm capping on a 5700mm² cross-section. For 100 by 75mm:

$$D = \frac{X}{75 \times 100^3} = 1.3 \times 10^{-8}\,X$$

For 150 by 38mm:

$$D = \frac{X}{38 \times 150^3} = 7.8 \times 10^{-9}\,X$$

The latter is much less; so a 150 by 38mm capping, provided that it was securely fixed against buckling, would be much stiffer than a 100 by 175mm. This is despite the fact that it would only contain three-quarters as much timber.

In the example given in **Fig. 5.10**, a wide capping sized 150 by 38mm is used. This, in turn, carries the tops of the posts making door jambs. On the left-hand side, a long dado rail spans between the door posts and wall post; there is a long glazed frame above and a panelled frame below.

Fig. 5.11, in the section **A–A**, shows how the capping is built up to a decorative and solid looking appearance by introducing sprung mouldings with intermediate cross-grain packings. These are at 600mm intervals so that a recess is formed to take the top rail of the glazed framing.

The lower member of the sprung moulding over the

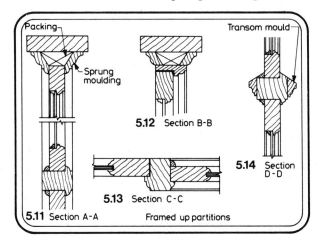

5.11 Section A-A Framed up partitions

5.12 Section B-B

5.13 Section C-C

5.14 Section D-D

door is removed to take a rebated narrow member to act as a door head (**Fig. 5.12**). **Fig. 5.13** shows a horizontal section through the door and door jamb.

CEILING-HEIGHT PARTITIONS

Fig. 5.15 shows the layout of the posts, head and transom only of a partition taken to the full height. By extending all the posts through to the ceiling, a greater rigidity is obtained permitting a comparative light fill-in of glazed and panelled frames. To maintain the apparent landscape proportions, the transom rail is made to appear prominent and continuous by mouldings planted on both sides of the rails over the framing. This section **D–D** is shown in **Fig. 5.15**.

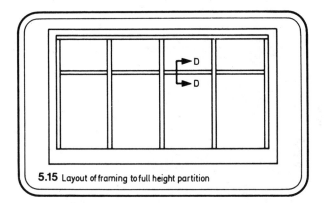

5.15 Layout of framing to full height partition

Fig. 5.16 is the elevation in basic outline of a full height partition, panelled up to the frieze, glazed above and with a central door. The diagonal dotted-line crosses indicate the separate frames considered to be the maximum size which can be given access to

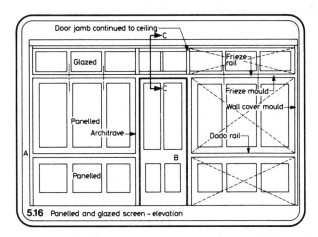

5.16 Panelled and glazed screen – elevation

the compartment. In **Fig. 5.17**, detail at **A**, the elevation shows how the cover mould and dado intersect with mitred mouldings. Details of moulds and clearances for ease of fitting are indicated in the horizontal and vertical sections.

In **Fig. 5.18**, the positions of the various members against the lock rail of the door are presented in elevation. The method of rebating the door flush into the main framing is apparent from the horizontal section. **Fig. 5.19**, section **C–C**, gives details of the glazed framing above the transom.

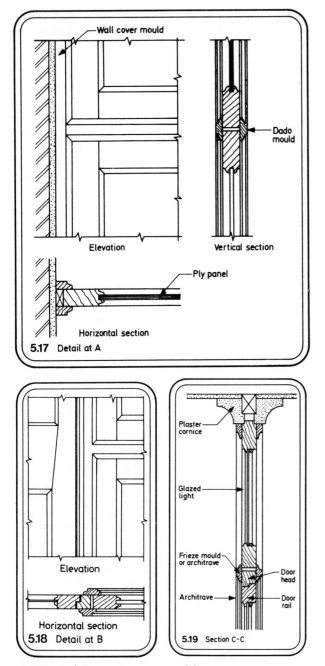

5.17 Detail at A

5.18 Detail at B

5.19 Section C-C

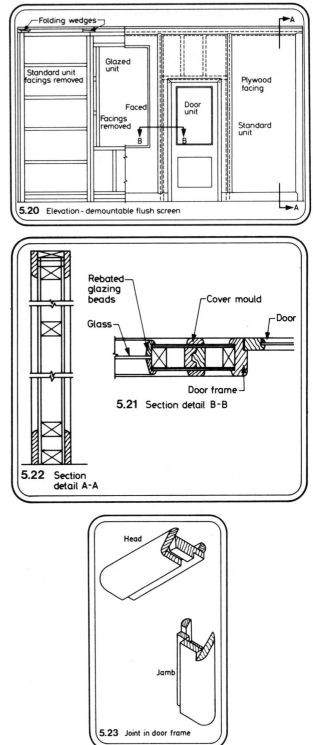

5.20 Elevation - demountable flush screen

5.21 Section detail B-B

5.22 Section detail A-A

5.23 Joint in door frame

Ceiling-height temporary partitions

Fig. 5.20 gives selected elevational details of a full-height temporary partition, capable of being erected and dismantled without any damage to wall or ceiling. It consists of units about 1.2m wide, flush on both sides with hardboard or plywood. There are plain or hardwood veneered facings according to the standard of finish demanded. The units are tightened down from a head board (placed to protect the plaster ceiling) by means of folding wedges. If the ceiling is delicately textured, it may be necessary to line the head board with felt.

Fig. 5.21 is a horizontal section giving (with details) the finish to the glazed unit, junctions between door frame and unit, and junctions between consecutive frames. **Fig. 5.22** is a vertical section giving head, intermediate and floor level details. **Fig. 5.23** illustrates how the door frames are tongued together at the head to show a mitre on the face.

Where screens have to be fire-resisting, they may be solidly constructed of a resistant timber – such as teak, gurjun or karri – with tongued-in panels at least 50mm thick and framing the same or thicker. Door rebates should be 25mm deep. Alternatively, they may be built up with sandwiched layers of plywood and a fire-resisting sheeting such as plasterboard, asbestos board or its substitute. Doors should preferably be self-closing. Plastic materials, such as nylon, should not be used for hinges or furniture in fire-resisting construction.

Although some degree of sound-proofing is advantageous with most full height partitions, it is difficult to achieve this to a high standard without adding considerably to the weight, which is contrary to the other purposes of the design. Layers of felt in the perimeter joints will, however, help to isolate the partition and reduce the transmission of sound to and from the main structure. Reverberation produced by sounds, such as of typewriters within a compartment, may be cut down by lining the partition with a soft material such as insulation board.

WALL PANELLING

Wall panelling is the general name given to wood facings to wall and to reveals in door and window openings which are used for a decorative effect. Traditionally it consists of panelled framing tenoned together. The enrichments are obtained largely by the use of mouldings to framing with flat or raised panels, dry grooved into framing and of limited size to accommodate and yet reduce moisture movement. The development of stable manufactured boards – such as plywood, multi-ply, laminboard, blockboard and more recently chipboard – has enabled these to be used as large panels in otherwise similar framed construction.

Raised panels may be formed with wide lippings tongued and mitred around to contain the raw edges and receive the required veneer facings. Afterwards they are moulded as required. However this is not advisable with chipboard, which is subject to some overall moisture movement.

The alternative, and more general, approach is to use the panels without framing, giving an overall flush appearance. Decoration and enrichment depend entirely upon the beauty of the grain of the veneered panel, which is heightened by the use of cross-banding or other patterned arrangements.

Insulation and moisture control
The risk of decay or mould discoloration from damp which penetrates the walls or exudes from the drying brickwork, must be countered by the application of bitumen or another waterproofing compound. The panelling itself, being a natural heat insulator, isolates the walls from room heat and encourages condensation on the cold surface.

Spacing at the back of panelling should, therefore, be ventilated to allow air movement. For these reasons also, panelling should not be fixed, or even brought on site, until the central heating has been in full operation for a reasonable length of time.

Measuring up
The work should start with actual detailed measurements on site. Separate elevations of all walls should be drawn from fully-dimensioned sketches. The measuring should include a datum level taken all round the room, from which measurements should be made up and down from ceiling to floor levels. Corners and openings should be checked for plumb. Details of any particular items with which the panelling has to link up, should be noted. For example, door and window frames should be measured in

detail. A note should be taken of the means of access and a maximum size for individual components decided on.

The panelling will be fixed to timber grounds, consisting of vertical and horizontal members, which are usually ex 75 by 20mm softwood halved or mortise and tenoned together. The timber should be pre-treated with a suitable preservative.

The grounds will be fixed to the wall by screwing or nailing to either twisted wood plugs into brick joints or timber, or proprietary fibre or plastic plugs placed in holes drilled into the bricks. If the plugs are inserted into the wall first, the exact position of each nail or screw in the ground can be defined using a template (**Fig. 5.24**). Mark its position on the wall with a pencil point on the plug, and then place it over the ground on the marked position, dotting the point for the nail with the pencil.

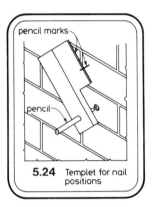

5.24 Templet for nail positions

Full-size setting-out rods should be made from the site drawings, with details taken from the architect's drawings. Advantage should be taken of the positions of mouldings, such as neck mould, dado rail, and architrave, to joint the panel units behind them. Grounds must then be placed centrally behind each joint. It may be safer to set out and fix the grounds only, and then check again on site before setting out the actual panelling.

Traditional framed wall panelling
Fig. 5.25 (the elevation of a section of full-height traditional framed wall panelling) shows the cornice, friese, neck mould, pediment over door, architrave moulds, dado rail and skirting. Each of these covers a means of fixing, and so will give the positions of the grounds. **Figs. 5.26** and **5.27** are horizontal and vertical sections through the framed panelling around the door. The door lining is brought to the face of the panelling. The architrave, which stands forward from this, varies in width to give an inset outline surmounted by a further mould. This then receives the convex frieze and cornice to the pediment.

Fig. 5.28 shows the position of the fixing grounds to receive the joints, **a** to **f**. As well as being accurately positioned, the grounds should be straight and flat on all faces and plumb at the angles and openings. Packings should be used, where necessary, to ensure this.

Fig. 5.29 shows the elevation of detail around a window. **Fig. 5.30** gives large scale section detail. A horizontal section through the jamb would be the

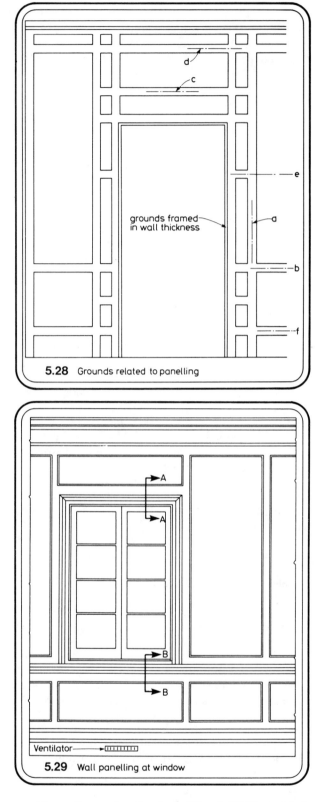

blocking   cornice

neck mould   frieze

d

B   c

pediment

B

A   A

e

architrave

a

dado rail

b

f

skirting

5.25   Elevation of wall panelling around door

5.26   Section A-A

5.27   Section B-B

d

c

e

grounds framed
in wall thickness   a

b

f

5.28   Grounds related to panelling

A

A

B

B

Ventilator

5.29   Wall panelling at window

same as **A–A**. Generally speaking, to look right, all parts of the framing should have the same width showing on face. The part hidden must be added to the standard width. The dado rail runs past and forms a finish to the window board.

Figs. **5.31**, **5.32** and **5.33** give typical detail of panelling around a fireplace. The distance **d** in **Fig. 5.32**, from the face of the ground to the tile or marble facing, governs the minimum projection of the pilas-

ter. The rail over the fireplace (**Fig. 5.33**) fits behind the pilaster, and lines up with the marble facing; the joint is covered by a moulding. The rail over the mantelshelf is wide to form a background to the usual display of ornaments. The shelf is jointed in two to reduce the risk of shrinkage distortion from heat.

Fig. 5.34 is the elevation of part of the dado panelling, which follows the stairs from ground floor to landing with pilasters at the two levels. For a uniform

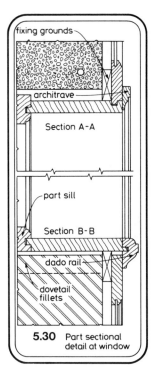

5.30 Part sectional detail at window

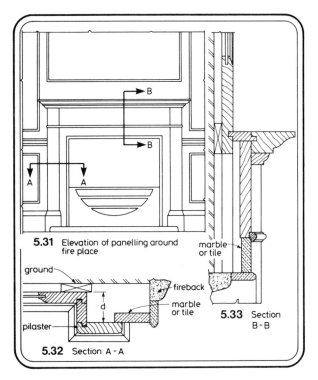

5.31 Elevation of panelling around fire place

5.32 Section A-A

5.33 Section B-B

appearance, the width of the string over the terrazzo-faced steps needs to be adjusted so that its mitre, with top and bottom skirtings, comes in half the going from the face of the first and last riser respectively.

The mitres of the dado rail should be vertically above those of the skirting. This is achieved by adjusting the height of the rail on the raking panelling. The panel line of the end stiles should follow from these. The standard face width of the stiles will then give the positions of the pilasters.

The dado rail is mitred around the pilasters with a filling piece to make up the extra width. **Fig. 5.35** is a vertical section through the panelling in the level position. **Fig. 5.36** is a horizontal section through a pilaster and part of the panelling.

The steps are presumed to be terrazzo-faced concrete, so the string must be scribed over them. **Fig. 5.37** shows a jig made for marking the scribe. A grooved stock is secured to a sliding fence by means of a wing nut which is set from it in a vertical position. A stem with a projecting bottom metal plate slides in the stock as an easy hand fit.

The jig is set in as many positions as needed. With the plate end in contact with the step, a prick or pencil mark is made against the V-notch for each setting. These points, once joined up, will give an exact reproduction of the step outline on the string. If carefully cut, it should fit first time.

Moulding finishes for panels
Fig. 5.38 shows a section of a simple ovolo moulded panel finish. **Fig. 5.39** shows a raised panel, which is fitted into a groove formed between a bolection mould on the face rebate, and a rebated retaining fillet on the back. This gives a maximum depth of finish in a minimum thickness of framing.

Fig. 5.40 shows the capping or rail to a dado panel-

ling in section. The panel is fixed to the grounds behind the dado rail, which is pinned and stopped in. The upper member of the mould is taken back to the plaster. **Fig. 5.41** shows a dado rail to full height panelling, the fixing screws again being concealed. The top panel is secured by dowelling to the lower one at about 250mm centres.

Forming angles
Fig. 5.42 shows various methods of forming internal and external angles. With the tongued and grooved internal angle in laminboard, the tongue should be less than half the board thickness. There are also other methods of forming a cove angle with either solid or loose tongues. A tongue should never be formed in multi-ply unless it includes the outer veneers. There are methods of jointing laminboard and multi-ply to solid timber to form a rounded corner. Other examples in **Fig. 5.42** include a tongued mitre and a recessed corner using lipped laminboard.

Methods of fixing panelling
Fig. 5.43 is a section through a built-up skirting. The bottom member tongued into the floor conceals the shrinkage possible in both skirting and floor joists. The skirting is pinned to the bottom rail of the panelling. It is supported by soldiers cut to fit over the grounds and to receive the skirting and fixed at about 600mm centres. **Fig. 5.44** shows a moulded dado rail recessed flush with panelling. **Fig. 5.45** presents a recessed skirting with a cove flowing to meet parquet flooring.

Fig. 5.46 illustrates a method of secret fixing for pilasters. Tapered blocks are screwed to the end stiles of the panelling and correspondingly tapered and notched buttons are screwed to the backs of the

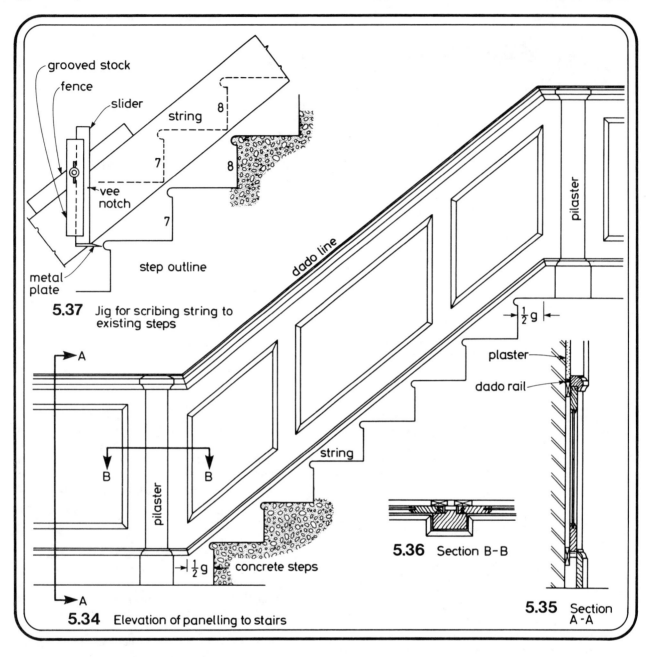

5.37 Jig for scribing string to existing steps

5.36 Section B-B

5.35 Section A-A

5.34 Elevation of panelling to stairs

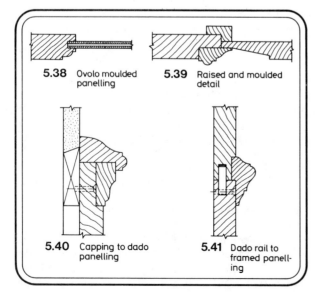

5.38 Ovolo moulded panelling

5.39 Raised and moulded detail

5.40 Capping to dado panelling

5.41 Dado rail to framed panelling

pilaster. The pilaster is forced down so that the button tongue clips down behind the block and tightens with the taper.

Architraves, when large, are best assembled with some type of construction joint such as a halving or loose tongue. **Fig. 5.47** gives pictorial views of a mitred halving and the joint between architrave and plinth block.

Semi-flush panelling

When large panels of multi-ply or laminboard are framed up with shallow projecting features, this is known as semi-flush panelling. An example is shown in **Fig. 5.48**. Cross-banded fillets are housed into the panel faces, while the vulnerable veneer edges are protected by narrow lippings. **Fig. 5.49** is a horizontal section giving details around the door opening. The back of the door is ovolo moulded to suit the external finishes.

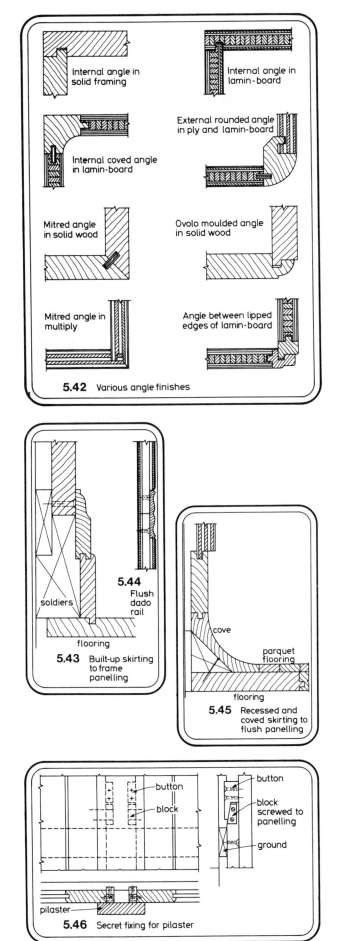

5.42 Various angle finishes

Internal angle in solid framing

Internal angle in lamin-board

Internal coved angle in lamin-board

External rounded angle in ply and lamin-board

Mitred angle in solid wood

Ovolo moulded angle in solid wood

Mitred angle in multiply

Angle between lipped edges of lamin-board

5.43 Built-up skirting to frame panelling

soldiers

flooring

5.44 Flush dado rail

5.45 Recessed and coved skirting to flush panelling

cove

parquet flooring

flooring

5.46 Secret fixing for pilaster

button

block

pilaster

button

block screwed to panelling

ground

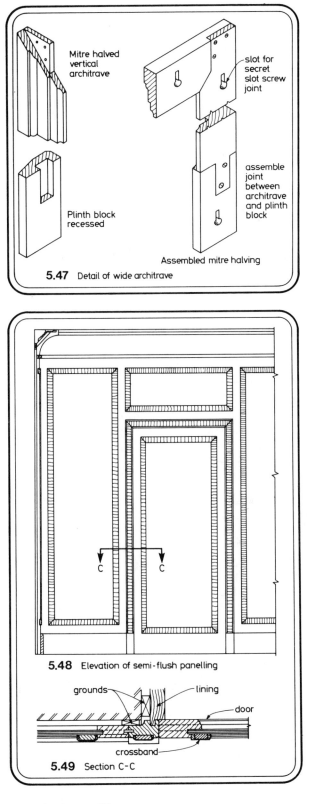

5.47 Detail of wide architrave

Mitre halved vertical architrave

Plinth block recessed

slot for secret slot screw joint

assemble joint between architrave and plinth block

Assembled mitre halving

5.48 Elevation of semi-flush panelling

C   C

5.49 Section C–C

grounds

lining

door

crossband

Fully-flush panelling

Fully-flush panelling is fixed with a surface level over all the joints, no framing being necessary. Special concealed fixings therefore become necessary. Examples are given in **Figs. 5.50** to **5.54**.

In **Fig. 5.50**, the bevelled cleats screwed to the back of the panels tighten down on to the bevelled grounds which are fixed to the wall. In **Fig. 5.51**, tapered tongued buttons clip down behind the bevelled

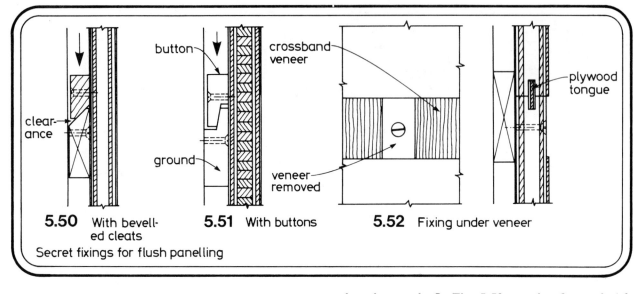

5.50 With bevell-ed cleats   **5.51** With buttons   **5.52** Fixing under veneer

Secret fixings for flush panelling

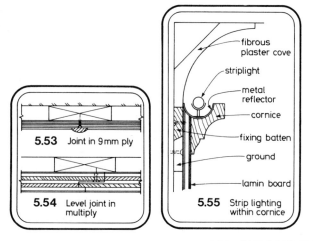

5.53 Joint in 9 mm ply

5.54 Level joint in multiply

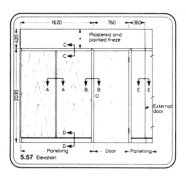

5.55 Strip lighting within cornice

rebated grounds. In **Fig. 5.52**, a strip of cross-band veneering is carefully removed. The fixing screw is inserted and the gap made good.

Fig. 5.53 is a section through a joint between 9mm plywood panels. As this is to be covered with a bead, the fixing can be concealed. The panels are lapped under the same screw. They are also rebated together, the rebates being tapered to avoid weakness at the shoulders. **Fig 5.54** shows a matched joint in multi-ply with a wide rebate in the one piece to take the fixing screw. This is flanked by a groove to take the tongue of the following panel.

Fig. 5.55 gives details of the provision for concealed strip lighting within the cornice of full-height panelling. The light is reflected by a fibrous plaster cove. Note the method of secret fixing.

QUESTIONS FOR CHAPTER 5

Question 12

Fig. 5.56 shows the dimensions of a public inquiry counter and screen in an office. The hardwood screen is 94mm thick. The counter is formed with 18mm thick chipboard and the top is covered with plastic laminate. The screen and counter are to be made in the shop.

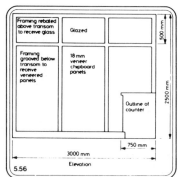

5.56 Elevation

a. Draw a section through the transom. Scale 1:2.
b. Sketch a vertical section through the counter showing the method of construction.

City & Guilds of London Institute Examination, Purpose-made Joinery, June 1978. No. 4.
Time allowed: 12 minutes.

Question 13

A manager's office is required to be panelled out in polished 6mm veneered plywood and finished with moulded mahogany trim as indicated in **Fig. 5.57**.

5.57 Elevation

a. Draw scale 1:1, sections at A–A, B–B, C–C, D–D and E–E showing construction and fixing.
b. Explain how the mouldings would be cleaned up by hand suitable for finishing with French polish. Give reasons for the methods described.

Institute of Carpenters' Associate Examination, 1975. No. 5.
Time allowed: 30 minutes.

CHAPTER 6

Staircases

It is not possible to cover all aspects of this subject in the space allotted. It is therefore assumed that the reader will have access to standard works on joinery covering the subject. The information provided therein will only be covered briefly here, detailed attention will be confined to the points requiring special consideration.

In this category may be included the application of the Building Regulations 1985 – Section K, Stairways, Ramps and Guards.

It is essential that the person who is responsible for their design and construction should consult these regulations in detail. They cover stairs in all types of buildings and for the purpose stair construction is given in four groups. i.e. Group 1 – Private stairs, i.e. domestic stairs for the use of one occupancy.

Group 2 – Common Stairs, i.e. domestic type stairs for the use of more than one occupancy.

Group 3 – for use in institutional buildings and buildings of assembly.

Group 4 – Stairways not described in any of the three groups above. Whilst some of the regulations are easily understood and applied, others are rather complex, not only in their legal phraseology, but also in the way in which they are inter-related. This can present what sometimes may appear to be insurmountable problems to the designer and joiner who has to fit a staircase into a limited space with specific floor levels.

In general, the Regulations cover staircase minimum widths, maximum and minimum overall dimensions and pitches of steps, head room, balustrades and handrails. There are some special Regulations with regard to winders, which are referred to as tapered treads. The definitions in general agree with those traditionally accepted but should be checked against them.

The modifications required to cover stairs used in the eight different purpose groups of buildings are mainly numerical and regulate step size, pitch, etc. The principles used in their general application are substantially the same. The examples given here will be confined to private and common stairs. The same logical approach can be used with buildings of other purpose groups, but the reader should consult the

Regulations to obtain the particular values he will have to use.

The following rules (see Table to H3) apply to all stairs:

Twice the step rise plus its going must not be less than 550mm or more than 700mm.

$(2R + G = 500 - 700mm)$.

Minimum step rise = 50mm.

Minimum head room = 2000mm.

Handrails must have a vertical height minimum 840mm and maximum 1000mm.

The maximum step rise and minimum step going varies with different situations, as does the maximum permitted pitch.

Taking the Regulations for private stairways the following rules are specific.

Maximum permitted pitch of stairs = 42 degrees.

Minimum step going = 220mm.

Maximum step rise = 220mm.

(Note the maximum rise cannot be used with the minimum going or the pitch would be 45 degrees.)

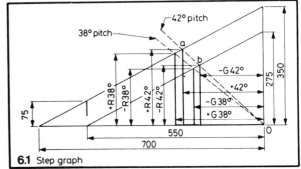

6.1 Step graph

The step graph in **Fig. 6.1** gives the maximum and minimum step size for any given pitch to conform to the rule:

$$2R + G = 550 \text{ to } 700mm.$$

The explanation is as follows:

Moving from right to left and assuming no pitch limitations if the going = 0 rise at point 0

$$= \frac{550}{2} - 0 = 275mm \text{ minimum, and}$$

$$\frac{750}{2} = 350mm \text{ maximum.}$$

Thus measuring from point 0 a vertical from any point on the horizontal line giving the going, will give the maximum and minimum permitted rise. A raking line from 0 to any given pitch will give the maximum and minimum step size, the step proportions then being unalterable.

The minimum pitch for domestic stairs for common use is 38 degrees and for private stairs 42 degrees. These are shown in **Fig. 6.1**: the − and + signs indicate minimum and maximum values. The graph does not take account of the maximum permitted rise and the minimum permitted going. These must set a point somewhere between the raking graph lines.

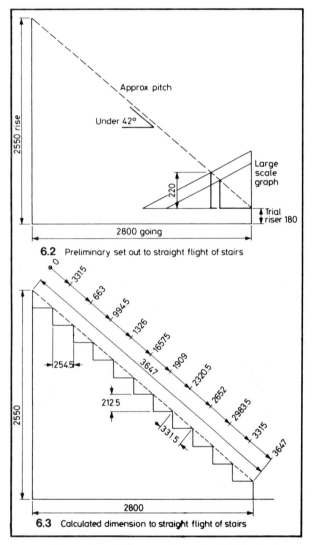

6.2 Preliminary set out to straight flight of stairs

6.3 Calculated dimension to straight flight of stairs

Fig. 6.2 and **6.3** illustrate a method of designing a straight flight of stairs with an established going and rise. It will be appreciated that the pitch of a stairs is not its going by its rise but the going by the rise minus one riser (see **Fig. 6.2**). The true pitch of the stairs cannot be truly established until the precise step rise is known. However, if an average riser is inserted, the difference between this and the ultimate true riser, spread over the height of the stairs will be negligible.

If the pitch is above 42 degrees, the job is not acceptable.

Calculating risers
Having set up the pitch to a small scale, the graph can be drawn on it as **Fig. 1.6** to a large scale as in **Fig. 6.2**, and this will immediately give maximum and minimum risers. A small electronic calculator can be brought in at this stage. Assuming that as few steps as permitted are intended, divide the stair rise by the maximum riser (as shown) of 220mm.
Then number of risers
$$= \frac{2550}{220} = 11 + \text{rem.}$$
So the minimum number of risers = 12 and the step rise
$$= \frac{2550}{12} = 212.5\text{mm.}$$
There will be 11 treads, so the step going
$$= \frac{2800}{11} = 254.5\text{mm.}$$

Check for the overall step limits. The rise of 212.5 is less than maximum and the 254.5 is more than the going minimum.

At this stage the traditional procedure in setting-out is to make separate applications of the pitch board along the nosing line on the string. Any error will be repeated for as many times as there are steps; however, with the electronic calculator, all dimensions for setting-out may be obtained to any degree of accuracy:
Length of pitch line (nosing line)
$$= \sqrt{G^2 + R^2}$$
This can be worked out on the standard scientific calculater as 3647mm.
and length of pitch board on rake
$$= \frac{3647}{11} = 331.5\text{mm}$$

Multiples 1 to 11 may now be read off by single operation giving the accumulating totals, as shown in **Fig. 6.3**. If these are marked from one end with a tape, it eliminates all risk of progressive errors. Familiarity with the calculating machine will enable these and more elaborate calculations to be done in a few minutes.

OPEN NEWEL STAIRCASE

Fig. 6.4 is a sketch plan of a staircase, indicating that it has to be built with open strings and two half-space landings. The object is to design the stairs to occupy as little floor space as possible. By the Regulations, all steps including those between landings have to be the same size. The tread sizes and the landing (and therefore stair) widths must be inter-related.

First of all, keeping stair widths to a minimum will allow more steps between landing. Assuming the stairs are to be used for private domestic buildings,

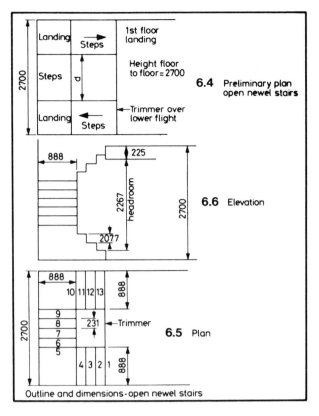

Outline and dimensions - open newel stairs

6.4 Preliminary plan open newel stairs

6.6 Elevation

6.5 Plan

then the minimum permitted widths between hand-rails = 800mm, say 850mm to centre of newel. Then maximum possible length between landings

$$= 2700 - 2 \times 850 = 1000\text{mm}.$$

Total stair rise = 2700mm. Maximum permitted step rise =220, therefore minimum number of risers

$$= \frac{2700}{220} = 12 + 1 = 12 + 1 \text{ remainder} = 13 \text{ risers}.$$

Therefore actual maximum step rise

$$= \frac{2700}{13} = 207.7\text{mm}$$

The maximum permitted pitch = 42 degrees. Therefore the minimum step going

= 207.7 × cotan 42 degrees.
= 207.7 × 1.1106 = 230.7mm.

Then the maximum possible number of steps between landings

$$= \frac{1000}{230.7} = 4 + 1 \text{ remainder}$$

There is now the choice of increasing the tread widths to take up the remainder which means increasing all tread widths; or of increasing stair widths. Assume the latter is decided on, then landing (and stair) widths

$$= \frac{2700 - 4 \times 230.7}{2} = 888\text{mm}$$

This is only 38mm above minimum.

Now the question of the number of steps in the return flights, along with the position of the trimmer. Assuming that as much room as possible will be required on the upper floor, the minimum number of treads will be allowed in the upper flight. But the headroom under trimmer must be a minimum of 2000mm. If the floor thickness = 225mm, then the distance from the upper floor level to the nosing

under the trimmer must be at least 2250mm and number of risers =

$$\frac{2250}{207.7} = 10 + R$$

so there must be at least 11 steps down. As an odd number is not possible, 12 steps down will give head room of 2267mm. This will require the layout shown in **Figs. 6.5** and **6.6** (plan and elevation).

DOGLEG STAIRS

This procedure may be carried out in buildings of other purpose groups, only numerical values needing to be changed. The traditional dogleg stairs, shown in **Fig. 6.7** (outline plan and elevation), are characterised by the outer string of the upper flight being directly over the outer string of the lower one. This means that the handrail of the lower flight dies out on the underside of the string of the upper one several steps short of the landing.

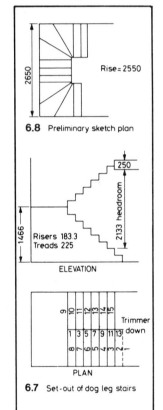

6.8 Preliminary sketch plan

Rise = 2550

Risers 183.3
Treads 225

2133 headroom

ELEVATION

Trimmer down

PLAN

6.7 Set-out of dog leg stairs

As the Building Regulations require that the handrail shall be continuous for the full length of the flight, this is no longer permissible unless a separate handrail is provided inside the balustrade. As the stairs would have to be that much wider, if planned to be of minimum dimensions, it seems simpler to separate the strings with two newels on the half space landing. This then becomes an open newel construction.

If, however, solid balustrade construction is envisaged this can be in the form of stud partition. Then the string is partly housed into the studding and rebated on the top edge to take the sheet facing material, plywood or hardboard. The handrail is of an undercut section to give a grip when fixed direct to the balustrade.

When stairs come off a half-space landing, there may again be the problem of providing sufficient head room under the floor trimmer. This is easily calculated if it is realised that step level differences increase by two for every one away from the landing. The minimum number of steps in the upper flight may therefore be obtained as before (see **Fig. 6.7**). Assuming the step rise = 183.3, then the number of step risers down to the nosing under the trimmer

$$= \frac{2000 + 250}{183.3} = 12 + R$$

or 13 risers giving six treads and seven risers in the upper flight.

STAIRS WITH WINDERS

Stairs with winders present problems because of the special requirements of the complex Regulations governing them. Two examples of design will be given relating to stairs in buildings of purpose groups I and III when the notional width is either less or more than 1m. Stairs for other purpose groups vary mainly in numerical values of accepted pitch tread and riser sizes, taper of winders, etc.

Notional width under 1 metre
First taking stairs of notional width of less than 1m: the following rules apply to winders (phasing is the writer's own.)

1. The minimum going at the newel shall be 50mm.
2. The going of all winders measured at the centre of the notional width must be the same.
3. The step rise of winders shall be the same as that of all other steps in the flight.
4. The equation 2R + G = 550 to 700mm measured on the line of travel at the centre of the notional width must also apply.

Fig. 6.8 is a preliminary sketch plan. The rise is 2550mm and, as there will be 13 risers in the flight, each riser

$$= \frac{2500}{13} = 196.2mm$$

If the maximum pitch of 42 degrees is aimed at, a step going of 218mm would give this. So the minimum accepted step going of 220mm is satisfactory.

The winders cannot, however, now radiate (as in the past) from the centre of the newel; so the first and last riser of the turn are stepped outwards more than 50mm (say 80mm) from the central newel point. The going of the fliers, therefore, measured to the centre of the newel, will be

$$3 \times 220 + 2 \times 80mm$$

and stair width to centre of newel

$$= \frac{265 - 820}{2} = 915mm$$

Using these dimensions, the whole stair plan may now be set out (**Fig. 6.9**) with the exception of the intermediate risers to the winders. The step pitch, size and proportions are now checked on the centre line of going, the curve being divided into three to give 307mm.

$$2R + G = 2 \times 196.2 + 307 = 699.4mm$$

which is just within upper limits.

The pitch is obviously less than 42 degrees, which is satisfactory. The narrow end of the kite winder must be at least 50mm wide so the ends of the risers are drawn tangent to an 80mm diameter circle in the newel, giving the final set-up in **Fig. 6.10**. The step lines represent riser lines as is usual and not nosings.

Notional width over 1 metre
When, however, the stair (notional) width becomes more than 1m, the rule for 2R + G must be applied, not at the centre of width, but 270mm from each end of it. This controls the amount of taper on each winder very tightly so that more than three winders are

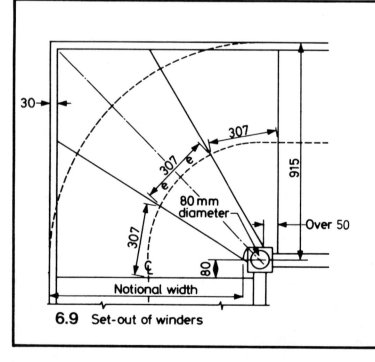

6.9   Set-out of winders

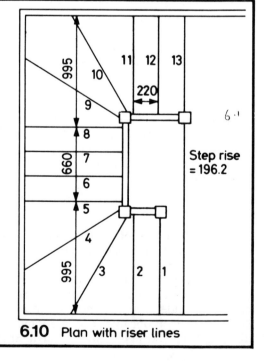

6.10   Plan with riser lines

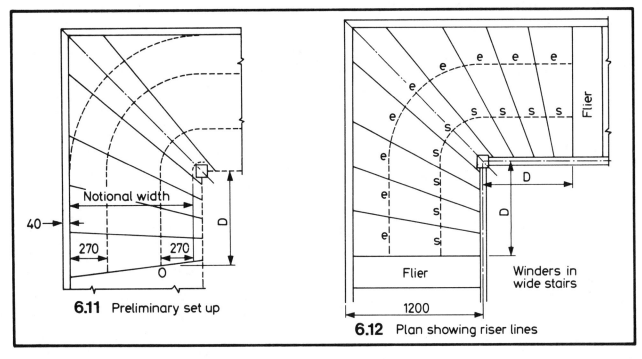

6.11 Preliminary set up

6.12 Plan showing riser lines

required to a right-angled turn. In consequence, this must be carried well beyond the newel.

Fig. 6.11 shows the preliminary set-up. As the string is presumed to be more than 30mm thick the notional width must be taken inside it. The intermediate lines to which the step rule is applied, are now drawn and taken round the 90 degree turn. It is obvious that, in order to obtain the maximum permitted amount of taper to each winder, the maximum limit for the rule must be applied on the outer going line and the minimum limit on the inner line. In the latter case, the going must be not less than 220mm. Assume the rise is fixed at 190mm.

By the 2R + G step rule therefore, the going on line **e–e**

= 700 − 2 × 190 = 320mm

and going on line **s–s**

= 550 − 380 = 170mm

But another rule says that the minimum going must be not less than 220mm so this rule also applies. Thus all winders on the line **e–e** must have a going of 320mm; and all winders must have a going of 220mm on the line **s–s**.

By these rules, the centre winder is set out and the goings stepped away from it until the right-angle turn is passed (**Fig. 6.11**). A riser line is then drawn through point **0** shortening the going of the last step on the outer dotted line. The same procedure is repeated on the other flight giving dimensions **D–D** from the centre. The foreshortened goings of all the winders on the dotted line **e–e** (**Fig. 6.12**) are then equally divided to make all the winders identical.

HALF-TURN OPEN NEWEL STAIRS

Figs. 6.13 to **6.19** are sketches dealing with the construction of half-turn open newel stairs. The lower flight starts with a bullnose step. Steps are housed and wedged to the wall and outer strings and glue blocked

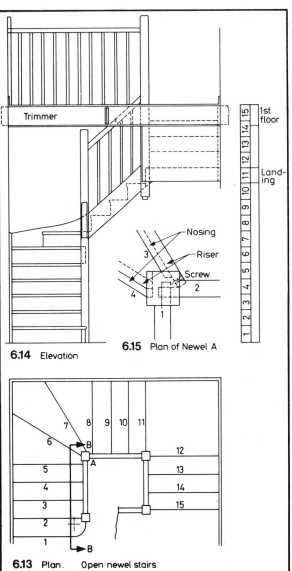

6.14 Elevation

6.15 Plan of Newel A

6.13 Plan. Open newel stairs

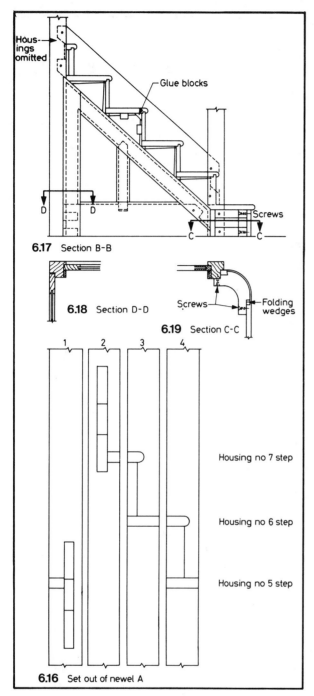

6.17 Section B-B

6.18 Section D-D

6.19 Section C-C

Housing no 7 step

Housing no 6 step

Housing no 5 step

6.16 Set out of newel A

The setting-out of straight flights may be done directly using a pitch board with tread and riser templets, using information obtained from the storey rod brought direct from the site. Where there are winders it is better to set them out full size.

Fig. 6.15 is a large scale plan of the newel post. Note that rise No. 7 (see **Fig. 6.13**) is notched and screwed to the post. The marking-out of the housing for the nosings on the newel is better done from the actual nosing itself when at an angle to the post. **Fig. 6.16** shows the four faces of the newel marked for housing with information taken from **Fig. 6.15**. The tenons into the post in **Fig. 6.15** are barefaced; this keeps the bottom of the step housings clear of the tenons.

Fig. 6.17 shows the panelling, known as spandrel framing, viewed from the inside. **Fig. 6.18** shows a section through the corner post with the spandrel rebated into the post with a stop bead. The back door is also fitted into a rebate.

The wall strings against the winders will have to be widened to accommodate them. **Fig. 6.20** shows the strings set out as on a drawing board.

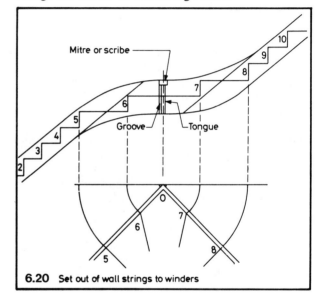

6.20 Set out of wall strings to winders

The details of step construction may vary from one maker to another. As the writer sees it, some provision for shrinkage should be made where possible. In **Fig. 6.21** three treatments are shown.

To form a satisfactory junction the handrail must

(see **Fig. 6.17**). The wall strings are fixed by nailing to plugs in walls and the outer strings are tenoned to the newel posts. The mortises should never be undercut but the tenons should be squared back to fit them. The bullnose riser may be cut from preformed plywood sheets but the traditional type is shown in **Fig. 6.19**.

The block supporting that part of the riser which is reduced to a veneer, should be carefully prepared with its curved face square to the flat faces. It is commonly laminated in three layers, the angles of grain being different to avoid short grain. If however, the grains are at 45 degrees to each other (rather than the centre layer being at 90 degrees) without being unduly weakened, there is less risk of shrinkage lines subsequently showing through the veneers.

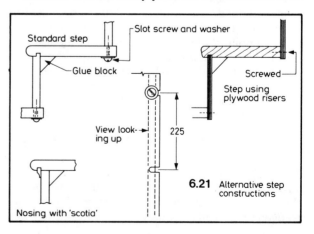

6.21 Alternative step constructions

come into the capping on a level plane. To do this it must be swept up at the bottom of the flight to the horizontal. However at the top it must first of all sweep up so as to bring it vertically to the cap level and then on to the horizontal. Two methods of doing this are shown in **Fig. 6.22**.

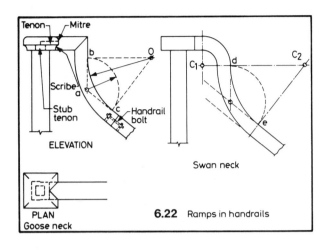

6.22　Ramps in handrails

OPEN STEP STAIRS

Fig. 6.23 shows a part elevation of an open step staircase. The strings are formed with full outer members. The centre laminate is reduced to accommodate the end of the step brackets. Additional fixing to the tread is by means of a steel angle. This is shown in **Fig. 6.24**.

To conform to the Regulations, the stairs to any building likely to be used by a child under five years of age must not have a space within the balustrade through which a 100mm diameter sphere may be passed. The exception is where there are open steps;

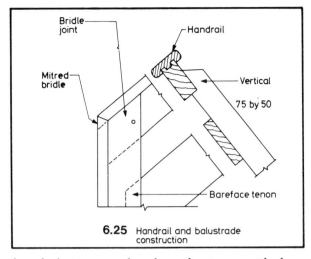

6.25　Handrail and balustrade construction

then the bottom member above the steps must be less than 50mm clear. This is shown in **Fig. 6.23**.

The handrail is a flat member ex 100 by 30mm which gives a hand hold and also provides extra stiffness to the balustrades (see **Fig. 6.25**).

GEOMETRICAL STAIRS

'Geometrical' stairs is the term given to staircases in which the outer string, and handrail over it, run continuously from floor to floor without any intermediate newel posts. Both are swept around a curve (usually circular) to the same plan centre at each change of direction. To set out and construct the stairs requires the application of advanced solid geometry, hence the name. In their simpler form, the flights themselves may be straight on plan with standard wall strings. The special construction of the outer strings is confined to the areas where they turn: i.e. at landings and winders. The curved parts of the

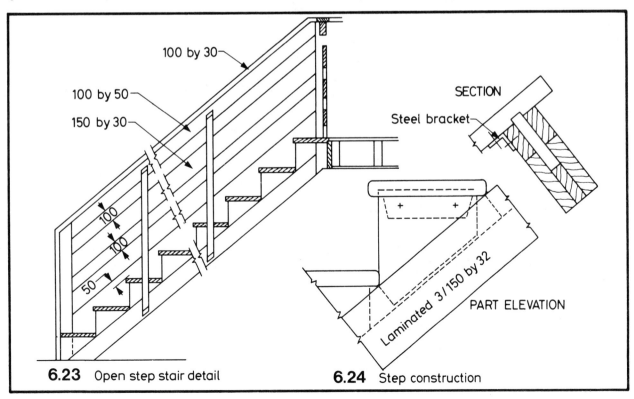

6.23　Open step stair detail

6.24　Step construction

strings and of the handrails are known as 'wreaths'; they are always formed separately and afterwards are jointed to the straight strings of the fliers.

The method of joining the steps to the strings by housing and wedging would be very difficult with the curved faces of the wreaths. It is therefore common to use cut strings: i.e. the strings are cut out to the step outline. Strings may be either cut and mitred (see **Fig. 6.26**) or cut and bracketed as in **Fig. 6.27**. Cut strings may also be used, instead of closed, for ordinary open newel stairs. The construction of the straight flights are the same. An additional precaution which must be taken, however, is to provide support in the form of rough carriages, because more than half the strength is taken away by forming the step outline. There is an even greater loss of strength in the wreaths.

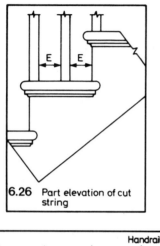

6.26   Part elevation of cut string

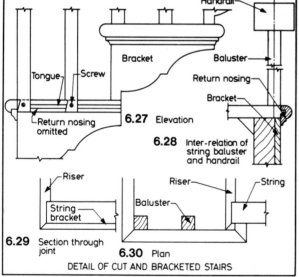

6.27   Elevation

6.28   Inter-relation of string baluster and handrail

6.29   Section through joint

6.30   Plan

DETAIL OF CUT AND BRACKETED STAIRS

Figs. 6.27 to **6.30** give details of a cut and bracketed string. In the elevation (**Fig. 6.27**), it will be seen that the lower member of each bracket lines up with the one below it. The tread is extended so that it lines up with the face of the bracket; the balusters finish to the same face. **Fig. 6.28** shows the relationship between the string, baluster and handrail. When the width (going) of each step end is reduced, as will occur where there are winders, then the width of each bracket will have to be reduced with members in the same proportion without altering the depth.

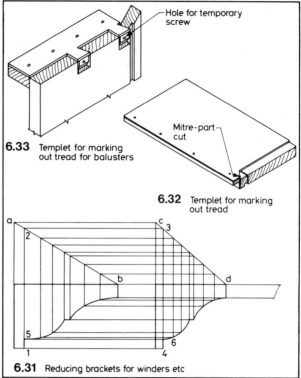

6.33   Templet for marking out tread for balusters

6.32   Templet for marking out tread

6.31   Reducing brackets for winders etc

Fig. 6.31 shows how this reduction is made. On the left is the standard bracket for fliers and on the right the one reduced to fit the winder. A raking line, of any convenient pitch, is drawn over the bracket winder. The width end of the reduced bracket is also drawn as shown with a raking line to the same height **c**.

Projectors are then drawn from the salient point in the one to give the corresponding points in the other. One series of projectors is shown, numbered in order of procedure to illustrate the method. Thus a vertical line is drawn through points to illustrate the method. The line is drawn through points **1** and **5** to cut the first raker at **2**, thence horizontally to the second raker at **3** and from thence a vertical to point **4** or beyond. Horizontals from points **1** and **5** then give the points **4** and **6** on the bracket. The same procedure is used for all other points which are then joined up with fluent curves or straight lines as indicated.

It will be seen from **Fig. 6.26** that the balusters are carried by the treads and therefore their spacing must be related to the step going. If they are to be equally spaced, it is usual to make one baluster in line with the face of each riser and one other between. The tread is carried through to the face of the string and finished with a return nosing mitred to the tread nosing and returned in itself at the back. The nosing may be slot screwed to the tread. As the screws are to be driven into end-grain, they should be longer than usual depending also upon the hardness of the timber.

The small return on the back end of the return nosing may be formed in the solid or mitred. The treads and riser may all be cut to length on the dimension saw. **Fig. 6.32** shows a templet used for marking out a tread to receive the mitred return nosing. The mitre should only be partly cut away in the initial stages leaving the more vulnerable part protected. The cutting away of the waste can be done on the bandsaw and, by using a suitable jig, finished on the router as far as the mitre.

Fig. 6.33 shows a templet for marking out the dovetail recesses for the balusters. These are initially sawn in and partly chopped away at the shoulder as shown. The risers are cut to length on the dimension saw. The mitre and rebate to the string may then be done on the tenoner.

Assembling cut string stairs

The procedure in assembling stairs with cut string is to fit the steps to the outer string and then wedge and cramp them into the wall string. The outer string is placed in the bench vice, supported level on blocks screwed to the bench front (see Fig. 6.34). A bearer is then levelled in on the back of the bench so that, when each step is in position, it rests on the bearer.

The treads and risers are assembled into steps which are fitted one at a time to the string. Temporary fixings are obtained for the treads by screwing

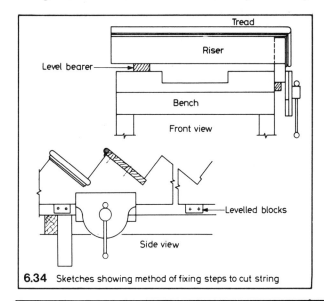

6.34 Sketches showing method of fixing steps to cut string

through the waste left in the dovetail notches. After that, the stairs may be turned over and permanently glue blocked from the inside. The old fashioned animal glue is still best for rubbed-in glue blocks.

Glue blocks should never be nailed in position for two reasons:

1. The impact of the hammer on the wood forces the glue out of the joint and leaves it starved, and

2. The nail emerging from the glued face of the block tends to lift a splinter and reduces the close fit.

In the final stage, the other ends of the steps are fitted and wedged into the wall strings. Packings are used when cramping to avoid damaging the projecting return nosings.

Reinforcing the handrail

Where cut strings are continuous for the full length of the stairs without newel posts, some additional reinforcement is necessary to the handrail beyond that provided by the wooden balustrade. This is achieved by introducing occasional steel balusters of the same pattern as the wooden ones.

Fig. 6.35 shows the fixing of a steel baluster to a cut and mitred string. The bottom end is cranked so that it may be taken back, housed and screwed into the inside of the string. When the string is cut and bracketed, the brackets may be used to conceal the lower part of the baluster. This may be recessed into the outer string face, as seen in Fig. 6.36.

A method sometimes adopted to avoid the use of steel balusters is illustrated in Fig. 6.37 showing the baluster fixed to the face of the string. The end of the tread is finished with a solid nosing with a scotia (concave) mould planted underneath it. The balusters are then cut back into the nosing and screwed to the string. The screws are concealed by pelleting or by decoratively turned buttons. The bottom of the baluster is finished with a suitable return mould. In this

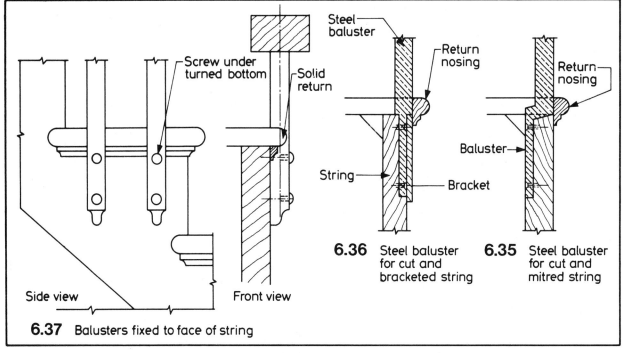

6.36 Steel baluster for cut and bracketed string

6.35 Steel baluster for cut and mitred string

6.37 Balusters fixed to face of string

case balusters are best set centrally to each tread in pairs. Although of sound construction, this method is considered to appear clumsy.

A PRACTICAL EXAMPLE OF GEOMETRICAL STAIRS

In describing geometrical stairs, it was decided to take as an example a half-turn staircase with a quarter-space landing and quarter-space winders. There is a starting newel, D-end and bullnose steps at the bottom. The outline plan is shown in **Fig. 6.38**. **Fig. 6.39** shows detail of **A** (**Fig. 6.38**).

The bullnose step is standard construction with most traditional stairs. The block for the D-end is shown with the grain of alternate layers at 45 degrees to each other. This will help to avoid joint lines showing through the veneer due to uneven shrinkage. As an alternative to the D-end, the first step can be a curtail one but this usually follows the outline of a handrail scroll over and will be dealt with later.

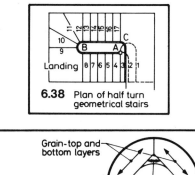

6.38 Plan of half turn geometrical stairs

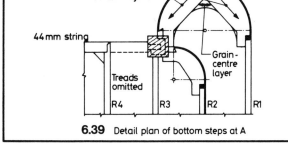

6.39 Detail plan of bottom steps at A

Forming the wreath

The first wreath in the string occurs at **B** (**Fig. 6.38**). The wreath includes the length of one flier above and below the springing. The method of forming the wreaths depends upon the radius of the curve and the quality of finish required. Where the radius is small, and the job is to be finished by painting, the wreath may be formed in solid timber, rebated or tongued to receive the strings, as shown in **Fig. 6.40**. The change of grain from the strings makes this unsuitable for

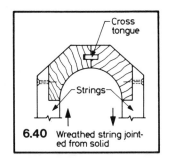

6.40 Wreathed string jointed from solid

polished or natural finished work and, for large curves, shrinkage would introduce problems.

For wreaths of large radius, say 500mm or more, the strings may be laminated, being built up to the required thickness in layers thin enough to be bent cold to the required curve. These are likely to be met where the stairs themselves are curved on plan.

For wreaths of radius of up to about 200mm, the best way to form them is by the veneer and stave method. The curved part of the string is reduced to a veneer. This is then bent around a drum of the desired radius at the requisite pitch. It is then backed up to the original thickness with vertical staves, fitted with close glued joints all round the curve between springings. The staves are made longer than required and screwed through the waste wood into the drum above and below the veneer. As soon as the glue has set, the backs of the staves are cleaned off and a stout canvas is glued over the surface. This has the effect of stabilising the work and reducing shrinkage movement and splits through loss of moisture. The wreath is then cut away to the outline of the steps and stair soffit and incorporated in the stairs.

Calculating the stretch-out of the wreath

The first procedure is to set out the stretch-out of the steps in the wreath full size. The stretch-out of the wreath at **B** (**Fig. 6.38**) is shown in **Fig. 6.41**. In the plan (**Fig. 6.42**), the curved well and the position of the landing and three winders are shown. A quick, but approximate method of obtaining not only the stretch-out of the curve, but also the position of the winders on it, is shown in plan.

A line at an angle of 60 degrees (θ) is drawn from the springing to intersect the centre line and a tangent parallel to the springing. Then the approximate length of the quadrant $= a_i - d$. If, from point **0**,

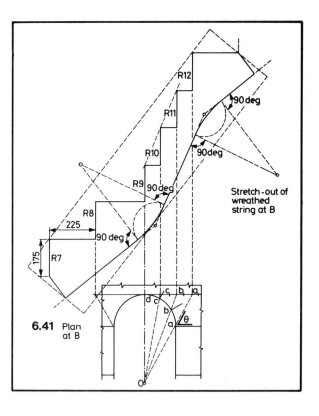

6.41 Plan at B

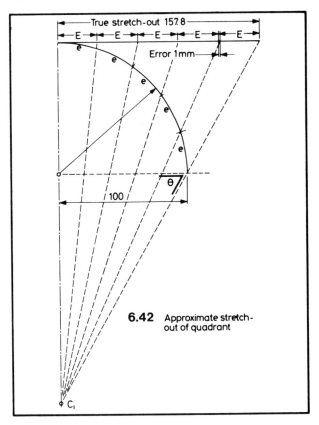

6.42 Approximate stretch-out of quadrant

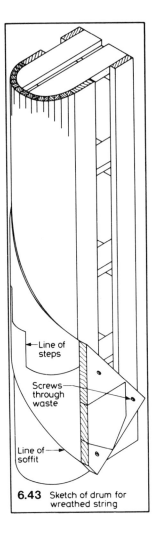

6.43 Sketch of drum for wreathed string

radiating lines are drawn through points **b** and **c** to cut the tangent again, the b_i and c_i will give the relative positions of the winders on the stretch-out.

As trial and error should play a small part in staircase work (or in any joinery for that matter), it is advisable to know the possible degree of error in approximations. For the full stretch-out, the true length and the drawing-board projected length can be separately calculated and compared.

If the radius of curvature is then taken at 100mm, the error, in mm, becomes a percentage of the radius; assuming this, the error to any radius can easily be calculated (see **Fig. 6.43**). Taking the radius of curvature of 100mm, therefore, the true length of quadrant

$$= \frac{\pi \times 100}{2} = 157.079\text{mm}$$

By the drawing board method, calculated radius = 100 (1 + cotan 60°)
= 100 (1 + 0.5774) = 157.74.
Therefore error = 157.74 − 157.079 = 0.66mm or the error is in excess of 0.66 per cent of radius. So, for a radius of 300mm, error will be 1.98 (say 2) mm.

Calculating riser positions
We now come to the drawing-board method of subdividing the stretch-out to give riser positions. This is also only approximate and an approximation taken from an approximation may be unacceptable. However, by altering the angle from 60 degrees the original error may be eliminated. The true length is 157.079, so the cotan of the angle θ

$$= \frac{157.079 - 100}{100} = 0.57079$$

From the trigonomical tables, the angle corresponding with this is 60.32 degrees or about 0.3 degrees over 60 degrees, which can be estimated as a variation from 60 degrees even without a protractor with high degree of precision.

In **Fig. 6.43** this angle was used at θ instead of 60 degrees. The stretch-out and the original curve were separately divided into five equal parts. Radiating lines were then drawn through the curve **e–e** to cut the tangent with its divisions **E–E**.

The maximum error proved to be 1mm or again 1 per cent of the radius. This error would not normally be noticeable, provided the tread width was adjusted to suit. Otherwise the nosings would have an uneven overhang on the riser.

Setting out step outlines
Figs. 6.41 and **Fig. 6.42** also illustrate the method of setting out the step outline to be marked on the plank from which the wreath is to be cut. Start with the last flier in the lower straight flight and finish with the first flier in the upper flight. Riser numbers should be compared with those in **Fig. 6.38**. The step and landing outlines should be drawn first.

The overall width, rise and going will give the pitch and string widths to agree with the upper and lower straight flights. A parallel to the nosing line of the three uniform winders will give the width of the wreath below them. The three straight lines are then joined by tangent curves by the method on **Fig. 6.41**. This should be self explanatory.

The width and length of the plank from which the wreath must be formed may then be drawn in as shown by the dotted lines (**Fig. 6.41**), enclosing the development. The plank is then set out from the drawing. It is as well to clean up the outer surface before marking out and working. It will be difficult to do this afterwards. Subsequent dirty marks due to handling may be easily removed afterwards.

The back of the plank is then recessed to veneer thickness between the springing lines on risers 8 and 12. It is bent around and fixed to the drum by screwing through the waste timber. None of the steps should be cut out at this stage. It is essential that the springing lines at risers 8 and 12 should be placed exactly over similar lines marked on the drum.

The drum is constructed of a number of rib frames covered with boards and staves and sufficiently solid to take the pressures in straining the wreath piece to the face, and to support the veneer against the pressure from the staves. **Fig. 6.43** is a sketch of the drum with the wreath piece wrapped around it before it is staved. The steps are shown on the back of the veneer purely to indicate their positions. They would, of course, be marked on the exposed face.

Fig. 6.44 shows the complete wreath removed from the drum and cut to the step and soffit outlines. If the steps are cut and mitred, the riser edges will have to mitre with the risers as shown for fliers. The canvas lining has been omitted, the better to indicate the vertical lines of the staving.

The joint between the straight string and the wreath is usually made with a tongue or dowels but is pulled up tight by means of a counter cramp (**Figs. 6.44** and **6.45**). Each member of the cramp contains a mortise; these are lined up when assembled to take a pair of folding wedges. **Fig. 6.45** is a section through

the actual mortises on assembly. The outer members are screwed to the right-hand side of the joint and the inner member to the left-hand.

When the wedges are expanded by tightening, the left-hand part of the joint is pulled to the right by pressure on the mortise of the central member and the right-hand part similarly to the left. Additional screws are driven in afterwards to give security. Although all three pieces are normally made the same width, it seems to be common sense to double the width of the central member. This will give it the same number of screws and the same bearing surface as the sum of the other two.

Figs. 6.46 and **6.47** show the plan and stretch-out of the wreathed string to the upper floor landing. The lines of the under edge of the string must agree with the string width on the rake, as well as with the depth of the apron lining (or fascia) to the landing trimmer from the underside of the nosing to the ceiling line.

The finish of the string at the top of the stairs is shown in **Figs. 6.48** to **6.51**. **Figs. 6.48** and **6.49** (elevation and plan) illustate the details of balusters and the method of spacing. The ultimate spacing distance of the balusters must be a factor of the ultimate overall length with a half baluster against the wall. However, it should be as near as possible to that on the stairs.

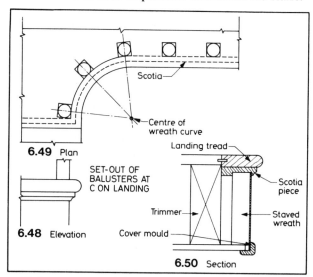

6.49 Plan

SET-OUT OF BALUSTERS AT C ON LANDING

6.48 Elevation

6.50 Section

Balusters around the wreath should radiate on plan from the wreath centre. As the string sweeps into the landing apron lining, its general section must agree with it because the nosing, scotia and stair soffit are continued to the end wall. **Fig. 6.50** shows a section through the wreath at landing level. The scotia mould is worked on a wide board which is housed to fit over the top edge of the string. This mould is then mitred to the step scotia (see **Fig. 6.51**).

Use of rough carriages

As previously stated, the cut and wreathed strings are not in themselves strong enough to carry the loads imposed on the stairs. Rough carriages are placed under the steps within the depth of the string in positions where they can take these loads and transfer them to the floor, walls and trimmers as may be convenient. They are secured by means of brackets (screwed to the steps and glue-blocked to the treads).

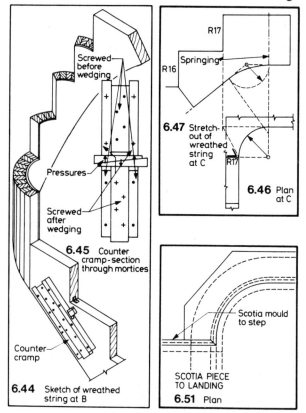

6.45 Counter cramp-section through mortices

6.44 Sketch of wreathed string at B

6.47 Stretch-out of wreathed string at C

6.46 Plan at C

6.51 Plan

The twisted or flued effect created by winders makes it difficult to show these precisely on a drawing. Their final position is best left to the joiner fixing the stairs.

Fig. 6.52 shows the plan and **Fig. 6.53** the section through the wreath and its support to the upper landing. Supporting the projection due to the wreath is no problem as the carriages may carry forward to the landing trimmer. The wreath is shown rebated to take the 25mm apron lining which is blocked off the trimmer.

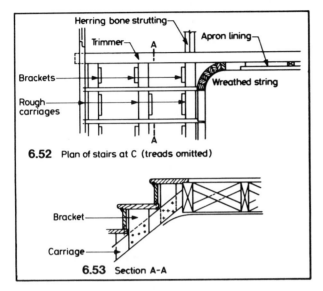

6.52 Plan of stairs at C (treads omitted)

6.53 Section A-A

Fig. 6.54 is a plan showing the possible disposition of the rough carriages and brackets under the stairs. The quarter-space landing is carried by trimmers built into the wall about 200mm. These should be tightly wedged and selected dry to avoid loosening through shrinkage. Carriages can often be arranged to give mutual support to each other at opposite ends. They ultimately have to carry the plaster soffit.

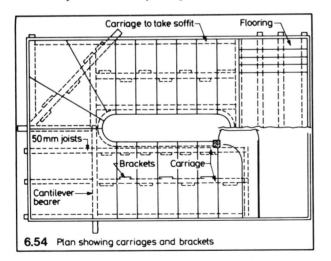

6.54 Plan showing carriages and brackets

CURVED STAIRS

Curved stairs are here defined as those which are curved in their general plan outline, as distinct from straight flights which are merely wreathed at the angles to give continuous lines of string and handrails. They involve problems, not only in geometrical design, but also in overall construction due to the difficulty of forming large curves in strings, etc, without destroying the graceful sweep of a curved soffit. The Building Regulations, 1976 which were obviously planned to promote the selection of straight flights with quarter space landings, also pose problems when related to winders. They are incompletely described in the Regulations as 'tapered treads'.

A quarter-turn curved staircase
Figs. 6.55 and **6.56** are the outline plan and elevations of a rather more than quarter-turn flight of stairs. Its shape is dictated by a curved wall of 2m radius. The staircase, being 1.2m wide, leaves 800mm radius for the outer or well string which forms 90 degrees of the turn. The total rise of 2,495mm, divided by the number of risers (16), gives a step rise of 156mm.

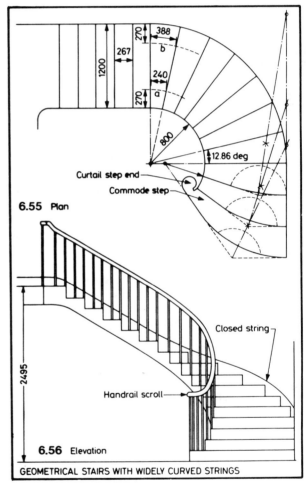

6.55 Plan

6.56 Elevation

GEOMETRICAL STAIRS WITH WIDELY CURVED STRINGS

The going of the fliers is taken at 267mm each =
$$2R + G = 2 \times 156 + 267$$
= 579mm which is satisfactory.

Pitch = angle with $\tan \dfrac{156}{267}$

= 0.597 or tan angle 30.30 degrees which is also satisfactory.

To have an average going to agree with that of the fliers 6 or 7 winders will be needed. Taking latter, these will taper

$$\frac{90}{7} = 12.87 \text{ degrees}$$

The width of each winder must be such that
$$2R + G \geqslant 550\text{mm} \leqslant 700\text{mm}$$
and maximum pitch = 38 degrees
apply on lines taken at 270mm from the inner and outer strings (see **Fig. 6.55**).

If these widths are taken as straight lines, they form isosceles triangles with the riser lines taken back to the centre of the string curve. These, when bisected, form pairs of right-angled triangles with base angles of

$$\frac{12.86}{2} = 6.43 \text{ degrees}$$

and hypotenuses of 1070 and 1730 respectively.

From this, using trigonometrical tables, goings on lines **a** and **b** =
$$2 \times \sin 6.43 \text{ degrees} \times 1070 =$$
$$0.2242 \times 1070 = 240$$
$$\text{and } 0.2242 \times 1730 = 388.$$

Both of these, taken with the rise of 156mm, will be found to come within the Regulation requirements as stated before.

In order to give a more convenient angle of approach, the winders are continued beyond the quadrant. The outer string continues to follow a curve, but the wall string becomes straight. In order to give a graceful fall to the lower part of the wall string, the goings of the steps are continued unaltered; but the radius of the curve to the outer string is shortened on a common normal, thereby further increasing the stair width and approach angle.

The risers are normal to both strings. The initially straight riser lines to each step meet at an angle which is bisected to meet the line of the wall string. They give the centres from which the curves giving the ultimate shape of the swelled risers may be struck. The bottom step should be finished with a curtail step to follow the shape of the handrail scroll above.

Semicircular staircase

Fig. 6.57 is the outline plan of a semicircular curved staircase in a semicircular ended well. The taper on the winders will again meet the design requirements with something less than 15 degrees taper.

In the example given, there are 13 risers, giving a taper of

$$\frac{180}{13} = 13.85 \text{ degrees}$$

Taking the step goings at 270mm from each string as before, values of 351 and 228mm are obtained. These, taken with rises of 165mm, are satisfactory. Additional steps to make up the height must then be fitted in outside the semicircle.

The supports to the steps and outer (well) strings constitute a problem and must be done almost entirely by means of carriage pieces as shown. It is best achieved by offering up the timbers underneath

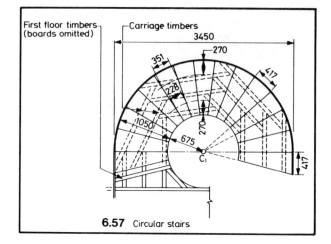

6.57 Circular stairs

the steps when the stairs are in position, placing them as nearly as possible so that they touch the step edge. The actual support is given to the steps by brackets screwed to the carriages (not shown).

It is better to work from the lower floor level, starting against the wall string. The right-hand carriage rests on the floor and is taken across to the wall string. The next up has its lower end nailed to the first and its upper end again taken to the wall. The procedure is repeated to the upper floor. The centre row of carriages take their first support from the outer carriages and their second from each other, the procedure being repeated against the well string.

Elliptical staircases

The set-out of elliptical stairs also involves some extra geometrical problems. **Fig. 6.58** is the outline plan of an elliptical staircase with a centre landing to avoid having more than 16 risers in one flight.

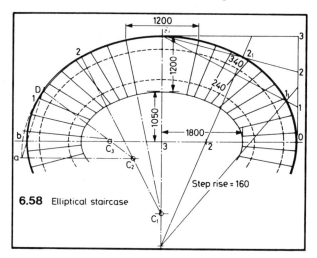

6.58 Elliptical staircase

The general requirement that the width of a staircase should be constant throughout its length precludes the use of a true ellipse for both outer and wall string as no two ellipses can be truly parallel. It must therefore be decided which of the strings must be elliptical or approximately elliptical, and then the other must be drawn parallel to it. In my opinion, it is better to use an approximate ellipse based on circular curves for the first outline. The other can then be drawn easily parallel to it from the same centres.

In **Fig. 6.58**, the outer wall curve is drawn as an approximate ellipse, the curves of the well string being constructed from the same centres. That outline is contained in a rectangle enclosing major and minor axes. On the right-hand side, the half major axis and outer vertical are divided equally into three. Radiating and converging lines respectively are drawn to intersect at points **1** and **2**, which would be points on the curve of a true ellipse. These points are repeated on the left-hand side.

So the setting-out of the curve is as follows: **3**–**2** is bisected with a line cutting the minor axis to give the centre for the first curve from **3** to **2**; **2** is joined to C_1; **2**–**1** is bisected to cut $C_1 2$ at C_2. C_2 is the centre to the next curve drawn to cut a horizontal from C_2 at **a**. A line is drawn from **a**, through the end of the major axis at **0** to cut the curve at **D**. A line drawn from **D** to C_2 cuts the major axis at C_3. From C_3, the final curve is drawn from **D** to **0**.

The outline of the well strings can also be drawn from the centres C_1, C_2 and C_3. As it would be tedious or impossible to calculate the lengths of the elliptical or approximately elliptical curves, it is easier to measure them with dividers, setting out to as large a scale as is convenient.

If the critical lines 270mm in from the strings are thus measured, step goings can be calculated by dividing by the number of treads, keeping (if possible) well within the upper and lower limits. In order to give a better outline to the stairs, the goings are divided equally along the outer and wall strings respectively, so that the stretch-out of each string will have straight edges and nosing lines.

The risers at the ends will not be normal to the plan curves of the strings and may have to be checked by measuring more nearly square across their widths.

Forming the curved strings

The problem in the construction of curved stairs lies in forming the long and widely curved strings. The method previously described of strings reduced to a veneer and backed with vertical staves, is not practicable. There would be insufficient strength where most was needed, and shrinkage problems would occur with the vertical staves.

One method of overcoming this problem is to build up 'brickwork fashion', as shown in **Fig. 6.59**, in layers to break joint. Afterwards both sides are veneered. Housing to take the steps or cutting and mitring is

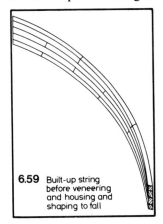

6.59 Built-up string before veneering and housing and shaping to fall

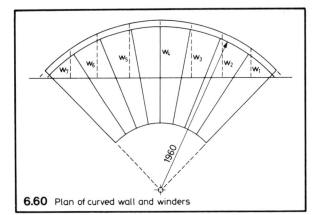

6.60 Plan of curved wall and winders

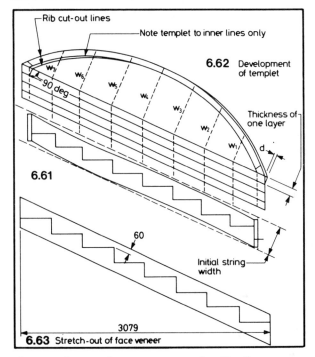

6.62 Development of templet

Note templet to inner lines only

Rib cut-out lines

Thickness of one layer

6.61

Initial string width

6.63 Stretch-out of face veneer

done to them as the case may require. For the purpose of reasonable economy, each layer needs to be in two or three lengths butt-jointed together. The assembled string will, in effect, be an oblique slice through part of a cylinder with walls equal to the string thickness. **Figs. 6.60** to **6.63** illustrate the steps in preparing and assembling the layers into the string.

The plan of the string and the position of the steps is first drawn (see **Fig. 6.60**). Lines from the riser faces can conveniently be drawn as ordinates, w_1 to w_7. Next, the elevation of the curved string is drawn (not its stretch-out), by first projecting the risers from the plan and then combining them with the step rises to produce the step outline (see **Fig. 6.61**).

The margin line width taken vertically will then give the elevation of the top edge of the string, while similar measurements taken below the steps will give the bottom edge. Raking parallel lines enclosing these limits will give the total width of build-up of laminations necessary to construct the slice of cylinder which will contain the string, also its pitch.

The outline elevation is repeated in **Fig. 6.62** and, suitably divided by parallel lines, represents the elevation of the parallel boards from which the slice of cylinder is built up. Projectors w_1 to w_7 are taken through to **Fig. 6.62** and squared over as shown. The ordinate widths, including string thickness, are marked on to give points through which the elliptical curves are drawn. This gives the true shape of the oblique section through the cylinder.

A templet is made to this shape and marked on a board. It is then slid the distance **d** parallel to the chord line and marked again. A templet is also made to this shape (i.e. the second templet will be wider at the ends). The pieces in each layer must be assembled with neat joints, marked out, cut and shaped overall to the larger templet. They must then be assembled on top of the templet. Next they will be marked from the second templet on both sides to give the waste to be cut away. In this case, it is by sliding the distance **d** to the left. The layers may then be assembled with screws and will form the cylindrical faces of the string.

It is then necessary to veneer both sides. Then the step outlines, the step housings and the falling lines of the top and bottom edge of the string may be marked and cut.

In this case all the step markings are presumed to be equal to the nosing line and top and bottom edge of strings will all be straight. As the radius is known and the string is a quadrant on plan, the horizontal stretch-out of string

$$= \pi \frac{1960}{2} = 3079\text{mm}$$

The going of each step will therefore be

$$\frac{3079}{8} = 385\text{mm}$$

If the goings of the winders vary, they will have to be measured separately; but it is still advisable to calculate the total stretch-out as a check. Where the curve is other than a quadrant, the going may be calculated as

$$2\pi r \left(\frac{\text{angle of turn}}{360} \right)$$

Laminating strings
Construction of strings by laminating is probably the strongest method but it may also be the most expensive, due to the need for a former for clamping the laminations during the process of gluing up. The thicker the laminations that can be conveniently used, the better. A general rule is to make them 0.01th part of the radius of curvature, but it depends upon the species of timber being used. It is worthwhile to test a sample piece of narrow width by bending it around the former, making allowance for the extra effort which will be needed for bending the full board.

If the thickness is taken at maximum to start with, it can, by trial and error, be successively reduced through the panel planer until the necessary flexibility has been achieved. As there is likely to be some spring-back, it is as well to make the radius of the former a little less than that of the actual finished curve. **Fig. 6.64** shows the former built up with staves nailed to framed centres and the string fixed in position at the necessary pitch.

The laminae are secured to the drum by means of clamps screwed in position, one of which is shown. The spacing depends upon the thickness of the

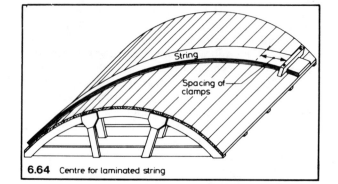

6.64   Centre for laminated string

laminae. If the top edge of the string is eventually covered, only the outer laminae need to be of the finished timber; the inner layers can be of softwood. As the gluing-up will be a long process and all the joints may not be 100 per cent perfect, it is as well to use a slow-setting gap-filling glue such as resorcinal formaldehyde. Long strings should be made in several lengths and assembled afterwards with tongued or dowelled joints. Generally each section should not be more than a quadrant on plan.

Housing of the strings to take the steps will be a long and expensive process, if carried out by hand. It may be possible to use a pair of jigs, one within the other, on the router with the compound table. The first one has a flat bed secured to the table and an upper concave cylindrical face fixed with its axis parallel to the line of travel of the table. On this, another cylindrical unit fixed to slide at right-angles to the axis, is so arranged that the string rests in it with stops keeping it to the required pitch to the axis of the cylinder.

For housing for the riser, the whole system is locked together and fed forward against the cutter. The table for the tread housing the string is fixed to the top cylindrical unit only. This is moved around the curved base at right-angles to its axis. Alternatively, the string can be fixed in a jig in the drilling machine and the waste drilled out. This leaves the outlines to be chopped by hand.

HELICAL STAIRS

Where circular stairs are free standing and more or less a complete circle on plan, they are often (erroneously) known as spiral stairs. The correct term is 'helical' stairs. A spiral curve reduces continuously towards its apex or eye.

The normal type of curved string cannot carry its own weight and the weight of the steps under load. The staircase must either be reinforced with continuous newels to the outer string at suitable intervals, or the stairs must be built around a centre newel in the form of a post or drum. The traditional method of using the solid post with a diameter of about 600mm is not permissible today due to the restrictions imposed by the Building Regulations. Two examples are given of how the Regulations affect design.

Taking private and common stairs and average storey heights the taper of the winders can again be rather less than 15 degrees. This can also be influenced by the radius of the inner string, column or newel post and the width of the stairs measured radially as well as the necessary step rise. The most economical helical stair design will require the maximum permitted step rise, the minimum step going and the least permissible radius to the outer string and centre newel.

Taking the common stairway. Effective width of winders = 900mm. The minimum going taken on the inner walking line 270mm from string or newel = 240mm and the maximum pitch = 38 degrees. The maximum walking line 270mm from the outer string must be such that 2R + G ≤ 700mm.

Pitch of step = 38 degrees so if going = 240mm 240 × tan 38 degrees equals 187.5mm. Applying the rule 2R + G ≤ 550mm 2 × 187.5 + 240 = 615mm which is satisfactory.

The going on the outer line 270, from the outer string must be such that it satisfies the rule 2R + G ≤ 700. Therefore the maximum going must be 700 − 2 × 187.5 = 325mm. Then from **Fig. 6.65** it will be seen that the effective radius of the drum or inner string

$$= \frac{325}{325-240} \times 360 - 630mm = 746$$

which must be the least radius of the drum to conform to the Regulations. It would require a built up drum or a string supported by continuous newels.

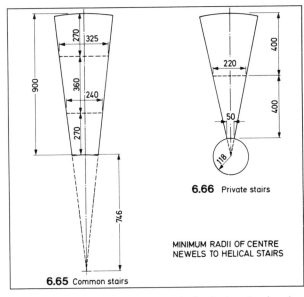

6.65 Common stairs

6.66 Private stairs

MINIMUM RADII OF CENTRE NEWELS TO HELICAL STAIRS

Taking private stairways, their design is simpler. Assuming that they conform to the rule for winders, the minimum radius of the flight has to permit the centre width of the winder to be at least 220mm and the minimum width to be 50mm.

Then minimum radius of the centre newel

$$= \frac{220}{220-50} \times 400 - 400 = 118mm$$

Within reason therefore the size of the centre newel or post can be at the discretion of the designer. **Figs. 6.67, 6.68**.

The elevation is drawn by projecting from the plan for the width of each step and combining this with step rise, to give step outline on string, column, etc. The stretch-out of the outside string (away from the centre) and step lines on the centre drum are all based

on straight lines, measuring the stretch-out of the plan going horizontally and the step rise vertically.

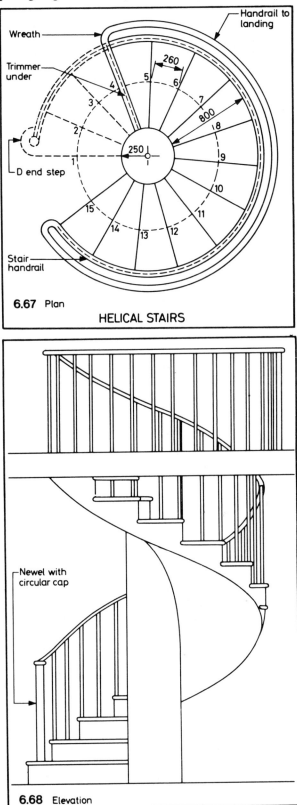

6.67 Plan

HELICAL STAIRS

6.68 Elevation

The continuous handrail follows above the outside string from a circular newel over a D-end step at lower floor level up to landing balustrade height. There it does a U-turn and caps the balustrade around the circular well hole to the straight balustrade over the trimmer.

The radius of the circular well over the landing is 180mm greater than that of the outside string. The outside string may be built up and veneered or laminated as already described but the centre drum (a solid newel would not be practicable) needs special consideration as it has to carry 100 by 50mm bearers cantilevered from the drum under each tread. These bearers carry the weight of the steps and the outer string and provide a fixing for the laths for the flued plaster soffit.

Figs. 6.69, **6.70** and **6.71** show details of the construction of the drum taken at the bottom of the stairs. The drum consists essentially of vertical staves, housed to built-up, horizontal, polygonal ribs framed in double layers of 30mm thick material and spaced at every fourth riser. A centre post of 100 by 100mm material is retained in position within the drum by

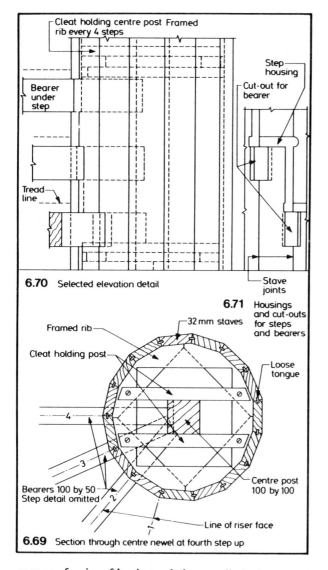

6.70 Selected elevation detail

6.71 Housings and cut-outs for steps and bearers

6.69 Section through centre newel at fourth step up

means of pairs of horizontal cleats nailed or screwed on each side and screwed down to the ribs.

The 100 by 50mm cantilever bearers are placed under the steps directly under each riser. The staves have been kept flat and there is one directly opposite each tread. They could, of course, be rounded to form part of a cylindrical drum but this would be more expensive and housings would be more difficult. The

staves are notched around the bearers and housed for the steps as shown in **Fig. 6.71**. The horizontal bearers are taken through to the centre post and notched into it. The staves are fitted with loose tongues and dry joints to allow shrinkage, although they may be glued to the ribs. In some cases, the bearers may slightly foul the holding cleats; in that case they may be notched around them.

HANDRAIL SCROLLS

When geometrical stairs are constructed with continuous strings and handrails, and without intermediate newels, the bottom of the handrail may terminate in a capping to a bottom newel. However the most logical and graceful finish is a handrail scroll, followed closely in plan outline by a curtail end to the bottom step. The handrail scroll is first set out in relation to the step position and then the step itself is set out following the curves closely from the same centres.

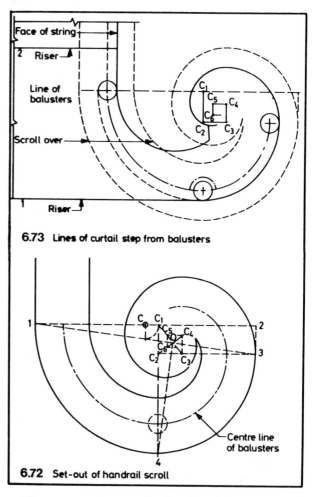

6.73 Lines of curtail step from balusters

6.72 Set-out of handrail scroll

There are various methods of setting out a scroll but the one shown (**Fig. 6.72**) gives a graceful shape, while being sufficiently robust to withstand the rigours of common usage. Procedure is as follows:

1. Mark out line **1–2**, 4 times the handrail width;
2. Draw line **2–3** one-half the handrail width and join **1–3**;
3. Draw a vertical line through the middle – **C**. Using **C** as a centre, swing the short distance up

on to line **1–2**. Then C_1 is the centre for the first quadrant;

4. From **3**, draw a horizontal to give centre c_2, which is the centre for the second quadrant;

5. From point **4**, draw a line at right-angles to **1–3**, cutting it at point **0**. Draw diagonals through **0** from c_2 and c_3.

Successive horizontal and vertical lines taken around these diagonals as shown will give centres for additional reducing curves as required. It will be seen that line c_2–c_3–**3** is a common normal. This continues with all other centres. Each reducing radius is used for an exact quadrant. The inside curve of the handrail follows from the same respective centres.

Curtail steps

Fig. 6.73 shows how the curtail step is set out in relation to the scroll. The inner curve is a continuation of the line of the outer string, the line of balusters coming against this as shown. The line of balusters continues to follow the first curve of the scroll from centre c_1 and disects the face of the riser to the step. Then the outer curve of the curtail follows with tangent curves from centres c_2, c_3, c_4 and c_5. The inner curve of the curtail is drawn from a convenient centre on line **1–2** so as to leave a suitable width of neck at the narrowest part. Balusters are positioned to agree approximately with their spacing on the stairs.

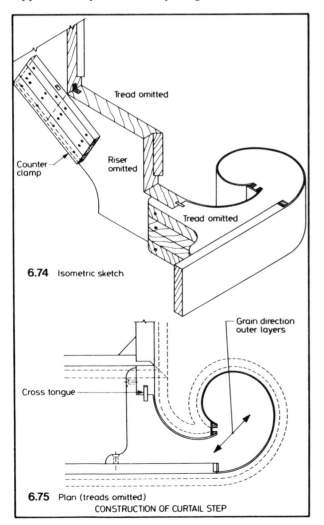

6.74 Isometric sketch

6.75 Plan (treads omitted)

CONSTRUCTION OF CURTAIL STEP

Figs. 6.74 and **6.75** show the construction of the curtail step. The shaped end is formed by the riser reduced to a veneer. This is glued around a block built up in three layers with different directions of grain. The end of the riser board, reduced to a veneer, is glued and damped on the back, wedged into the block and then laid flat on the bench with the block overhanging. The block is then rolled on to the veneer end, keeping it pulled tight to prevent crippling, and wedged and screwed into position. The bottom part of the string is jointed at the back of the second riser.

The short piece of string is reduced to a veneer which is wetted, glued and cramped into the concave part of the riser block using a shaped hot caul. Finally, the step is jointed to the main part of the string by means of a counter cramp.

Commode steps

Commode steps with swelled risers and D-end or curtail ends may be formed in several different ways. They can be built up and veneered (as described for a string), or laminated using a former, or be faced with plywood, as thick as will satisfactorily bend to the curve, fixed to framed-up ribs. **Figs. 6.76** to **6.79** show this method, incorporating a D-end.

The flexibility of plywood (in relation to its thickness) varies with the species of timber, numbers and thicknesses of plies, etc. Before finally selecting the ply, it is safer to test two or three strips of different thicknesses. The block forming the D-end is incorporated into a frame consisting of horizontal ribs suitably curved with stub-tenoned vertical soldiers. The part of the plywood riser to fit around the block is reduced in thickness to two plies. A short piece of the back end is left at full thickness to check into the block.

The ribs are notched to take folding wedges and accommodate a vertical cleat pre-glued to the riser as shown in **Fig. 6.76**. The block with the ribs attached is rolled on to the reduced end, tightened with folding wedges, and held there temporarily with packings and gee cramps. The rest of the riser is then glued and held in place against the ribs using shaped packings and gee cramps. If the waste from cutting the ribs is assembled as shown in **Fig. 6.79**, it can be used for this purpose.

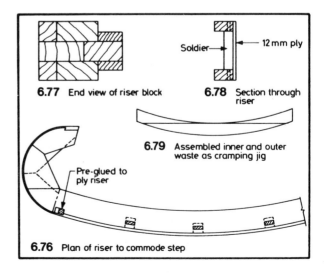

6.77 End view of riser block

6.78 Section through riser

6.79 Assembled inner and outer waste as cramping jig

6.76 Plan of riser to commode step

QUESTIONS FOR CHAPTER 6

Question 14
An open newel stair is shown in **Fig. 6.80**. The stair is for private use.
The total rise is 2340.
Newel posts = 100 by 100mm.
Strings = 38mm thick.
Treads = 32mm thick.
Risers = 15mm thick.

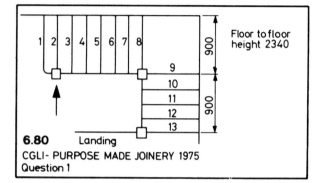

6.80 Landing
CGLI- PURPOSE MADE JOINERY 1975
Question 1

    a. Calculate the step rise and determine a suitable step going.
    b. Draw an elevation in the direction of the arrow of the bottom three steps, showing the joint between the string and the newel post. Scale 1:5.
    c. Set out the four faces of the newel post to show positions of treads, risers and mortises for the string.
    d. Sketch the construction of the bullnose step.

City & Guilds of London Institute Examination, Purpose-Made Joinery, 1975. No. 5.
Time allowed: 30 minutes.

Question 15
Fig. 6.81 shows the plan of a geometrical stair. The wreathed string is cut and bracketed. Given that the width of the fliers is 300mm, and the width of the tapered steps at their narrow ends is 125mm, draw a development of the wreathed string when the rise is 190mm. Scale 1:20.

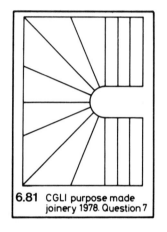

6.81 CGLI purpose made joinery 1978. Question 7

City & Guilds of London Institute Examination, Purpose-Made Joinery, 1978. No. 7.
Time allowed: 12 minutes.

Question 16
To a scale of 1:20, draw the development of the well string in **Fig. 6.55** and indicate the joint lines.

(I was not able to find a suitable question available in past papers and have therefore presented my own.)

CHAPTER 7

Handrails

GEOMETRICAL HANDRAILS

Geometrical handrails invariably form part of a geometrical staircase as described in Chapter 6. Being continuous from floor to floor, they give the user the advantage of uninterrupted support. This makes them suitable for public buildings and where there are elderly and infirm people. They are, in some cases, fixed to walls with bullnose or rounded quoins. There are two recognised systems of producing geometrical handrails. The most commonly known is the square-cut and tangent system, which will be demonstrated here, and the normal section method. Each have their own advantages and disadvantages.

Handrailing is probably the least understood of all the processes coming under the heading of 'joinery'. The drawings necessary in producing a handrail wreath may appear very complex to the uninitiated observer but, when taken carefully and step-by-step, the work breaks down into a fairly simple series of logical processes.

Setting out a wreathed handrail
It is important that the setter-out should understand how the handrail is related to the staircase. Its position on the stairs must, first of all, be ascertained in relation to the balusters as carried by the (usually) cut string. The handrail will follow the straight flights in the normal way but a wreathed (or curved) rail is jointed between the straight rails on the bends.

The wreath will follow round the same plan centre as the wreathed string under. In **Fig. 7.1**, which is the plan and vertical section of the stair string, baluster and handrail, it will be seen that the radius of curvature is dictated by the position of the handrail in relation to the string. The radius of curvature is given by the centre line of the handrail coinciding with the centre of the baluster.

If a vertical axis is taken up from the plan centre, the handrail swings around this axis at a constant plan radius. Or, to put it another way, the centre line of the handrail climbs around a vertical cylinder within the positions where the straight rail centre lines meet it at a tangent.

In the square-cut and tangent system, the inner and outer faces of the handrail also coincide with vertical cylinders about the same axis, the difference in radii being the handrail width on plan (see **Fig. 7.2**). As the handrail wreath must follow from, and meet with, the lower and upper straight rails, then (like them) its top and bottom faces must be level on all lines normal to its vertical faces: i.e. on lines radiating from the axis. The lines placed on the cylindrical faces giving this are shown in **Fig. 7.2**. The completed wreath (before moulding) is sketched on **Fig. 7.3**.

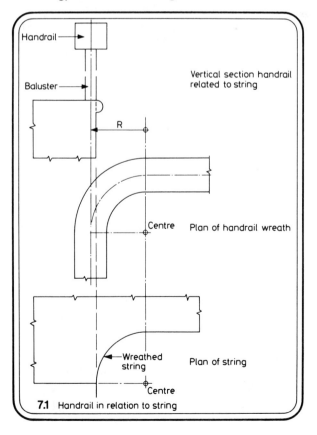

7.1 Handrail in relation to string

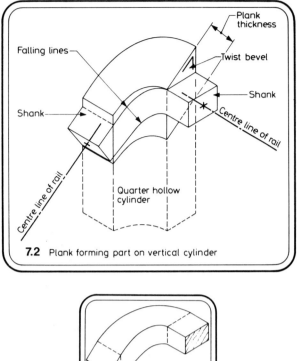

7.2 Plank forming part on vertical cylinder

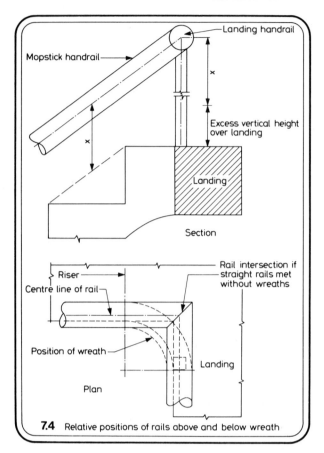

7.4 Relative positions of rails above and below wreath

7.3 Squared wreath ready for moulding

The wreath must start with a flat plank, which must be of sufficient thickness to accommodate the twisted upper and lower faces. **Fig. 7.2** shows the plank with shanks cut to meet the straight rails. The sketch is made to illustrate the cylindrical principle involved and, as shown, would be wasteful of timber. The centre line of the handrail in the wreath will lie in a flat plane, two sides of which will be formed by the lines of the straight rails above and below the turn being continued. As they form oblique sections through a cylinder, the curves in the centre-line plane will be truly eliptical. The continuing straight lines must meet.

The easiest way to think of the situation is to imagine first that the handrails are taken into the corners without wreaths (see **Fig. 7.4**) and then to cut them away and put in the wreaths afterwards. This would, of course, never be done in reality.

One point it is important to emphasise is that the position of the upper and lower straight rails must be adjusted to give this intersection of the centre lines. **Fig. 7.5** is a sketch illustrating this centre-line plane. The continued centre lines of the straight rails (called 'tangents') and the limiting plan radii ('springings') are continued in vertical planes to form a box called the 'prism'. The top of the prism is the centre-line plane. It may be said to contain the cylinder which penetrates the plane to give the centre line of the handrail.

Fig. 7.5 illustrates the prism and centre line of a handrail to a wreath joining a rail from the stairs to an upper landing with a right-angle turn. The height of landing balustrade permits the tangents to coincide at b_i. The springings O_i-C_i and O_i-a_i will be half major

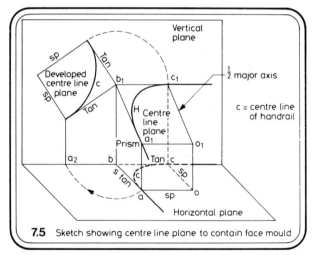

7.5 Sketch showing centre line plane to contain face mould

and half minor axes of the quarter ellipse **H** forming the centre line of the handrail.

When drawn in orthographic projection, the side a-b-b_i is hinged back against the vertical plane, **a** moving to a_2. The method of obtaining the developed centre-line plane should be self-evident. **Fig. 7.6** shows the method of obtaining the facemould which should be studied in conjunction with **Fig. 7.5** in which o-a-b-C is the plan of the prism and the pitch of a_i-b_i is the pitch of the stairs. Projectors from the plan on to the raking line give the width of the shank at **C**. As the facemould at a_i is level at the springing, the shank is the plan width.

The facemould curves are quarter ellipses and can be drawn by any known geometrical method to complete the facemould. The lower part of the wreath will be parallel to the plank (**Fig. 7.2**) and, as the upper part will be level, the twist bevel will be the pitch of the stairs. If the handrail section is drawn horizontal, lines touching its corners at the same pitch will give the plank thickness. **Fig. 7.7** shows the face mould as it would be over the plan of the wreath.

Fig. 7.8 shows the first stage in cutting out the wreath on the band saw. It is marked from the templet and the tangent lines put on. It is then band-sawn 3 or 4mm outside the lines, but the ends are shot and finished dead square to the face as well as dead square to the tangents. The exact centre of the thickness of plank is marked both ends and the sections of the shanks are marked on; the lower one is parallel to the face, and the upper one is set to the pitch bevel.

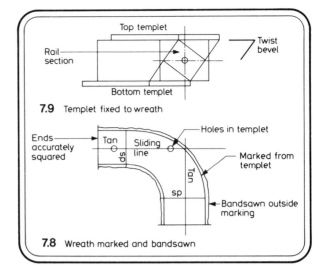

7.9 Templet fixed to wreath

7.8 Wreath marked and bandsawn

The templets are then placed, one forward and one back, as shown in **Fig. 7.9** to coincide with the pitch bevels and so that the lower tangent agrees with the templet tangent or (in this case) the sliding line.

The shanks are squared up first, and then the cylindrical faces are trued up. This should always be done parallel to the theoretical vertical axis and not straight across.

Finally, the falling lines are put on and the top and bottom surfaces completed. This can be done geometrically but is more often put on by the joiner himself to give a better line. As a check, a square held vertically and firmly against the cylindrical faces, so that the blade follows the radius, should fit all the way.

Rake to rake wreathed handrail with equal pitches
The next type of wreath to be discussed is the rake to rake with equal pitches. This occurs on a quarter-space landing where the pitch of the handrail is the same above and below the wreath. Although all the fliers in a flight should be equal, and the pitch above and below the landing should be the same, equal pitches are only possible in the wreath when the tangents (which are the continuation of the centre lines of the handrails) can be made to meet at the corner of the prism without adjustment of the straight rail.

Fig. 7.10 is the plan of the steps around a quarter-space landing in which the treads are 240mm wide but are spaced 120mm from the corner of the prism. The lower flight is hinged back about point **b** against the vertical plane and the stretch-out drawn as in **Fig. 7.11**. It will be seen that the distance on the stretch-out between risers **9** and **10** is 240mm – the same as the fliers – and, consequently, the nosings are in a straight line. Thus the pitch of both handrails will be the same. This will occur in any situation where the two distances **9-b** plus **b-10** equal the going of a flier.

In this case, in order to develop the facemould and obtain the bevels, some new geometrical principles have to be introduced. It is necessary:

1. To obtain the shape of the centre-line plane,
2. To obtain the width of the shanks on the face mould, and

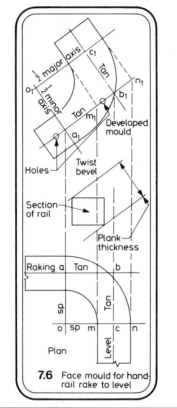

7.6 Face mould for handrail rake to level

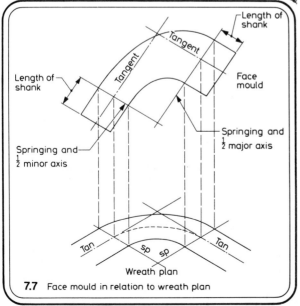

7.7 Face mould in relation to wreath plan

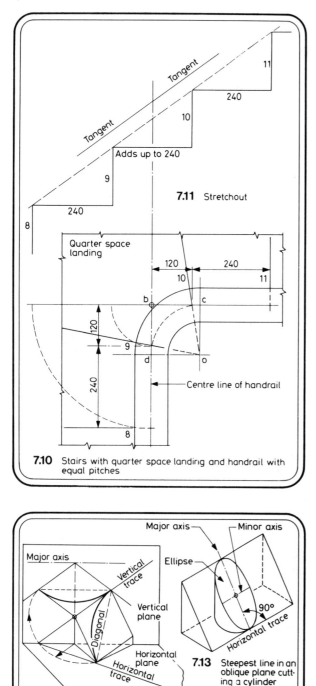

7.11 Stretchout

7.10 Stairs with quarter space landing and handrail with equal pitches

7.12 Oblique sketch showing geometrical principles

7.13 Steepest line in an oblique plane cutting a cylinder

3. To obtain the positions and length of the major and minor axes.

Figs. 7.12 and **7.13** illustrate the application of these principles. Being drawn in oblique projection, angles, etc are a little distorted. As the pitches are equal, we know that tangents and springings are all equal and are given in true length in the elevation and stretch-out of the prism. In order to draw the centre-line plane we then only need to know the diagonal. As the wreath contains part of a vertical cylinder, the major axis will be parallel to the steepest possible line in the centre-line plane. If this plane is continued to cut the horizontal plane, then the steepest line will be square to the horizontal trace.

In this case, as the centre-line plane will be a rhombus (equal-sided), the horizontal trace will be at 45 degrees to the vertical plane and the diagonal will be the steepest line in plane. A line passing through the centre parallel to the steepest line will contain the major axis and a line square to this or parallel to the horizontal trace passing through the centre will be the minor axis (see **Fig. 7.13**).

Now consider **Fig. 7.14** which shows a method of obtaining the facemould and bevels for rake to rake wreath of equal pitches. In the diagram, $o-a-b-c$ is the plan of the prism. The diagonal is $a-c$ on plan and goes from a_1 to c_2 in elevation. With the compasses from centre c on plan, $c-a$ is swung on to the $x-y$ line in plan and projected to m in elevation, giving C_2-m as the true length of the diagonal. From b_2, a_2-b_2 is swung up to meet c_2-m from c_2 and so give the tangents and diagonal. The springing lines are parallel to the tangents. The major axis passing through O_i will be parallel to the diagonal and the minor axis will be at right angles to it.

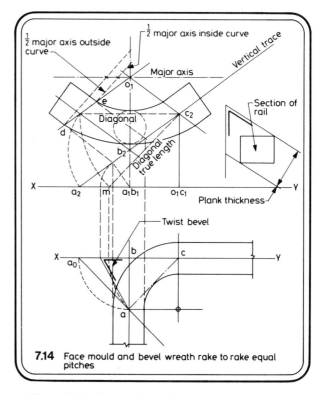

7.14 Face mould and bevel wreath rake to rake equal pitches

The width of one shank is obtained by projecting from the plan on to the tangent and then parallel to the other tangent to cut the springing. The points d and e are therefore points on the ellipses of the facemould. Half of the minor axis always equals the plan radius, but the length of the major axis is not known.

Refer now to **Fig. 7.15** and use the trammel method to draw an ellipse to find the major axis. If a trammel (or tick strip) is marked with half the major axis and half the minor axis respectively from the same end, and it is placed so that the minor axis point is on the major and the major axis point is on the minor, the end of the trammel marks a point on the ellipse. In reverse, strike off a distance equal to the minor axis from any known point on the ellipse to cut the major axis. Draw a line from the source through this intersection and continue it to cut the minor axis, this will effectively be a trammel and will be equal to half the major axis.

In **Fig. 7.14**, this has been done for both inner and outer curves. From the information thus provided, the elliptical curves may be drawn by one of a number of different methods; the most convenient is to continue by the trammel method. The shank at each end is now required. It is parallel to the tangent in each case and square to the tangent at each end. The effective length of the shank is measured on the centre (tangent) line and the length of the straight rail is the distance between springings less this amount at the ends.

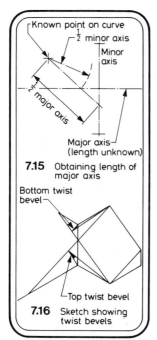

7.15 Obtaining length of major axis

7.16 Sketch showing twist bevels

Fig. 7.16 illustrates the method of obtaining twist bevels. As the shank is cut square to the tangent, then the twist bevel for marking on this shank must also be taken on a plane square to the tangent. In the present case, the top and bottom twist bevels are the same. The latter is obtained in the same way as for the top twist bevel in **Fig. 7.16**. If **Fig. 7.14** is studied in conjunction with this, the method should be easily understood.

Rake to rake wreathed handrail with unequal pitches
We shall now consider a wreath to a quarter-space landing where the nosing lines of the upper and lower flights do not intersect on the prism (see **Fig. 7.17**). The going of the fliers equals 240mm, but the landing rises **10** and **11** come on the springing lies of the wreath giving an overall stretch-out of 400mm.

In order that the tangents may intersect on the prism, therefore, either the bottom tangent must be lowered or the top one lifted. This would mean that, in either case, a short piece of handrail, curved in elevation only, would have to be fitted between the wreath and the straight rail.

The wreath will be rake to rake unequal pitches. In **Fig. 7.18**, information as to pitches is taken from the previous drawing. The prism is **a–b–c–0** on the plan.

In the elevation, the lower tangent **a–b** in plan, is swung into the vertical plane at a_2–b_2. The vertical trace of the upper tangent continues to cut the **x–y** line at **k**. Projected down on to the plan **x–y** line, it gives a line passing through point **a** which is the

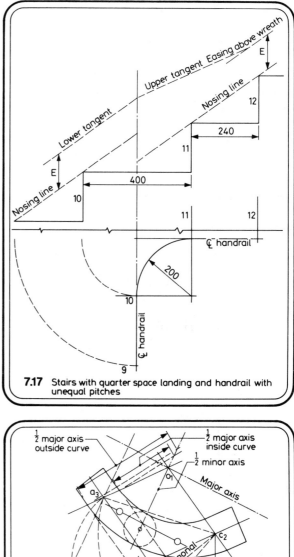

7.17 Stairs with quarter space landing and handrail with unequal pitches

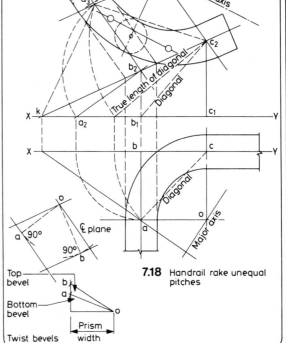

7.18 Handrail rake unequal pitches

horizontal trace. Note that the diagonal is not square to the horizontal trace on plan. The plan of the diagonal is swung from **c** back to the plan **x–y** line and projected up on to the elevation **x–y** line. It is joined to C_2 to give the true length. The diagonal is then swung from centre c_2 to intersect the lower tangent. This is swung from a_2 to give the junction between diagonal and lower tangent at a_3. The parallelogram which is the centre-line plane may then be completed.

The major axis has now to be found. The horizontal trace is **a–x** and becomes **k–a$_3$** in the development. The major axis passing through 0_i is square to this. The thickness of the facemould at a_3 is projected from the plan and gives points on the inner and outer elliptical curves of the facemould. From this the semi-major axes are found, enabling the curves to be completed and then the other shank. The minor axis and the width of the facemould on it are plan dimensions.

A method of obtaining the twist bevels (they will be different) is shown in **Fig. 7.16**. The top twist bevel, as previously described, will be the angle between the centre line plane and the vertical plane; but the bottom one is the complement of the obtuse angle between the centre-line plane and the lower tangent plane. The lower tangent is taken behind the vertical plane and swung up into the vertical plane. If **Fig. 7.16** is studied, **Fig. 7.19**, giving the actual true angles, should be intelligible.

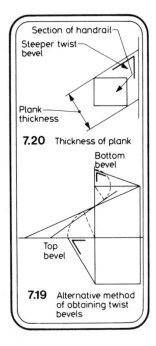

7.20   Thickness of plank

7.19   Alternative method of obtaining twist bevels

An alternative method of obtaining the bevel, given with **Fig. 7.18**, is to take the dimensions square to the tangents from point **0** on the centre-line plane. Then cut them off on to a right angle with the base equal to the prism width. This is probably the simpler method but, with the same degree of precision, is less positive. The thickness of the plank is always given by setting the steepest twist bevel against the section of the rail, as shown in **Fig. 7.20**.

ORTHOGRAPHIC PROJECTION FOR HANDRAILS

It is essential to the proper understanding of geometrical handrailing that the principles of orthographic projection, as applied to solid geometry, are fully understood. These principles, when combined in their application to one drawing, may result in diagrams of some complexity. This is increased by the fact that they have to be superimposed over some preliminary staircase details, but taken individually and isolated, they are quite simple in their application. Many of these principles, although initially learnt or understood, are often ignored through lack of familiarity. A few of them relevant to handrail setting out are as follows.

To draw a horizontal trace, it is only necessary to find two points where it touches the horizontal plane. The horizontal and vertical trace where angled must meet on the **x–y** line. Any line in a plane, which is parallel to its horizontal trace, must also be horizontal so its height remains constant. This fact may be used to obtain unknown heights.

The steepest line in a plane must always be at right angles to its horizontal trace, but otherwise it can be in any position. If it passes through the axis of the vertical cylinder, which contains the handrail, then it will contain the major axes of the ellipses which, with the shanks, constitute the facemould.

If a line is known to be horizontal or can be seen by its elevation to be horizontal, it will be at its true length and shape in plan. If a line or shape is known or seen to be parallel to the vertical plane, its elevation will be its true length or shape. If a line inclined to the vertical plane, as seen in plan, is swivelled to a position in plan parallel to the vertical plane, its new elevation will give its true length and inclination to the horizontal.

The shank of a facemould is nearly always parallel to the tangent and its end is square to the tangent. The length of a handrail, including easings, between wreaths is the length between springings (as seen in elevation) minus the centre-line lengths of the shanks.

The twist bevels are always the dihedral angles between the vertical planes containing the tangents and the inclined planes containing the centre line of the handrail. The minimum thickness of plank is given by the distance between two lines, at an angle to the vertical of the steepest twist bevel, enclosing a horizontal section of the squared handrail.

Handrail wreath for a half-turn staircase
Fig. 7.21 is the plan of a half-turn stairs with quarter-space landing and quarter-turn winders. **Fig. 7.22** shows the preliminary work necessary to enable the handrail wreaths to be set out and constructed. The centre line of the handrail has an initial radius of 200mm. The nosing line of the winders to the upper flight is projected direct from the plan, but the upper and lower flights are hinged back against the vertical plane. It will be seen that the nosing lines to the upper and lower flights meet the centre line **c–c$_1$** at different levels.

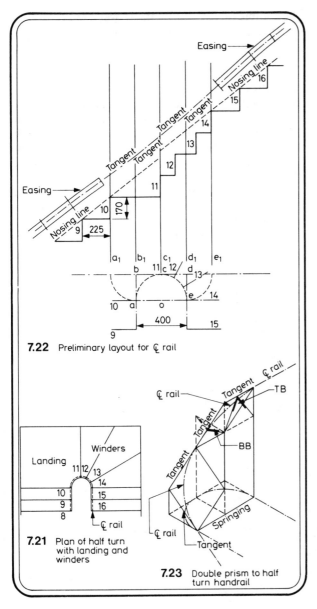

7.22 Preliminary layout for ℄ rail

7.21 Plan of half turn with landing and winders

7.23 Double prism to half turn handrail

given on another drawing. The setting-out details for the lower wreath, which follows the line of a previous example has been omitted. Generally speaking therefore, the construction shown (**Fig. 7.24**), relates to the upper wreath only.

The centre-line planes will be parallelograms with springings equal and opposite to the respective tangents. If therefore the length of the longer diagonal is found, the true shape of the parallelogram may be obtained: **f–h** is the true length of the upper tangent and **j–f** the lower one. The plan of the diagonal is **c–e** and its height is **h–l**. Therefore the plan length of the diagonal marked off from **1** to **m** gives **m–h** its true length. This is then swung up from **h** to intersect the true length of the lower trace (**f–j**) swung up from **j** to **g** about point **f**. The centre-line plane may now be drawn in.

Next, the major and minor axes are required, so that the inner and outer curves of the face mould may be drawn. As the prism is the opposite way about (**Fig. 7.23**), there is some difficulty in obtaining them. It will be appreciated that the tangent **f–h** in elevation is folded back and its real position is h_0–**p** so that, if the vertical plane to the upper prism is taken as passing through **O–e** on plan, then line k_0–**p** (continued to cut x_1–y_1 at **s** and projected on to **a–O** will give the horizontal trace at **r–c**. At right angles to it, the plan of the major axis through **O** will be found. As **r–c** is the horizontal trace, and **u–e** (being parallel to it) is also horizontal, the height of point **u**, (which is level

It will be necessary to have two handrail wreaths meeting on line **c–c₁** but, as they must join continuously without shanks, their tangents must also be a continuous straight line. The position and inclination of this line is at the discretion of the setter-out. In **Fig. 7.22**, it is adjusted so that easings in the straight rail at the top and bottom are not too obvious, while the handrail follows the nosing line reasonably well.

The work will therefore have to be formed with the lower wreath having a flatter pitch tangent at the bottom and the upper wreath with a steeper pitch tangent at the top. The work will have to be based on a double prism (**Fig. 7.23**), with centre-line planes in opposite directions. The lines of the tangents, extending into the shanks, give the pitch to the inner ends of the easings in each case.

In practice, the layout of the stairs and all the detail of the upper and lower wreaths would be carried out on one full-sized drawing. Coloured pencil is introduced in preliminary details which will later become redundant. To avoid confusion, here likely to be increased by limitations to black-and-white and small-scale work, the preliminary stair detail was

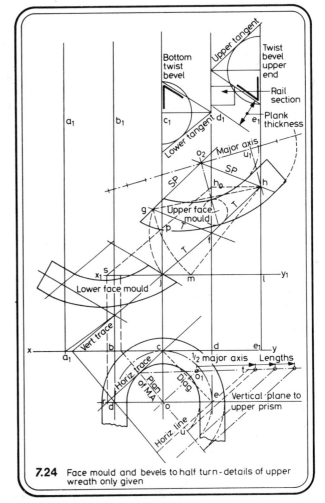

7.24 Face mould and bevels to half turn - details of upper wreath only given

with **e**) is the distance **h–l** above the **x–y** line. This, laid off from **u** as in a vertical plane, gives the point **t** through which the major axis may be drawn.

The plan of the wreath carried round to cut the plan of the major axis, gives a point which may be projected up to give the lengths of the major axes as shown. The distance **u–e** from the plan (marked off **h–u₁**, elevation) and the distance **O₁–t** marked off on the major axis, gives the point **u₁** through which the major axis may be marked off. From thence the curves of the inner and outer ellipses can be drawn. The minor axis is square to the major axis at O_2, the lengths being plan radii. The shank of the upper end may then be drawn and the steepest line in plane marked on in a convenient position, parallel to the major axis.

The upper twist bevel lies in the prism, as shown in **Fig. 7.23** and is the dihedral angle between the centre-line plane as labelled. The lower twist bevel is

the complement to the angle between the centre-line plane and the lower tangent plane, but is taken by continuing the vertical plane above the centre-line plane surface.

Wreathed handrail in an acute turn
Fig. 7.25 deals with facemoulds and bevels to a handrail wreath to a stairs with the outer strings at an acute angle and with a landing between two flights. The lines of the strings are presumed to have given the centre line of the handrail as shown. The centre line of the rail to the lower flight continues to point **b**. Risers **5**, **6** and **7** are swung into the vertical plane with the landing continued; while the risers **8**, **9** and **10** are taken on again and the nosing lines are drawn in.

The centre lines of the handrail will follow equidistant from the nosing lines and are shown as being a long way from meeting on line **b–b** of the prism. The pitch lines have been adjusted to give as smooth a run

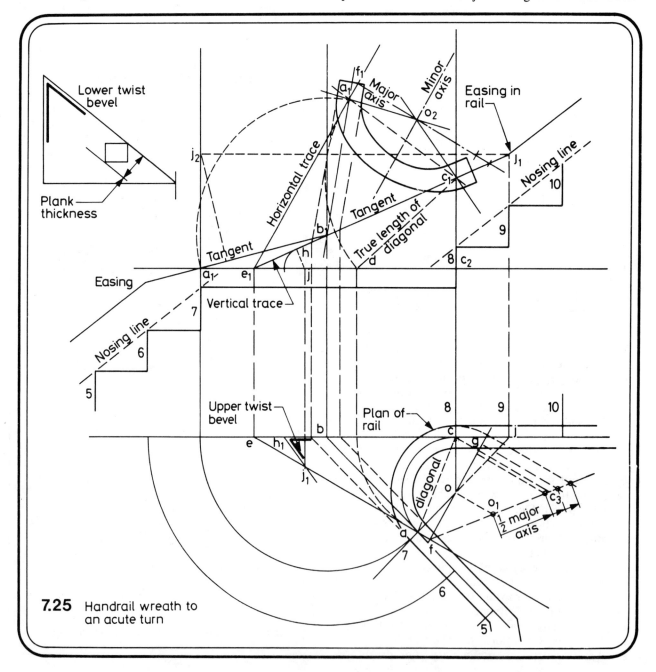

7.25 Handrail wreath to an acute turn

as possible without too pronounced a bend in the easings to the straight rail. The prism is a trapezium on plan and not a square. The two long sides, **a–b** and **b–c**, are the tangents, while **a–O** and **O–c** are springings. The easings would be formed into a smooth curve tangent to the wreath and to the straight rails.

To develop the centre-line plane, the tangent a_1–b_1 is swung about point b_1. It intersects the diagonal c_1–**d**, swung about c_1, at a_1, giving the two sides of the trapesium as a_1–b_1–c_1. The horizontal trace is now obtained by continuing the upper tangent in elevation to cut the **x–y** line at e_1, projecting down to the **x–y** line on plan to a point **e**, when **e–a** becomes the horizontal trace on plan. The distance **e–a** is taken from the plan and swung from point e_1. The elevation should again cut the centre-line plane at a_1 and so give a check on accuracy.

As **f–g** on plan passes through the plan centre of the cylinder, and is at right angles to the horizontal trace, it must contain the plan of the major axis. If the vertical line (**c** on plan, c_1–c_2 in elevation) is redrawn from **c** square to the plan of the major axis, so that **g**–c_3 is equal to c_1–c_2; then a line drawn through **f**–c_3, regarded as in a vertical plane, will contain the true lengths of the major axis, the point **O** and the handrail curves continued round and projected up on to **f**–c_3 to give the lengths required.

The distance **a–f**, marked on the plan of the horizontal trace, is a true measurement; so it may be marked off a_1–f_1 on the centre-line plane. The distance **f**–O_1 is also a true measurement and, squared off from f_1, it will give the point O_2 to complete the centre-line plane. The major axis may now be marked in, the minor axis drawn and the facemould completed. The steepest line in plane may be drawn on the facemould parallel to the major axis.

Fig. 7.26 shows how the upper and lower twist bevels are related to the prism. The upper twist bevel is the dihedral angle between the centre-line plane and the vertical plane of the upper tangent. As shown, the inclined plane is taken down to form a trace on the horizontal plane. The distance **j–h** in elevation is laid on the plan so that h_1–j_1 forms the bevel required with the **x–y** line. The lower twist bevel is also pictured in **Fig. 7.26**.

If the plan of the lower springing is continued from **O** to **j**, and projected up, the elevation of the upper tangent can be continued back to meet it at j_1. From

j_1, a line is then projected across to j_2 and a measurement is taken back square to the tangent, which really lies in a position **a–b** on plan. This measurement, squared off the length **a–j**, gives the pitch bevel as in **Fig. 7.25**. As this is the steeper pitch, it may be used to obtain the plank thickness as shown.

Handrail wreath for an obtuse angle staircase

Figs. 7.27 to **7.31** give details of the setting-out to a wreath where the stair strings from an obtuse angle over a landing. The plan of the handrail prism is again a trapesium but in the reversed position. The plan of the strings or rather the centre line of the handrail over the strings is drawn (**Fig. 7.27**) and is continued to meet at point **b**.

The elevations of the upper steps and the lower steps, folded back into the vertical plane, are drawn; then the nosing lines are drawn in. It is seen that they do not intersect on line **b–n**. In this case, both straight rails are stopped 200mm back from the springing at **e** and **f**. A continuous straight line is drawn, defining the wreath as rake to rake with equal pitches. Therefore the lower tangent, when folded back, coincides with the continued trace of the upper tangent; **g–a**, continued, forms the horizontal trace of the centre-line plane. It follows that **g–a** is a true length as is g_1–b_1 in elevation. Therefore **g–a**, swung (from g_1) to meet g_1–b_1 (swung from b_1) defines the tangent at their true angle at a_1–b_1–c_1.

As **g–a–k** is a horizontal trace, it (and the positions marked on it) are true lengths. A line from **k** at 90 degrees passing through **O** contains the plan of the major axis. The inner and outer curves may be delineated on this by continuing the plan of the wreath beyond the springing. As **c–m** is parallel to

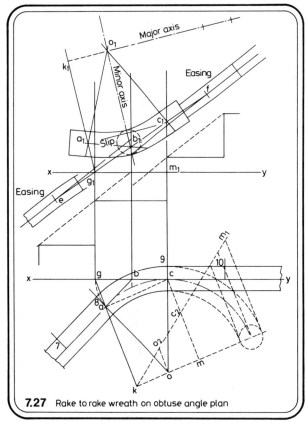

7.27 Rake to rake wreath on obtuse angle plan

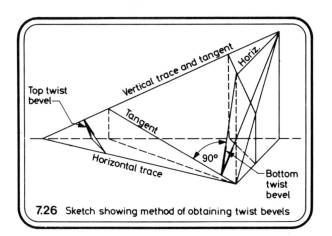

7.26 Sketch showing method of obtaining twist bevels

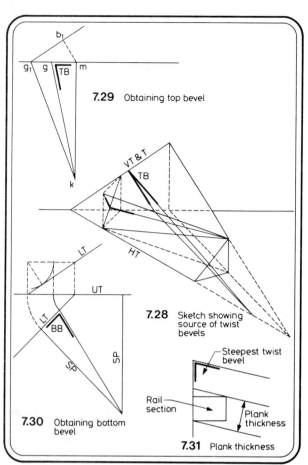

7.29 Obtaining top bevel

7.28 Sketch showing source of twist bevels

7.30 Obtaining bottom bevel

7.31 Plank thickness

THE NORMAL SECTIONS METHOD

The square-cut and tangent system, which has been dealt with so far, is based on the principle that the sides of the rail are vertical and form part of a hollow cylinder. Also that the centre of the rail coincides with a line formed by a middle cylinder cutting an inclined plane. The straight-line boundaries of this are tangent to the mid-thickness and continue as axes of the straight rail above and below the wreath. The top surface of the rail is level on all radii to the common vertical axis of the wreath. By this system, the hand-rail may be symmetrically positioned over the string so that the vertical balusters can be centred on the string and undersurface of rail.

However it does have the disadvantage that only the vertical section of the rail is rectangular. A normal section to the rising curve means that it is hollow on the inside (towards the central axis) and rounded on the other. This distortion is increased when the hand-rail rises steeply to follow the line of consecutive narrow winders; and some adjustment is necessary to the moulding of the rail in order to produce an acceptable section.

By the normal sections method, the initial preparation is the same as for the production of the upper and lower pitches of the straight rail, or easing, as the case may be. Meanwhile the centre line of the rail still forms an elliptical curve lying in the centre-line plane. However the rectangular sections (taken vertically in the tangent system) are normal to the actual centre line of curve in the method of normal sections. One should imagine a wire bent to the elliptical shape for the centre line, and a number of squares threaded on this through their centres normal to the curve in every way, but with their top edges level. Then, with four wires smoothly bent and welded consecutively to the corners, the result will be a skeletal outline of the wreath.

$g–k$, which is horizontal, the height of m is the same as c. The height of c_2 from m in the vertical plane is the same as c_1 above m_1 in elevation; $k–c_2$ continued will contain the major axes.

The length $g–k$ in plan is transferred to $g_1–k_1$ in elevation, with the measured distance $k–O_2$ taken square off it at O_1. This will then be the centre of the ellipse and $k_1–O_1$ continued will contain the major axis dimensions of which may be taken from $k–m_1$. The minor axis will be square off this at plan radii. The elliptical curves and the shanks of the wreath may now be drawn and the steepest line in plane marked in parallel to the major axis.

Fig. 7.28 shows a diagram of the handrail prism, the extended centre-line plane and the position of the twist bevels. The upper twist bevel is the dihedral angle between the centre-line plane and the vertical plane.

In **Fig. 7.29**, $g–k$ is the horizontal trace and $b_1–g_1$ is the vertical trace. If $k–m$ is drawn square to the $x–y$ line at random, $b_1–m$ is drawn to meet it square to the vertical trace, it will give the bevel required. The bottom bevel (**Fig. 7.30**) is the complement of the obtuse dihedral angle between the centre-line plane and the lower tangent plane. It is suspended from a horizontal over the springing line to meet the lower tangent at right angles. **Fig. 7.31** shows the minimum plank thickness, as indicated by the twist bevel.

In this example, as both pitches are known to be the same as also are the pitch bevels, the centre-line plane will be symmetrical (a kite) as also will be the face-mould. These conveniences have been ignored so as to show the procedure when the pitches are different.

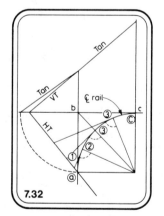

7.32

Fig. 7.32 is an introductory drawing showing, by the accepted method, the plan of the prism and centre line of the rail. The lower tangent is swung back into the vertical plane, and the trace of the upper tangent cuts the X–Y line. This enables the horizontal trace of the centre-line plane to be drawn through point a of the prism on plan. Sections of the rail are placed at $a–1–2–3–c$. As these are normals, they must radiate to the centre on plan. The tangents to the curve will be square to the respective radii on plan and they will all lie in the centre-line plane. Each normal section must be square both ways to its tangent, in order to be normal to the curved centre line.

Setting out the normal sections

The procedure in setting out the normal sections follows. The centre-line plane and horizontal trace are drawn as in **Fig. 7.32**, and the tangents and vertical trace as dictated by the existing conditions. Points in the curve are selected for placing normal sections and the plans of their tangents drawn square to the radii at **a–1–2–3–c**.

The plan of the steepest line in plane (S.L.I.P.) is drawn square to the horizontal trace (**Fig. 7.33**). The true S.L.I.P. sets off this by making **f–e** square to **d–f** and equal to **c–c₁** and then joining **d** to **e**. In **Fig. 7.34**, d_1–e_1 is drawn parallel to **d–e** and points **a–1–2–b–3–c** projected to **d–e** and square to d_1–e_1. If the S.L.I.P. is now hinged vertically, so that **e** lies over **f** and d_1–e_1 (**Fig. 7.34**) is placed over **d–e** (**Fig. 7.33**); the horizontal trace a_1–d_1 (**Fig. 7.34**) will lie over **a–d** (**Fig. 7.33**). Then, if level projectors (in **Fig. 7.34**) parallel to horizontal trace, 1–1_1, 2–2_1, etc (and equal to 1–1_1, 2–2_1 in **Fig. 7.33**) are taken back from **d–e**, they may

then represent the centre-point line of the handrail as it lies in the centre plane.

Point **b** projected in the same way and joined to **a** and **c** in **Fig. 7.34** gives the tangents of the prism. If the points **g–m–n** are taken from **Fig. 7.33** and plotted in **Fig. 7.34** and joined respectively to **1–2–3**, they will represent the tangents to the curve at the selected points for normal sections as they lie in the plane. The normal sections will therefore be square to them. This applies also at the springing. The lower half of **Fig. 7.34** is a repeat of the upper, as also is **Fig. 7.45**.

The reader is now asked to appreciate that the plank from which the wreath is to be cut lies with the centre of its thickness in the centre plane of the prism. Each tangent to a section also lies in this plane. The tangent itself must also be considered as lying in a vertical plane. The plane which contains the section must be square to that and also square to the tangent as seen on this vertical plane. The plane containing the normal section will have its horizontal trace square to the vertical plane.

Setting out the twist bevels

The plank faces are parallel to the centre-line plane. Each twist bevel must therefore be given by the intersection of three planes:

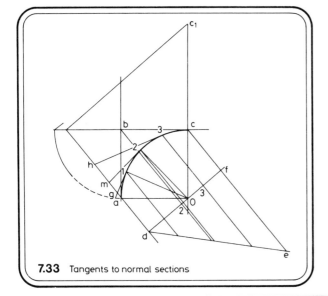

7.33 Tangents to normal sections

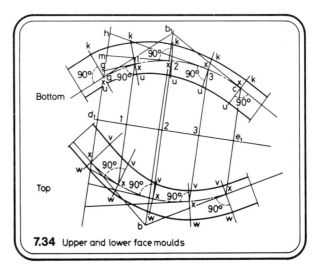

7.34 Upper and lower face moulds

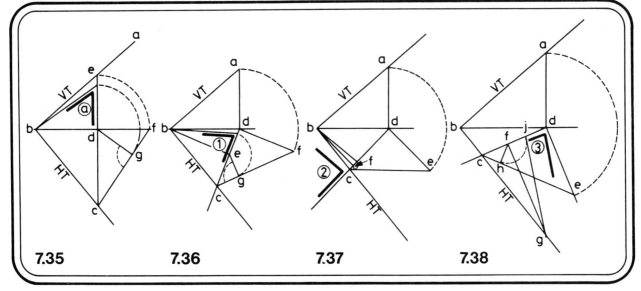

7.35   **7.36**   **7.37**   **7.38**

1. The vertical plane containing the tangent;
2. The plane with its horizontal trace square to the vertical; and
3. The centre-line plane as it is cut by 1 and 2.

There are five twist bevels involved, corresponding to points **a–1–2–3–c**. **Fig. 7.35** gives the twist bevel at (**a**), **Fig. 7.32**. The vertical trace is **a–b**; **b–c** is the horizontal trace; **e–d** the elevation; and **d–c** the plan of the plane containing the tangent. Its true shape is **d–c–f**. The plane containing the normal section cuts the vertical plane at **d–g** and the horizontal plane at **b–d**, giving the twist bevel at (**a**), as shown.

Fig. 7.36 gives the twist bevel at (**1**), **Fig. 7.32**. Parallel to the plan is **c–d** of the tangent at (**1**). The horizontal trace of the plane containing the normal section is **b–e**. The vertical plane containing the tangent is **d–c–f**. The height of the triangle for the twist bevel in (**1**) is **e–g**.

Fig. 7.37 gives the twist bevel at (**2**) **Fig. 7.32**; **c–d** is the plan of the tangent and **c–d–e** is the true shape of the vertical section containing the tangent. The horizontal trace of the plane containing the normal section is **b–f**, and from a very short line square to **c–e**, swung up to **c–d**, the bevel (**2**) is obtained. As the section is nearly parallel to the horizontal trace, it is nearly square to the centre-line plane.

Fig. 7.38 gives the twist bevel at (**3**), **Fig. 7.32**. The plan of the tangent is **c–d**, and **c–d–e** is the vertical plane containing the tangent. The horizontal trace of the plane containing the normal section is **f–g**, cutting the horizontal trace the other side. The square section, **f–h**, is swung up to **j**, giving bevel (**3**) which goes the other way.

Finally, **Fig. 7.39** is the twist bevel at the upper springing. The horizontal trace of the normal section plane is **c–d**, and **a–b–d** is the vertical plane containing

the tangent, while **e–d** swung down gives the twist bevel (**c**).

It is now necessary to produce three different facemoulds: one for the bottom face of the plank, one for the top and one to which the plank may be economically cut. As already explained. **Figs. 7.34** and **7.45** contain the true shape of the centre line of the wreath in repetition. This centre line occurs in its proper position in the centre of the thickness of the plank only, and the facemould is offset from it in both top and bottom faces.

Setting out facemoulds

To understand how the facemoulds are set out, suppose that the plank is squared to length. Then the centre line is marked on one side, squared over and marked on the other side. Take each twist bevel and set out off the vertical as in **Figs. 7.40** to **7.44**. Giving the point in the centre-line plane to each normal section, draw the section of the rail with vertical sides to the steepest pitch and obtain the plank thickness as in **Fig. 7.40**. Draw the other sections and enclose them centrally within the same thickness of plank.

Produce the sides to cut the top and bottom plank faces. Draw lines square to the plank face through the centre of each section (see **x–x**, **Fig. 7.40**). Then this line coincides, in each case, with the selected points in the centre line marked on the top and bottom of the plank. The points formed by the extended sides of the rail sections are set off from **x**, in each case, to give the points through which the curves of the facemoulds are drawn. Thus for the bottom facemoulds, **k** and **u** are marked off from **x** consecutively; while for the top, **w** and **v** are marked. The shanks are square to the tangents at the ends.

Finally, to avoid wastage in material, a cutting mould is used to mark out the plank. **Figs. 7.40A** to **7.44A** are **Figs. 7.40** to **7.44** repeated. But, in each case, the plank width is reduced by the squared lines to just enough width to enclose the rail sections. The centre line will be in the centre in each case. **Fig. 7.45** shows the cutting mould.

Cutting the wreath

Having prepared the necessary templets and bevels of the wreath, the plank is marked for cutting on the band saw. The ends are accurately squared, and then the centre line of the wreath is squared across them. These lines then give the position for fixing the

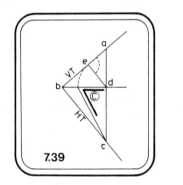

7.39

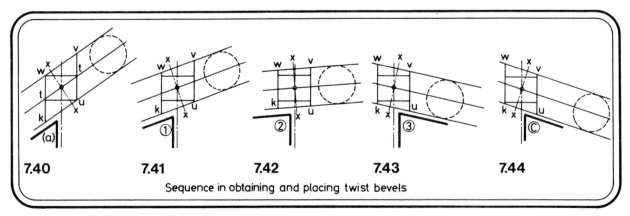

7.40   7.41   7.42   7.43   7.44

Sequence in obtaining and placing twist bevels

facemoulds to the wreath, flush at both ends. The handrail may then be cleaned back to the facemoulds; not following the vertical axis of the cylinder, as in the square-cut and tangent system, but square to the pitch.

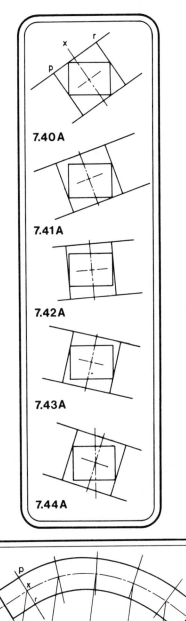

7.40 A

7.41 A

7.42 A

7.43 A

7.44 A

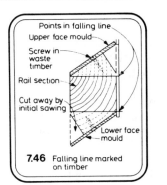

7.45 Cutting mould

Points in falling line
Upper face mould
Screw in waste timber
Rail section
Cut away by initial sawing
Lower face mould

7.46 Falling line marked on timber

Band-sawing to the cutting mould will have removed some of the waste above and below the rail section, as shown in **Fig. 7.46**. The surface will be twisted, and the falling line is best marked on from points plotted directly on the timber.

The lines of the normal sections are joined from each facemould across the thickness. Referring to **Figs. 7.40** to **7.44**, points marked on these lines are taken from inner and outer vertical lines giving point **s** on line **w–k** on the outside curve and **t** on **v–u** on the inside curve, and so on. These points are joined up with a smooth curve giving precise outlines.

EASINGS

The normal procedure in the design of handrails, as already explained, is to keep the centre line of the handrail within the centre-line plane bounded by the upper and lower tangents and the springing. Adjustments are then made to the pitch so that the eventual fall of the rail will follow as nearly as possible parallel to the nosing line of the winders, following around the wreathed string.

In most cases this will require that an 'easing' is inserted above or below the springing of the wreath to bring the pitch back to that of the straight flight.

The alternative to this is to insert an easing within the wreath itself, so that the wreath may be joined direct to the straight rails. This is particularly desirable when there is a large and abrupt change in the pitch. The falling line can then be adjusted within the whole of the turn.

In the example given, stairs rise from a level landing around winders to meet the straight rail at a normal pitch. The setting-out related to the stairs is shown in **Fig. 7.47**. The plan of the turn is drawn within the prism, the size of which is dictated by the radius of the string as before. From this, the elevation stretch-out of the nosing line is obtained. It should be noted that this follows the plan curve of the centre line of rail from **1** to **7** and not the tangents **a–b** and **b–c**. The central falling line is then drawn in. The top is curved to meet the pitch of the upper flight; and the lower one is swept out to meet the rail on the level landing. This rail is presumed to be 80mm higher off the landing than the handrail is off the stairs.

As the easing continues outside the springing at both the top and bottom before it sweeps in to the desired pitch, the initial upper and lower tangents will have to be extended beyond the springings so that the easings can be continued into the shank. To satisfy economic requirements that the plank shall be as thin as possible, the pitch of the upper and lower tangents must be so arranged that the falling line, as it sweeps around, shall coincide as nearly as possible with the centre-line plane. That can only be done by trial and error. Draw trial upper and lower tangents as m_1–b_2–h_1. Note that they extend beyond the springing of the prism. Continue the upper tangent as the vertical trace to **p**, and swing m_1 round to **m** about **b**, to give the horizontal trace of the extended centre-line plane.

From point h_1, as nearly as possible where the falling line eases into the standard stair pitch, drop a

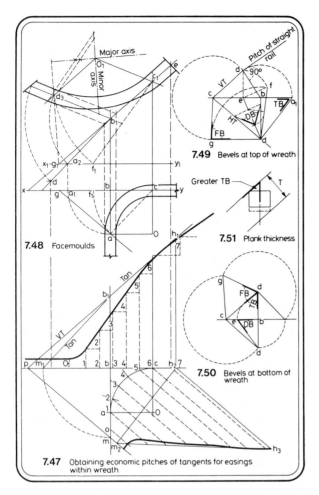

7.49 Bevels at top of wreath

7.51 Plank thickness

7.48 Facemoulds

7.50 Bevels at bottom of wreath

7.47 Obtaining economic pitches of tangents for easings within wreath

vertical on to the **x–y** line at h_2. Square a line back from h_2 to the horizontal trace at m_2. Then h_2–m_2 is the plan of the steepest line in plane. In other words, it presents an edge view of the plane. If now the selected points are squared across from **0–7** on to the S.L.I.P. as shown, and the corresponding heights are transferred from the verticals **X–Y** to the falling line, this will give its proximity to the S.L.I.P.

Several trials were made to achieve the results shown. It will be noted that the falling line stretch-out is nowhere near the lower tangent. This is because the former is the direct length from the plan curve, while the tangent is hinged back from **b**.

Once the pitch of the tangents has been decided, the facemould may be obtained. The curve of the facemould within the springing will be the same as for the square-cut and tangent system, but the lengths of the shanks are critical. Their ends are not square either to the face of the timber or to the tangents.

The prism and tangents are redrawn in **Fig. 7.48** to avoid confusion. The lower tangent is extended to **d**, and the upper to **e**, to give the lengths of the shanks. The geometry is now confied to the prism itself by hinging **a** from **b** and projecting up to cut the lower tangent at a_2.

A new **y** line, x_1–y_1, brings the problem back to standard dimensions. The plan of the diagonal **c–a**, hinged up to **f** and projected to f_2, gives the true length of the diagonal at c_1–f_1. This may be swung up from c_1 to intersect the length of the lowest tangent swung up

about **b** from a^2 to intersect at d_3. The major axis is square to this horizontal trace and passes through the point **O**.

The width of the shank is projected up from the plan to the vertical trace and over to the springing. The inner and outer radii cut off the major axis from the shank points and continue to meet the minor axis, giving the semi major axis length. From this, the elliptical curves of the wreath may be drawn by any method selected.

The bevels

Three bevels will have to be applied to each of the shanks. This is because, at both ends, the straight rails meet the wreath at an angle before the falling line is worked. The angles in each case are:

1.   The bevel to the tangent marked on the shank of the facemould;
2.   The joint bevel on the thickness marked on the unworked shank; and
3.   The twist bevels.

It is simpler to divorce these bevels from the wreath and consider them in relation to the different planes involved. Taking the top end of the wreath first (**Fig. 7.49**), draw the **X–Y** line and put in the vertical and horizontal traces **a–c** and **c–d**. Also put in the pitch of the upper straight rail. Then **a–b** is the elevation of the joint plane to the top rail, seen edge on, and **b–d** is its horizontal trace. So a swing out to a_1 from **b** gives the upper twist bevel **TB**.

The joint bevel, marked across the thickness of the plank as lined in on the square-edged timber, will be the dihedral angle between the centre-line plane **c–e–d** on plan, and the plane **e–b–d** on plan. They form the joint face against the square joint of the upper rail. The vertical-height plane **e–f–d** (height **e–a**) is intersected by the dihedral angle – the plane containing this angle has its horizontal trace square to the trace of the vertical plane – while being tilted squared to **f–d**, and giving the required angle as shown in **DB**.

The true angle for making the end of the top shank of the facemould will be at the top corner of the centre line, **c–e–d** on plan. The true shape of this plane will be represented by a triangle containing the true lengths. The vertical trace **c–a** and the horizontal trace **c–d** are the lengths of two of the sides, the other being **f–d**. Combined as shown, these give the actual shape of the centre-line plane and the face bevel **FB**.

Fig. 7.50 gives the bevels for the bottom shank. The vertical trace is **a–c**, and **c–d** is the horizontal trace of the centre-line plane. As the joint surface is vertical, it is parallel to the vertical plane (above the **X–Y** line). The face bevel is therefore the same as the angle between the springing and tangent. This again is the same as the angle between the lower tangent and the vertical trace, as shown in **FB**.

The twist bevel again, as the joint face is parallel to the vertical plane, will be the elevation of the vertical trace cutting the vertical side of the prism, as shown in **TB**.

The thickness bevel is a little more difficult to understand. It will be an obtuse angle taken from the

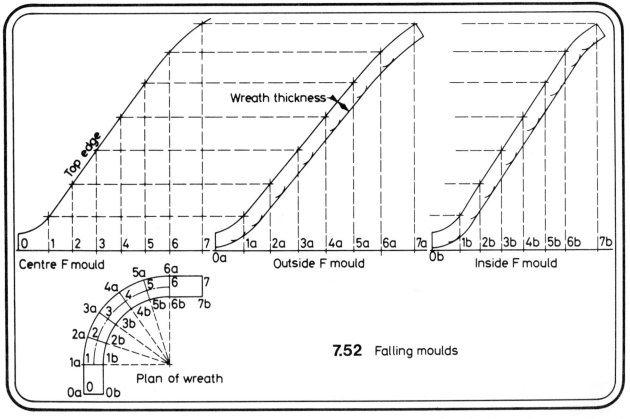

7.52 Falling moulds

top downwards. So it is best considered as an acute angle applied from the underside, rather than being the supplement of the other. This is then the dihedral angle between the centre-line plane and the vertical joint plane from the springing.

Remembering that, if an inclined plane intersects two parallel planes, the alternate dihedral angles will be the same; therefore the upper dihedral angle between the centre-line plane and the vertical-joint plane will be the same as the angle between the underside of the centre-line plane and the vertical plane on the **XY** line. The horizontal trace of the plane containing this angle will be **b–d**, and its height square to the vertical trace **a–c**, will be **e–b**, thus giving the thickness bevel **DB**.

The thickness of the plank will be obtained in the same way as for the normal square-cut and tangent system, with an allowance for the deviation, of the handrail from the centre-line plane, as in **Fig. 7.47**. The plank thickness equals **T** in **Fig. 7.51**.

The centre falling line is given developed in **Fig. 7.47** (elevation). If the strictly geometrical form were adhered to, the depth or thickness of the handrail would have to be plotted uniformly on vertical ordi-nates. In this case, all radical lines taken across the rail to the cylinder axis could be level on upper and lower surfaces. But, as the pitch of the rail increased, the normal section of the rail would be reduced, causing problems in moulding as well as leaving a question-able appearance.

A common way of setting out the falling mould for the inside and outside of the wreath is to give the stretch-out of the centre line of the wreath. Then the upper and lower lines of the mould are made tangent to a number of circles middled on the centre line. This has the disadvantage that a rising horizontal radial will no longer fit either top or bottom surface of the rail. For this reason, in the square-cut and tangent system, the falling lines are commonly put in freehand.

An alternative, in this writer's opinion, is to make the centre falling line the top middle falling line, keeping all radial checks strictly level. Then draw the bottom falling line tangent to arcs centred on the top line. This is shown in **Fig. 7.52**, which should be self-explanatory. It means that the full error is trans-ferred to the underface of the wreath, where some adjustment must be made in the fit of the balusters.

QUESTIONS FOR CHAPTER 7

Question 17

A handrail wreath is to be set out to suit the conditions given in **Fig. 7.53**.

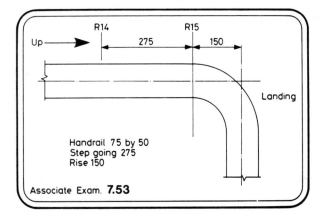

Associate Exam. **7.53**

a. Determine the shape of the facemould, and
b. The twist bevels and thickness of plank required. Scale 1:10.

NOTE: This question was originally given in imperial measure but has been converted to metric. Institute of Carpenters Associate Examination, 1969. No. 7.

Question 18

Taking the example on normal sections given on page 114, but assuming that both tangents are pitched at 38 degrees, obtain the twist bevel only.

Question 19

A staircase with upper and lower outer strings approaching at an angle of 60 degrees, is formed with the turn wreathed at 200mm radius. The step rise is 170mm and going to fliers 240mm. Set out the wreathed string in outline, designed so that the position of fliers and winders give a rake to rake handrail of equal pitches without easings.

CHAPTER 8

Glulam Timbers and Plywood Constructions

The construction of laminated timber beams is the process of building up structural units, such as beams, ribs and arches, from layers of thin boards or planks to any size or shape required. The development, during the latter half of the century, of glues which provide joint strengths equal or superior to the shear strength of the timber itself, has made the process possible. The 'laminates' (layers) are bonded together with parallel grain directions by being cramped up in special jigs arranged to provide the straight, cambered or curved outline required in the finished work.

The laminates may be side-jointed to increase the member width, and also spliced to increase the length. The depth of the member depends upon the number of laminates used. They can therefore be built up to any size, governed only by practical limits of assembly space, transport and handling.

It should be noted that each laminate, according to its position in the depth of the beam or arch, is subject to only a single stress of either tension, compression or parallel shear. The splices in the length must therefore take account of this. As the joints can be staggered throughout the length, they can have little, if any, weakening effect on the moment of resistance or section modulus at any point. This is unlike a solid beam, which can only be spliced or scarfed at points where the bending moment is low.

The thickness of each laminate, in the case of straight beams, depends upon the depth of the beam. There should be a sufficient number of layers so that a joint in any one board does not constitute a weakness. However, a laminate should not be so thick as to give it individual cross-grain strength to warp or perhaps split. No laminate should exceed 50mm thickness.

Where curved members have to be formed, the board must be flexible enough to bend easily, without being subject to stresses that could weaken it. Steam bending of the laminates is not permissible. It is generally accepted that their maximum thickness should be 1/150 of the radius of the sharpest curve.

Glued laminated constructions under load are generally likely to bend. The extreme fibres are subject to tension or compression respectively, according to the direction of the load. The middle ones shear as in **Fig. 8.1**.

Although the outer laminates may have to conform to, say, grade 75 of CP112, the middle layers (to about three-fifths of the depth) may be taken from timber grade MSS. This is because the shear strength of lower grade timber does not drop to the same degree as does that of tension and compression. The existence of knots tends to increase, rather than reduce, sheer resistance.

The ends of laminates can be jointed in various ways. Probably the best joint for tension members is the plain scarf, shown in **Fig. 8.2**, with a slope of 1:12 giving an efficiency rating of 88 per cent. Those in compression can be plain scarfs of 1:6, which in compression give a rating of 1.00. An alternative to this could be a finger joint (**Fig. 8.3**). The strength of this depends upon the thickness of the laminate, as this governs the glued surface areas. In some cases, butt

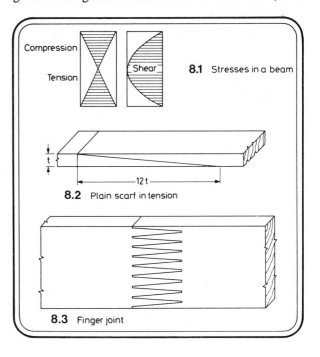

8.1 Stresses in a beam

8.2 Plain scarf in tension

8.3 Finger joint

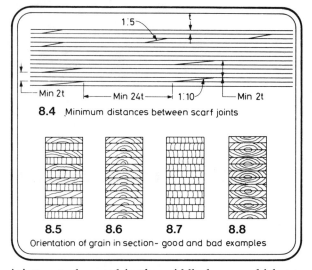

8.4 Minimum distances between scarf joints

8.5   **8.6**   **8.7**   **8.8**

Orientation of grain in section- good and bad examples

joints may be used in the middle layers, which are subject only to shear. Scarf joints in laminates to curved members, should be glued up and planed off before they are finally assembled.

The joints in laminates should be staggered, so that those in consecutive boards are at least 24 times the board thickness apart. No section through the member should show scarf joints less than two thicknesses apart (see **Fig. 8.4**). Where laminates are joined to width, consecutive joints should lap twice the board thickness, or one-quarter of its width, whichever is greater.

Preparing the laminates

Individual laminates require careful preparation. The moisture content of the timber is important. Any major absorption by, or evaporation from, the timber *in situ* will set up undesirable stresses in it. The laminate should be dried to the estimated percentage moisture content to which it would eventually settle *in situ*. This is known as the 'equilibrium mc', and is likely to be from about 12 to 15 per cent in normal buildings. An effort should be made to bring all the timber to about that value. Also, to avoid internal stresses being set up by the laminates one against the other, the maximum variation should be less than 5 per cent.

It is known that the moisture movement within the tree, as seen by a cross-section, varies in relation to its structure. Shrinkage around the tree (as seen in flat-sawn boards) is twice as much as from the pith to the bark (rift-sawn boards). It is thus better to avoid the combination of boards in section as shown in **Fig. 8.5**. **Fig. 8.6** is probably the best example of arrangement, as the natural moisture movement continues as in the original tree. Any subsequent shakes, being generally radial, would least affect the shear strength. **Fig. 8.7** is satisfactory; but **Fig. 8.8** is not so good, because the joints will tend to pull one against the other. These arrangements are not critical, when the percentage moisture content (mc) is not likely to fluctuate in the member *in situ*.

Cutting the laminates

The laminate should be planed accurately to thickness to tolerances of +0.4mm. The plane knives

should be sharp and should not be jointed, as this causes a slight hammering effect likely to produce a glazed surface. The feed speed should be such as to limit the depth of the cutter marks. This, in turn, is governed by the mark width. For the depth of 0.025mm, which is the criterion, the pitch of the width of the marks should be according to the diameter of the cutting circle, as shown in **Table 8.1**.

Table 8.1.

Diameter of cutting circle (mm)	Pitch of cutter mark (mm)
100	3.2
125	3.6
150	4.0
200	4.2

$$\text{Feed speed in metres per min} = \frac{\text{pitch} \times \text{no of cutters} \times \text{RPM}}{1000}$$

Thus, for a 150mm cutter block with three cutters revolving at 4500 for a pitch of 4.0mm,

$$\text{feed speed} = \frac{4 \times 3 \times 4500}{1000} = 54\text{m per minute}$$

Gluing the laminates

In order that the planed surfaces shall not become case hardened or contaminated, the gluing should be carried out not more than 48 hours after planing. The laminate should be checked for cupping just before gluing up. The permitted depth varies according to board width and thickness, as in **Table 8.2**.

Table 8.2

Thickness (mm)	Maximum cup (mm) Finished widths (mm)		
12	100	150	200
12	1.6	1.6	1.6
19	0.79	1.6	1.6
25	0.79	0.79	1.6
32	none	0.79	0.79
38	none	0.79	0.79
44	none	none	0.79

Gluing of each laminate is achieved by passing it between rollers in a special gluing machine. This may be adjusted to give the depth of spread required. The advice of the manufacturer should be sought on all matters related to the adhesive. The recommended spread of glue will be given, say, in kg/100m². The easiest way to check this is to pass a short length of board, of the same thickness as the laminate, having weighed it first dry, through the glue spreader. When glued, weigh it again. The difference in values will be the weight of the glue. This divided by the board area in m and multiplied by 100 will give the spread.

For example, assume the board is 1200×200mm, and the difference in weight is 0.9kg. Then weight of

$$\text{glue per } 100\text{m}^2 = \frac{0.9 \times 100}{1.2 \times 0.2} = 375\text{kg}$$

If the machine glues both sides at once, that value will have to be halved = 187.5kg.

Cramping

The cramping jig generally consists of vertical frames of steel angle (**Fig. 8.9**). They are set so that the lines of the vertical standards conform to the shape (straight, cambered or concave) of the member to be glued. The jig incorporates cramps. But additional cramps (**Fig. 8.10**) will have to be used inbetween, to provide the necessary continuity of pressure. This spacing depends upon the thicknesses of the laminate, the cramping head, and the caul (an outer board to help distribute the pressure), see **Fig. 8.11**. Spacing equals $2(B + C + D)$.

The cramping procedure is as follows. The inner caul board is placed on the jig, its surface treated to prevent adhesion. Then all the laminates are glued in their correct sequence on the jig, finally the outer caul is added. The whole is firmly cramped back to the jig in the centre. If the member is curved, the ends are pulled back roughly to the jig using a winch or block and tackle if necessary. Then the cramps are placed from the centre towards each end, using a powered nut runner to tighten them up.

A precise pressure is required, in the order of between 0.07 to 0.105kg/mm². Set the clutch on the nut runner to a little less than this, and add the final pressure with a torque wrench. It is essential that no cramps are tightened beyond the limit given, because it will be found, when they are released, that the joint will have been starved of glue.

Terminology of gluing

Certain terms are used in the glue procedure. The preliminary assembly of the collected board to determine positions of joints, etc, is known as the 'dry assembly'. The gluing and collection of the laminates on the jig before cramping is called 'wet assembly'.

The time interval between the gluing of the laminates and the application of pressure is known as the 'closed assembly time'. The 'cramping period' is the length of time for which the work has to remain under pressure: it depends upon the temperature, the type of adhesive and the shape of the member.

Curved work in which the laminates are under stress must stay on the jig for a longer period. After the work is removed from the cramps, it may still need time for the adhesive to develop strength to withstand the strains imposed by crane hauling and heavy machining. This is known as the 'conditioning period'.

Finishing joints

It will be appreciated that, in spite of the close tolerances to be observed in the preparation of the laminates, and the efficient cramping system used, it is still not possible to make joints with the kind of tight fit one associates with normal joinery work. The adhesives used must retain their full efficiency under these

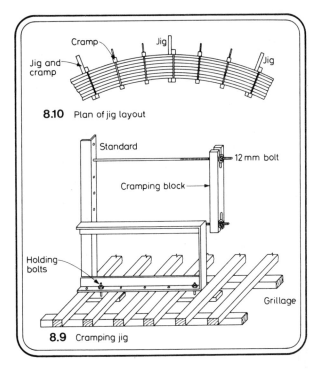

8.10 Plan of jig layout

8.9 Cramping jig

imperfect conditions. This quality is usually achieved by adding a filler to the glue, which is then known as 'gap-filling': the first requirement of all adhesives used for laminated work. This capacity varies, with the different adhesives available, from 0.75 to 1.25mm.

Finishing the units

The final process is the finishing of the laminated unit ready for delivery to site. The surplus glue should be cleaned off from the edges. Then the sides of the beam should be planed and sanded, possibly by passing it through a thickness supporting the ends on mobile platforms. Alternatively, a powered hand planer may be used.

Where the faces have to be tapered by stepping back the laminates, these will need to be cleaned off by passing them through the band-saw and finishing with purpose-made machinery.

The laminated units are usually finished in one of three grades. From lowest to highest:

GRADE I: Soffits and face boards to be free of dead or loose knots. No patching to be done and surfacing to edge laminations may allow an occasional miss.

GRADE II: The exposed edges of the laminates must be fully surfaced, no misses permitted. Small surface voids must be filled in, and larger ones patched with timber, care being used to match colour and grain. The member shall be wrapped or otherwise protected prior to delivery to preserve the finish.

GRADE III: Voids and defects on edges of laminates shall be patched with clear wood inserts with matched colour. Soffit and faceboards shall be clear and selected with care to match colour and grain at scarf and edge joints. All exposed faces shall be

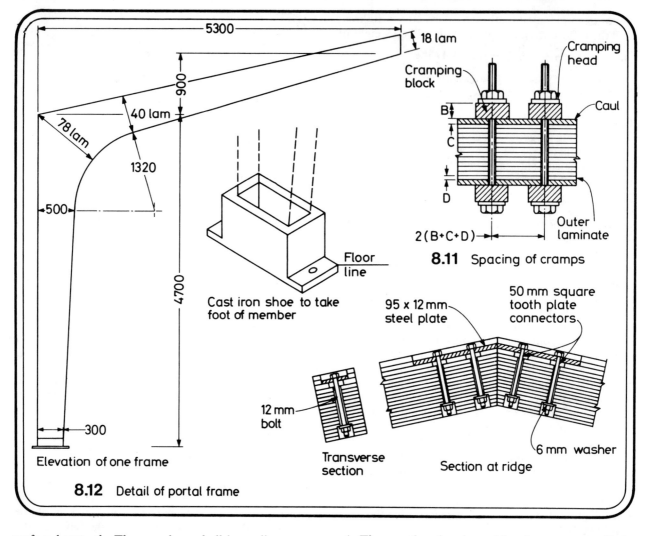

8.11 Spacing of cramps

8.12 Detail of portal frame

surfaced smooth. The members shall be well wrapped to protect the finish.

ADHESIVES

There are several adhesives used for laminate work. Most of them have characteristics which limit their suitability for use in unfavourable conditions.

The oldest known type is casein glue, which is made from sour milk. To be suitable, it should come within BS444, Type A. This requires that it should be treated against bacterial attack. Supplied in powder form, it is mixed with water and is available for use within 20 minutes. It is used cold and has ample strength, but is only suitable for dry situations.

Urea formaldehyde is a resin glue impervious to bacterial attack. All such glues, when supplied, are in a condition of slow continuous setting, and can only be kept for a certain period in the original containers before their reaction makes them unusable. This period is known as the 'shelf life' of the glue. They come under BS1204, Type MR/GF.

Before the resin glue can be used, it has to have a setting agent, known as a 'hardener', added. This speeds up the setting process to the hour or so needed for the gluing and assembling of the unit. The process, for urea, can be carried out in one of two different ways:

1. The powdered resin and hardener are supplied mixed together to the required proportions, and they do not start to react until mixed with water.
2. The resin and hardener are supplied in separate containers in liquid or powder form, the powder being mixed with water. The resin is then applied to one joint surface, and the hardener to the other. Reaction does not begin until the two surfaces are brought together.

This adhesive is moisture resistant, but should not be used under really wet conditions. It is also sensitive to heat and may lose its strength when subject to temperatures much above 40°C, such as under the direct rays of sunlight and, of course, in fire.

Resorcinal formaldehyde is by far the best adhesive, but also the most expensive. It will set in temperatures of 15°C; added heat will reduce the setting time. The resin and hardener are mixed together as before. It may be used to glue timbers up to 18 per cent mc. It is fully resistant to water and fire, and will endure as long as the timber itself.

Phenol formaldehyde is an adhesive with similar properties to resorcinal, but requiring a temperature up to 150°C. This cannot be economically achieved for large work. But the adhesive can be used for scarf joints, with radio frequency heating.

Phenol resorcinal adhesive is a mixture of the two

formaldehydes. It is cheaper than resorcinal, but requires a setting temperature of about 23℃.

All of these adhesives are made in slightly different mixes under various proprietary brands. When any particular adhesive is to be used, the manufacturer's instructions should be followed explicitly.

Setting times of the various adhesives do vary. But **Table 8.3** may be taken as a general guide. Cramping times of all types under normal temperatures should be about 16 hours.

Table 8.3

Casein	24 hours
Urea	48 hours
Phenol	7 days
Phenol resorcinal	7 days
Resorcinal	7 days

It is important that the temperature of the timber itself is at the required level. It should be subject to this temperature at least 24 hours before gluing. To maintain the mc at its original level, humidity should be kept between 55 and 65 per cent during the period. It is important for all occasions, when heat is to set the glue, that humidity of the air should be adjusted by means of steam jets. This prevents the drying-out of the timber from its surface.

PRESERVATION OF GLULAM WORK

The main causes for decay of timber in building are dry rot and wet rot. The former occurs when the mc passes 20 per cent; the latter occurs under really wet conditions, usually at ground level. The trouble usually starts when timber is wet 24 hours a day, with no chance to dry out. By the introduction of suitable damp-proof courses and the use of intelligent design, this condition can be avoided under normal circumstances. There are, however, occasions – perhaps in factories where processes involve great amounts of steam – where conditions of high moisture content cannot be avoided. The only answer then would be to treat the timber against fungal attack. If the preserva-

tive is to be applied before assembly, the vehicle used to carry it into the wood, or the preservative itself, may react unfavourably with the adhesive. This is a problem for the manufacturer's chemists. The adhesive used under these conditions will, in any case, have to be resorcinal, or a resorcinal phenol compound. If the adhesive is water-based, the moisture content will be raised.

Re-kilning is likely to cause distortion, which would indicate that the laminates should be planed to size after treatment has been carried out. If the treatment is applied to the finished job, it should only be after the glue has been fully hardened, or after the conditioning period.

Assembly on site
Fig. 8.12 shows details of assembling a typical portal frame. In order to accommodate the maximum bending stresses, the frame is thickened at the knee. The shape is achieved by stepping back the laminates towards the bend, and sawing and planing to shape afterwards. The portal frames are paired to give the building outline. Walls may also be of timber, if required, as the portal frames will give adequate support.

The protection of the feet of the frames from rising damp is important. The best method is probably by use of a cast-iron shoe, as in **Fig. 8.12**. The frames are connected at the apex by steel plates recessed in and bolted through timber connectors.

Fig. 8.13 outlines a bowstring roof truss with bracing. The diagonal braces are only necessary to resist unequal loading, wind or snow. **Fig. 8.14** shows the elevation of a truss with a low-pitched flat roof. This is much too large to be carried out in solid timber.

Laminated work should be designed as if it were of solid timber, but higher stress values may be used. There are four reasons:

1. No defects, such as large knots or shakes, can exist to weaken a large area;
2. Better quality material can be placed in positions of high stress;
3. There is full continuity of grain irrespective as to shape; and
4. All the timber can be seasoned to a tight moisture percentage.

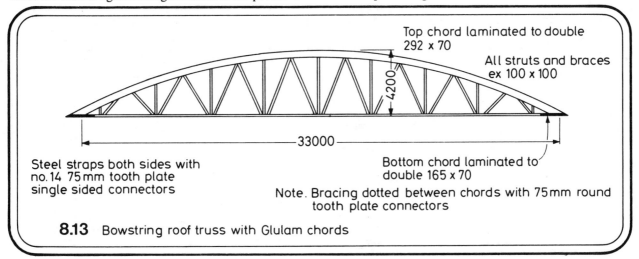

Top chord laminated to double 292 x 70

All struts and braces ex 100 x 100

4200

33000

Steel straps both sides with no.14 75mm tooth plate single sided connectors

Bottom chord laminated to double 165 x 70

Note. Bracing dotted between chords with 75mm round tooth plate connectors

8.13 Bowstring roof truss with Glulam chords

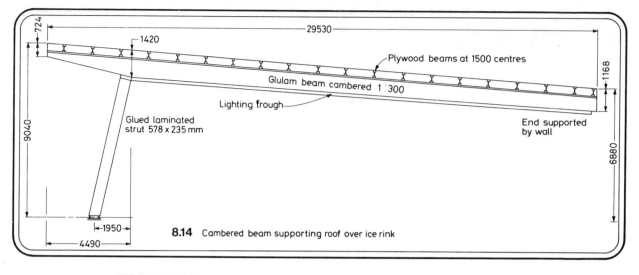

8.14 Cambered beam supporting roof over ice rink

PLYWOOD

The mechanical properties of plywood include high strength which is practically uniform in all directions; complete stability with virtually no moisture movement; and absolute freedom from splitting which allows it to take nails near its edges to any reasonable degree of close spacing. These qualities make it suitable for use, when stiffened, in any type of structural unit, acting as a beam in its widest sense. The plywood faces are either parallel to the load, accepting the shear stress, or normal to the load-taking tension or compression, according to its position in the structural unit.

The major requirement in all cases is that the marriage of the plywood with the solid timber – transferring the tension or compression in the flanges to the shear in the webs – must be provided with a properly-designed and carefully-prepared joint. This joint must resist the shear stresses to which it will always be subject. The stronger and more efficient is the joint, the more nearly the timber and plywood components will be able to be stressed to their maximum safe capacity. However, the ultimate strength in any joint between timber and plywood can only be obtained in carefully-controlled factory conditions with special adhesives, under proper conditions of temperature and pressure. So it is often cheaper, and certainly more convenient when considering the production of purpose-made units to sacrifice some of

that strength, and compensate with the use of thicker and heavier solid timber components.

Plywood firms often provide information on the construction and dimensions of units to cover a wide field of spans and loadings. The Plywood Manufacturers of British Columbia, for instance, have published information on fir plywood, while the Finnish Plywood Development Association has covered the use of birch plywood.

Alternative constructions are:

1. Glued joints secured while setting with closely-driven nails; and
2. Nailed joints only.

Glued and nailed joints

Fig. 8.15 shows the elevation, and **Fig. 8.16** the section, of a typical box beam, using solid timber flanges and plywood webs. The top flanges are subject to almost pure compression, and similarly the bottom flanges to tension; while the plywood webs take most of the shear.

Shear stresses must start in the joint between the webs and the flange. But, if ultimate shear occurs, this will be seen as a vertical fracture in the plywood webs (**Fig. 8.17**). The shear joint, when satisfactorily glued, will have its strength limited to the capacity of the timber which will be weaker. Shear which occurs parallel to or within the planes of the plywood, will take place in that ply or laminate normal to the line

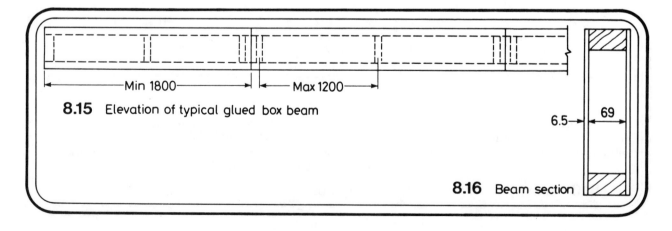

8.15 Elevation of typical glued box beam

8.16 Beam section

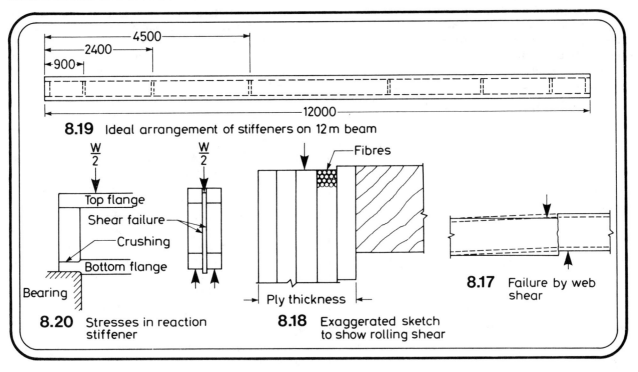

8.19 Ideal arrangement of stiffeners on 12 m beam

8.20 Stresses in reaction stiffener

8.18 Exaggerated sketch to show rolling shear

8.17 Failure by web shear

of force, but beyond the immediate support of its adhesive.

Failure will occur with the destruction of the normal cohesion between the fibres. This causes them to roll individually (**Fig. 8.18**). This is known as rolling shear, and is only about a quarter of that on a plane normal to the panel thickness, which is known as 'panel' shear. Resistance to rolling shear must govern the strength and the depth of the joint between flange and web and the end stiffener.

The shear strength in the plywood used in the webs is such that the minimum thickness of plywood necessary to provide it may be insufficient to prevent it buckling under the same load. Some vertical stiffeners between the flanges are then necessary to prevent this. In common with all uniformly-loaded beams, the greatest shear stresses are at the points of minimum bending near the supports. The stiffeners should therefore be placed closer together at the ends of a beam.

Fig. 8.19 shows the ideal position of the stiffeners in a beam 12m long. One stiffener is necessary at each end of the beam. This has to carry and transmit, through the bottom flange, half the total load (assuming this is uniformly distributed) carried by the beam. The width should be sufficient to give, with the depth, the necessary rolling shear areas to carry this load. The bearing area corresponding to the cross-section area of the stiffener should be sufficient to reduce the unit compression stresses imposed by the load to within the safe maximum allowed for compression perpendicular to the grain, see **Fig. 8.20**.

Nailed joints

When local conditions are not suitable for the use of glues, it is still possible to do the work using nailed construction only. But, as there is some sacrifice of strength and a greater relative deflection, the compo-

nents must correspondingly be heavier to compensate. When the joints are formed with nails only, the shear stresses are translated into transverse stresses on the nails. Values for these are given in CP112.

The Plywood Manufacturers of British Columbia can supply information on the construction of box beams using dry-nailed assembly. In the interests of economy and convenience in the use of readily-available materials, sizes are standardised: depths of beams (flange widths), given as approximate factors of available sheet widths, are tabled at 241mm, 305mm, 406mm, 508mm and 610mm. All flanges and stiffeners are formed with ex 100 × 50mm construction grade Douglas fir, duplicated or trebled as necessary where extra strength is needed. The specification adds:

1. Spacing of stiffeners must not exceed 1220mm.
2. No joints in the web must come outside the middle half of the beams.
3. Flanges not in one length must be spliced by a suitable splayed scarf or finger jointed to the necessary degree of strength.
4. Built-up flanges may be assembled with 75mm wire nails.
5. The plywood webs may be butt-jointed over the stiffeners. Nails are to be 50mm for 12mm plywood webs and 63mm for 19mm webs.

With this standardisation in assembly details, the strength of the materials will not be realised. But the losses will be balanced by ease of fabrication, and greater convenience in planning. All beams detailed have been made up, and responded satisfactorily to tests.

The range of beam sections comprises the following: 241mm deep beams with single flanges and 12mm and 19mm webs (two choices); 305mm deep beams with single or double flanges and 12mm or

19mm webs (four choices); 406mm, 508mm, and 610mm deep beams with single, double or treble flanges giving 18 choices of beam strengths. **Fig. 8.21** gives three examples of beam sections: light (**A**), medium (**B**), and heavy (**C**).

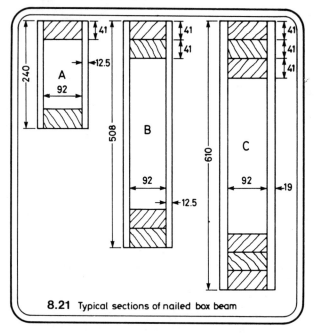

8.21 Typical sections of nailed box beam

The number of pieces in the reaction stiffeners is specified in each case. As seen in **Figs. 8.22, 8.23** and **8.24**, the spacing of the nails in the webs varies according to whether there are one, two or three pieces in the flanges. In order to give the increased shear strength needed, the nail pitch at the ends of the beam is half of that in the middle, the same pitch being used in each case in the enclosed stiffeners.

In building up these beams, where there is a choice, joints in flanges should be as near the ends as pos-

sible, and joints in the webs near the centre. The Finnish Plywood Development Association has produced a booklet which deals with stressed skin construction in beams and flat panels. This includes both box and I-beams in its designs. All work is glued and nailed. The main purpose of the nails in this case is to ensure close contact between the glued surfaces.

Thus the spacing of nails is standard with one or more staggered rows at 100mm centres (**Figs. 8.25** and **8.26**). Because the glued joint is more efficient than the dry-nailed, the timber and plywood itself may be more heavily stressed, allowing smaller sections to be used. The grain of the plywood webs is specified as being vertical.

The general conditions and arrangement of the joints is more stringent. Although the safety factor allows all stiffeners to be spaced at 1200mm, joints in webs must not be closer than 1800mm from the beam end. All splices in webs must be glued and formed with plywood splice plates; two stiffeners should be incorporated in the joint (see **Figs. 8.27** and **8.28**). Joints in the flanges should be splayed scarfs (see **Fig. 8.29**).

Recommended glues are urea formaldehyde for dry conditions, and phenol resorcinal formaldehyde for external use. Standard 6.5mm birch plywood is recommended for all box beams tabled with flange sizes varying from 69 by 44mm deep to 138 by 788mm deep, and with webs up to 1200mm deep, capable of carrying loads of up to 6000N per m run, and of up to 12.4m with spars. Intermediate stiffeners are standardised at 44mm thick with reaction stiffeners individually specified. Splayed scarfs, which are used to join flanges to one length, should be 12 times their thickness in length.

Figs. 8.30 and **8.31** give details of construction of I-beams with birch ply webs. As before, joints in the flanges should be of full strength and, if possible,

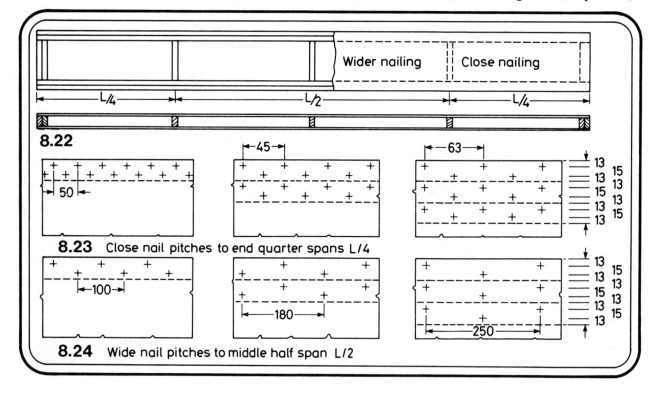

8.22

8.23 Close nail pitches to end quarter spans L/4

8.24 Wide nail pitches to middle half span L/2

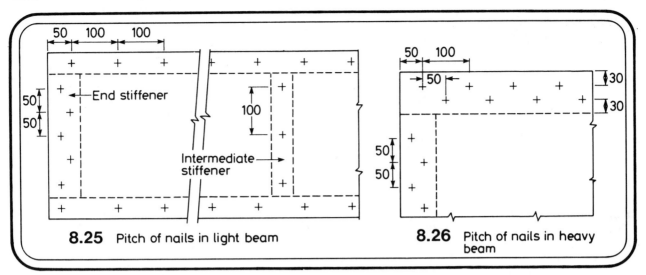

8.25 Pitch of nails in light beam

8.26 Pitch of nails in heavy beam

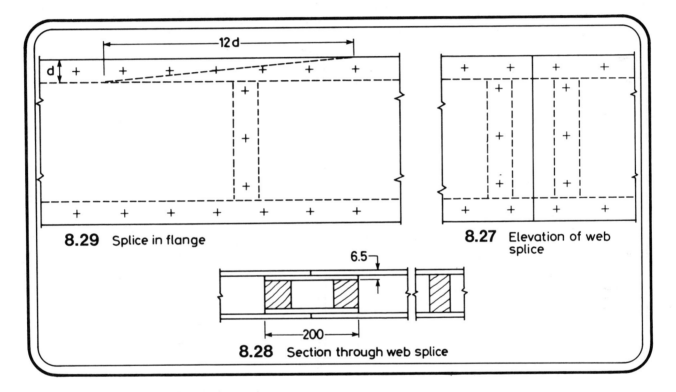

8.29 Splice in flange

8.27 Elevation of web splice

8.28 Section through web splice

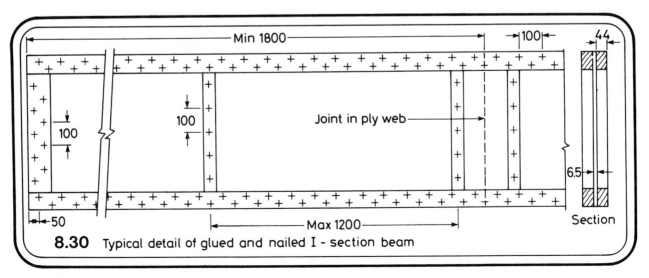

Joint in ply web

8.30 Typical detail of glued and nailed I - section beam

formed near the beam ends. Those joints in the webs should be away from the ends. Design thicknesses of webs rise from 6.5 to 12mm, and flanges from 19 by 44mm to 44 by 144mm. Nails used should be three-quarters the combined width of flanges and web.

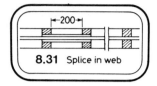

8.31 Splice in web

Single stressed skin panels

A nailed single stressed skin panel is shown in **Fig. 8.32**. The plan and elevation are shown in **Fig. 8.33**. The nails are spaced at 75mm centres as shown in **Fig. 8.34**. Plywood sheets closely nailed to the ribs or joist, become virtually integral with them, and so convert the whole panel into a compound of T-beams. In this case, the panel takes most of the compression in bending, transferred through the nails to shear in the ribs, the bottom set of which are in tension (**Fig. 8.35**).

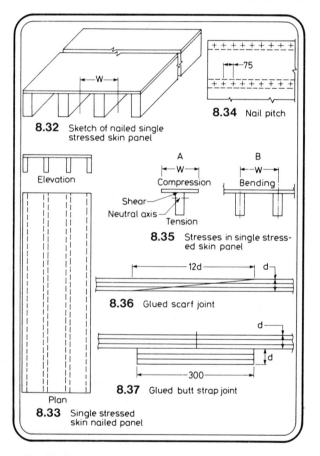

8.32 Sketch of nailed single stressed skin panel

8.34 Nail pitch

8.35 Stresses in single stressed skin panel

8.36 Glued scarf joint

8.37 Glued butt strap joint

8.33 Single stressed skin nailed panel

Both ribs and plywood panel must be in a single length, or effectively spliced, to take the load according to the position of the splice in the rib or panel. Splices in ribs should preferably be made at the ends of the span. **Figs. 8.36** and **8.37** show other methods of jointing the plywood.

Double stressed skin panels

Fig. 8.38 shows a double stressed skin panel. It is manufactured with various patented modifications by a number of timber engineering firms. This acts as a

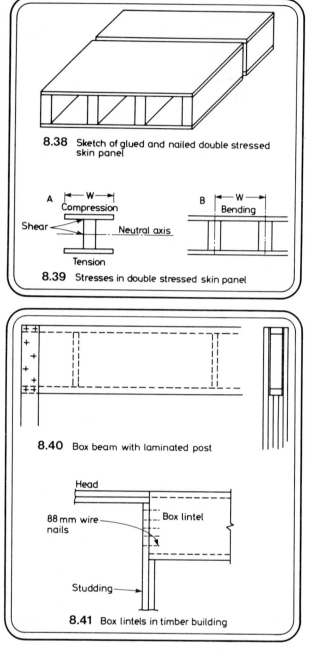

8.38 Sketch of glued and nailed double stressed skin panel

8.39 Stresses in double stressed skin panel

8.40 Box beam with laminated post

8.41 Box lintels in timber building

compound of I-beams, with the top skin taking the compression, the bottom skin the tension, and the ribs taking these stresses through to a central shear, as in **Fig. 8.39(A)**. In common with all level or inclined sheeted structures, the top skin or ply is also subject to bending between the ribs (**Fig. 8.39(B)**), and may be thicker in heavy units.

The Finnish Plywood Development Association publishes booklets which give values for panels with bottom skins of 6.5mm and top skins of 6.5, 9.13 and 12mm thickness; varying the rib spacing from 300, 400, 500 and 600mm; with ribs sized from 35 by 72mm to 47 by 244mm, with loads of up to 10.2kN/m², and spans of up to 6m.

Fixings are generally simple matters. Box beams may need support in the vertical plane with steel brackets to timber plates, or in the case of all timber construction, slotted into laminated posts as in **Fig. 8.40**. If the joints are well nailed or formed with tooth plate connectors, most of the load is taken in vertical shear. **Fig. 8.41** shows a box beam used in a timber building as a lintel.

Folded plate roofs

A development of the box beam and stressed skin panel construction is the 'folded plate' roof. This consists of a W-section timber roof formed by building up plywood panels into interconnected frames, with flanges and stiffeners at regular intervals.

It can be described as stressed skin construction in that the single or double skins – instead of being vertical as in box beams or horizontal as in stressed skin panels – are tilted, one against the other consecutively to create a saw tooth roof of equal pitches, as shown in **Fig. 8.42**. The actual pitch of each plane is governed by the available plywood sizes, each plate being tilted to agree with the required plan width cover.

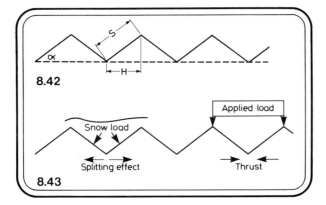

The imposed load (**Fig. 8.43**), generally given as a vertical stress component, creates bending stresses within (and parallel to) the panel as represented by w_2 in the triangle of forces (**Fig. 8.44**), and a horizontal thrust represented by w_h. The unit load over the roof surface must also be resolved into two components (**Fig. 8.45**), to give the stresses w_1 and the stresses in the roof plane.

The general effect of the imposed loads is to create thrusts; their horizontal components are taken by opposing panels acting as deep box beams within the roof planes. Thus, the weakness of one panel normal

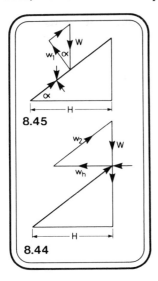

to its surface is countered by the adjoining one at ridge and valley acting within the roof planes. Secondary stresses are taken care of by stiffeners acting, with the plywood, as I- or T-beams which transmit the loads to the flanges.

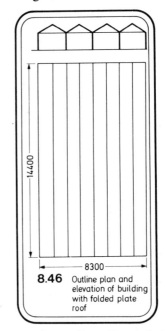

8.46 Outline plan and elevation of building with folded plate roof

For **Fig. 8.46**, the outline plan and elevation of a building with a folded plate roof, the skins would be formed with 1200mm wide Douglas fir plywood, with spans of 14.4m. **Figs. 8.47** and **8.48** show the plan and section of a folded plate construction. The upper and lower flanges are laminated from normal 100 by 50mm timbers, the double skins being 12mm Douglas fir plywood. The stiffeners are spaced at 600mm centres.

If the panel is regarded as a box beam, the flanges will take the bending stresses and the plywood skins, acting as webs, will take the shear. But the top plywood skins will also be subject to bending stresses under load as roof covering. They transmit this, in turn, to the stiffeners which will act as ribs or rafters integral with the sheeting as I-beams.

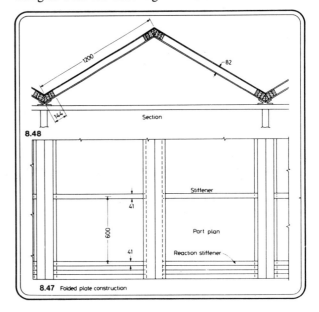

8.48 Section

8.47 Folded plate construction

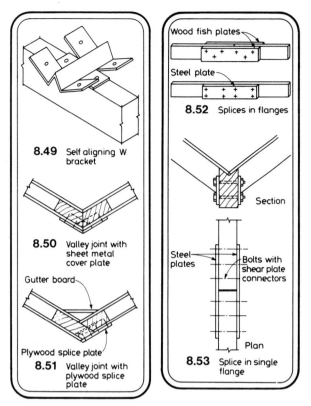

8.49 Self aligning W bracket

8.50 Valley joint with sheet metal cover plate

8.51 Valley joint with plywood splice plate

8.52 Splices in flanges

8.53 Splice in single flange

joints should also be considered in relation to bending stresses and shear. With twin plate construction, just sufficient ventilation to allow evaporation from any condensation, must be provided within the sealed cavities.

As an alternative to glued folded plate design with twin plywood skins, single plywood skins may be used. These are assembled by nailing only, generally *in situ*. Much heavier construction is used to compensate for the lost efficiency.

All nailing is best done with a nailing machine. Flanges may be joined lengthwise in various ways. Two methods are shown in **Fig. 8.52**. Single flanges also may be used at valley and ridge, the top edge being suitably splayed or V-recessed. **Fig. 8.53** shows a valley with details of a splice in length. **Fig. 8.54** shows a splice where twin flanges are used. This should be near to the supports, because the one flange must carry double the load at the splice.

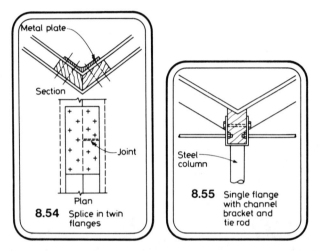

8.54 Splice in twin flanges

8.55 Single flange with channel bracket and tie rod

The framed plates are assembled into the roof, generally by close-nailed joints. The ends may be supported by purpose-made brackets (**Fig. 8.48**), or, where there is more than one span, by brackets as shown in **Fig. 8.49**. The joints at the ridges, being under simple pressure, present no problem. But the joints in the valley need nailing and possibly some additional support. In **Fig. 8.50**, a metal cover plate is used over the joint; while in **Fig. 8.51**, the flanges are lapped instead of being mitred, and the joint is covered by a plywood splice plate.

Flanges must act as single lengths over the whole of the span, and longitudinal splices must provide the necessary strength. The joints in the plywood skins should be made with equal care. The positions of the

At the ends of the spans or, if necessary, at intermediate points, the roof needs to be supported either on timber tie beams with props under, or with separate columns. **Fig. 8.55** shows the end of a flange carried by a steel column with a channel bracket connected to tie rods to take the horizontal thrust.

QUESTIONS FOR CHAPTER 8

Question 20

Straight glued laminate beams, 6m long, 120mm wide and 400mm deep, are to be made for use in a works kitchen.

a. What is the maximum thickness of laminate recommended?

b. Sketch types of longitudinal joints which may be used in the laminates.

c. What type of adhesive would you recommend?

City & Guilds of London Institute Examination, Purpose-Made Joinery, 1977. No. 4.

Question 21

a. What is meant by stressed skin construction?

b. Sketch details of a stressed skin panel, noting the important points of construction.

City & Guilds of London Institute Examination, Purpose-Made Joinery, 1977. No. 10.

CHAPTER 9

Veneers

The use of veneers in woodworking may be separated into three general classes: plain veneering, where wide panels of plywood and other manufactured sheeting has to be given a facing to match the grain of the timber in the rest of the job; veneers to shaped work, which is used to cover up the joints in a curved member, built up in pieces to avoid weak cross-grain; and purely decorative, where the veneer is especially selected for the look of the grain, and is put together in geometrical or other patterns. These form contrasts either by effect of light and shade on fibres at different angles, or by the use of different coloured timbers. In all cases, the veneered surface is likely to create interest and to come in for close inspection. All veneered work should therefore be immaculate.

There are two main types of veneer available: knife-cut, not more than 0.85mm thick; and saw-cut, which is about twice as thick. The latter must be cut to size and fit with a veneer saw (**Fig. 9.1**) which has fine teeth without set. The cuts should be made on a solid bearing against a straight edge which is better cramped into position. Curved cuts must be made with a fret saw. They are not used much today because they are too expensive. There is also more than 50 per cent wastage in sawdust. However, when a curved member has to be faced to match existing solid work, a suitable veneer may always be sawn in the mill.

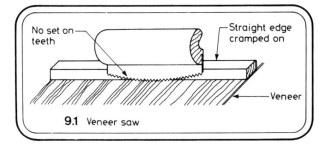

9.1 Veneer saw

Veneers should be kept in a humid atmosphere. If the ends are liable to split, they should be protected with gummed paper strips (**Fig. 9.2**). Veneers, when supplied in bulk, are parcelled in consecutive num-

bers as cut from the log (**Fig. 9.3**), and should be kept in this order, particularly those used for pattern building, so that identical figure formations may meet on a joint line (**Fig. 9.4**).

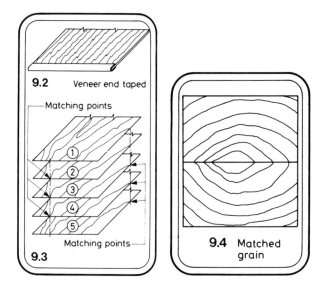

9.2 Veneer end taped

9.3

9.4 Matched grain

KNIFE-CUT VENEERS

Knife-cut veneers are sheared from the log in various ways to show a particular grain or figure (see Chapter 1). They may be cut with a thin-edged sharp chisel, or a knife. Cuts should be made against a straight edge or curved metal templet, held firmly in position, with the knife tight against the guide. Just sufficient pressure is used to cut through the veneer at one stroke.

A wide knife may be used for straight cuts, but for sharp curves, a thinner, narrower knife is more convenient. Knives with thin, replaceable blades may be purchased from tool manufacturers, but a worn-out kitchen knife (carbon steel, not stainless) is satisfactory. It should of course be sharpened to a thin razor-like edge, and frequently rubbed up. **Fig. 9.5** shows a knife suitable for straight cuts; **Fig. 9.6** shows a narrow one for curves.

Cuts across the grain should be made first so that

any breaking away would be in the waste at the side. Saw-cut veneers should have the rough on the glued side removed with a toothing plane (see **Fig. 9.8**) to provide a flat surface for bedding.

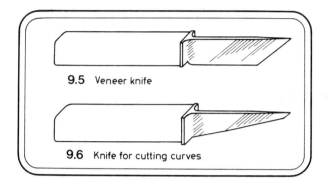

9.5 Veneer knife

9.6 Knife for cutting curves

PREPARATION OF THE GROUND

The part of the work to which the veneer has to be glued is termed the 'ground'. It may be a panel, a counter end, wall panelling, a drawer front or a curved rail. Its functional requirements will therefore govern its size, shape and construction, as well as the material from which it is made.

However, to provide a satisfactory ground for the veneer, it needs to be perfectly flat or smoothly curved, and accurately cut and shaped to the required dimensions. Defects, such as shakes, should be filled with wood feathers and cleaned off (see Chapter 1). Other mechanical defects, including knots, should be cut out and replaced with cross-grain wood pellets or little joiners (**Fig. 9.7**), and cleaned off.

The final preparation is to provide a matt surface to the ground to give a satisfactory key to the glued joint between ground and veneer. This may be carried out using a drum or wide belt sander and 80 grade grit. The abrasive surface should not be worn, or an undesirable burnished face will result.

Preparation by hand involves the use of a toothing plane (**Fig. 9.8**). This is similar to the traditional wood smoother, but has a single cutting iron. This is V-grooved on the back so that, when sharpened, it presents a toothed edge (**Fig. 9.9**). It is ground and sharpened in the usual way, but the wire edge is removed by driving its teeth into end-grain hard-

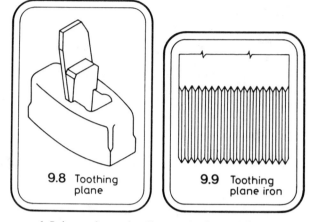

9.8 Toothing plane

9.9 Toothing plane iron

wood. It is used evenly all over the face of the ground, first at 45 degrees to the grain one way, and then at 45 degrees to the grain the other. The result is a level, accurate, matt surface.

Materials for the ground

The part of the work which forms the ground may be of solid timber or a laminated board, such as plywood or laminboard, or chipboard. The surface of the ground must be of uniform texture. This rules out the use of Douglas fir, due to its physically pronounced annual rings.

The ideal solid timber is Honduras mahogany, but it is expensive and difficult to get. Even-grained soft hardwoods, such as obechi or American whitewood, are also suitable. Mellow softwoods, such as yellow pine (though scarce), silver spruce, western hemlock or parana pine, are also satisfactory. European redwood (red deal) is suspect, having too much contrast between the texture of summer and spring wood.

When the ground is part of a structural unit with joints exposed on the face, no part of these should be end-grain. Any subsequent shrinkage will leave this standing proud, and the joint will show through the veneer. Thus a lap and not a through dovetail should be used on a veneered carcase end, see **Fig. 9.10**.

The choice of proprietary sheeting for veneer grounds depends partly upon other requirements.

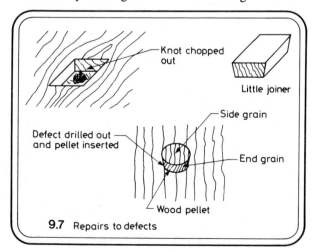

Knot chopped out

Little joiner

Defect drilled out and pellet inserted

Side grain

End grain

Wood pellet

9.7 Repairs to defects

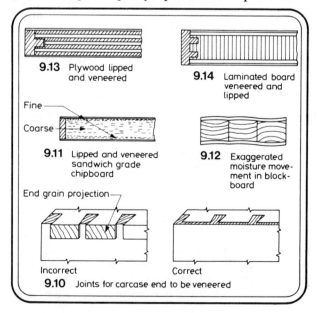

9.13 Plywood lipped and veneered

9.14 Laminated board veneered and lipped

Fine

Coarse

9.11 Lipped and veneered sandwich grade chipboard

9.12 Exaggerated moisture movement in blockboard

End grain projection

Incorrect

Correct

9.10 Joints for carcase end to be veneered

Laminated sheeting is probably more stable than plywood. But when, say, a carcase end has to be housed to take cleats or shelves, the core should always be vertical, as housing with the grain destroys its strength.

The most suitable chipboards are either the sandwich or the graded density types. The former (**Fig. 9.11**), is that where the density of the outer layer of chips is fine, and the middle ones coarse. The latter is that in which the chips are graded from fine on the outside to coarse in the middle.

Problems with boards

One disadvantage of boards with strip cores is that there is always the risk of some moisture movement causing distortion of individual strips, tending to produce a wavy surface on the outer plies. This is likely to be more prominent when the core strips are wider, and rules out batten board – and to a lesser degree blockboard (**Fig. 9.12**) – when the veneered face is likely to be given a high finish, or is a show part of the job.

Another problem is the risk of distortion to the veneered face, due to the drying shrinkage of the veneer itself, which causes the veneered surface to pull hollow. This can be minimised by using as little moisture as possible. It can also be countered in various ways: veneering on the heart side of the board in solid timber; veneering across the grain of the ground; veneering the back of the work to give balanced pulls; and by screwing cleats on the back of the ground before the veneer is laid, removing the cleats only just before fixing.

The grain of the face veneer should not follow the grain of the ply or veneer to which it is glued. When the plies of the laminated boards are turned off the log, they are bent away, with the result that fine cracks or 'checks' are formed over the inner face. Although the face is glued down to the core or inner ply, the checks do constitute a weakness. Subsequent sanding increases this by removing the more solid face. Under stress from the shrinking veneer laid with its fibres parallel, these checks will open, causing the veneer itself also to split. For this reason also, the sanding of all laminated boards should be minimal, only enough to smooth and flatten them.

Lipping exposed edges

Where the edges of the groundwork would be exposed, they should be lipped with solid timber. There is a choice of lipping first and veneering over the lipping (**Fig. 9.13**), or veneering first and lipping afterwards (**Fig. 9.14**).

The first method has the advantage that the veneer conceals the lipping on the surface, but leaves the veneer edge exposed. The second method, while showing the lipping on the face, does protect the edge of the veneer. If the lipping's appearance is acceptable, it should be used.

Chipboard may be lipped with a plain fillet glued and pinned to the edge and then veneered, or the veneer itself may be glued to the edge. Manufacturers of veneered chipboard supply glued edging, to be

added using a hot flat iron. Pressure is applied immediately as the glue cools and sets.

Laminated boards, due to their mixed grain construction (whether cored boards or plywood), cannot be veneered direct on their edges. They should preferably be lipped with one or more tongues on the lipping set into grooves in the board. The adhesive between plywood layers is generally highly abrasive, and the cutters will last longer if the groove is arranged so that the corners come into the middle of individual plies and not on the joint lines.

Occasionally, solid timber is specified for, say, the top of a unit. Then the grain of the veneer follows that of the timber core to allow unrestrained moisture movement in sympathy with other parts of the job. If the end grain edge has to be veneered, adhesion is likely to be uncertain, even after sizing. The best treatment is to house the end of the board, and insert a cross-grain fillet, which may then also be veneered cross-grain (**Fig. 9.15**).

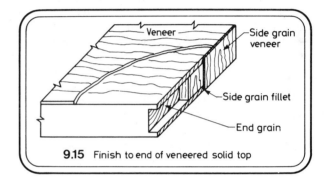

9.15   Finish to end of veneered solid top

ADHESIVES

The choice of adhesives used for veneering is governed by the method selected of sticking the veneer to the ground; the chemical composition of the timber, with the risk of staining reaction between glue and timber; the presence or absence of heat in the gluing process; and the durability needed – although decorative veneers are seldom exposed to the weather.

Animal glue is still satisfactory for use in dry positions, as are also the various proprietary pva adhesives, which are generally non-staining. Casein glue is a powerful adhesive and may be used cold, but cannot be used for acid timbers, as the acid reacts with the alkali in the glue to form dark stains.

Most of the resin glues are satisfactory; urea formaldehyde in its various brand forms being the best-known. The setting time of resin glues is related to temperature and the type of hardener used; these must be adjusted to allow sufficient time for assembly and clamping.

APPLYING THE VENEER

The simplest method of applying veneer, and that which needs the least equipment, is hammer veneering. A veneer hammer (**Fig. 9.16**), with a brass or other non-staining metal strip, and a domestic flat-iron (**Fig. 9.17**) are needed. In view of the wet conditions of working, an electric iron, however, would not be safe. Also required are a can of hot water, a clean swab and a pot of animal glue. Other types of glue are not suitable, as they are not sticky enough.

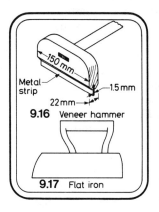

9.16 Veneer hammer

9.17 Flat iron

The glue should be prepared by soaking the glue cakes for 12 hours in cold water, and then heating the resulting jelly in a water-jacketed container to a temperature of about 70°C. It should not be boiled. The consistency should be such that it runs freely off the brush when held a little way off the pot, without breaking into droplets.

Assuming that the flat board, which is the ground, has been prepared and toothed and that it is going to be veneered with one sheet, the veneer is cut about 25mm larger each way all round. Glue the ground evenly all over and also the back of the veneer. It can be allowed to chill, as it will be reheated before pressing down. Place the veneer in position and press down overall with the hand.

Damp about half the back of the veneer with the swab and run the heated flat-iron over the damped area until the glue has fully melted. Then, with the hammer held more or less upright, press down firmly on the veneer and, using a zig-zag movement, force the glue away in front of the hammer until it is expelled at the edges. Work outwards from the middle. Damp the other half of the veneer and repeat the operation. The blade of the hammer should not be allowed to lie parallel to the grain, or it will be in danger of breaking the veneer.

Turn over the panel, and place one end half way on a planed batten. Press hard on the panel edge and, with the knife, cut away the surplus veneer (**Fig. 9.18**). Repeat for the other end, and then deal with the edges.

Turn the panel veneer-side up and test for overall

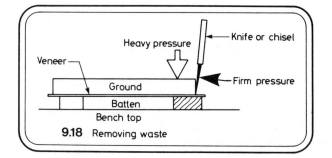

9.18 Removing waste

satisfactory adhesion by tapping with a fingernail. A hollow sound will indicate a blister. Apply local heat and press down again. Failing this, tack a small piece of ply over the blister with veneer pins with a sheet of paper to stop it from sticking. Finally, wipe off any surface glue with the clean swab, with the minimum of dampness.

When more than one piece of veneer is needed to cover the ground, one piece is laid as described; then the second is laid overlapping it by about 25mm. A straight edge is then held over the middle of the lap, with G-cramps if necessary, and the two veneers are cut through in one pass using a veneer knife or a chisel with a long thin edge (**Fig. 9.19**). The waste from the two veneers is removed. Then the length of the joint is reheated with the flat iron and pressed down with the hammer. Finally glue some gummed paper over the joint to keep the air from it and prevent it from prematurely drying and so shrinking open.

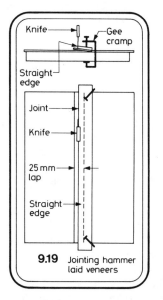

9.19 Jointing hammer laid veneers

PATTERN HAMMER VENEERING

A common decorative feature is obtained by putting a cross-band margin all around the panel. The panel is prepared as before, but the veneer is kept smaller so that it lies inside the edges. With a cutting gauge which is set to the width of the margin and works off the panel edge, cut the waste veneer and remove it by reheating with the flat iron and lifting.

The cross-bands are cut from the end of the sheet of veneer with a cutting gauge. The veneer is laid on a board, slightly overlapping the edge and held down by pressure on a batten. The gauge is held against the edge of the veneer; use just sufficient pressure to cut it through (**Fig. 9.20**). The inside edge of the cross-band must then be straightened on a shooting board with a plane, being held down by firm pressure on a batten as before (**Fig. 9.21**).

A number of veneers may be shot together by holding them in a vice between two battens, and planing veneers and battens together, see **Fig. 9.22**. The mitres in the banding may be cut against a mitre square, and the butt joints with a square on a flat

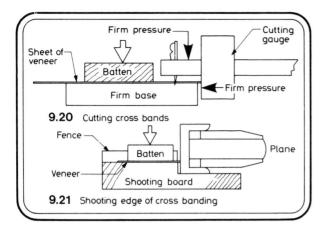

9.20 Cutting cross bands

9.21 Shooting edge of cross banding

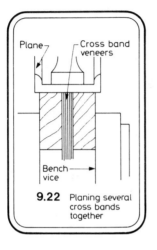

9.22 Planing several cross bands together

board. The cross-banding may be glued round the edge of the board using the peen of a warrington hammer to press it down. If hot glue is used, no reheating should be necessary.

Finally, all the joints should be covered with gummed paper strips. **Figs. 9.23** and **9.24** show the various stages.

Rounded corners

Where a panel has rounded corners, it becomes a little difficult to hold the cutting gauge always towards the centre as it should be. If, however, a hardwood fillet is pinned to one edge (**Fig. 9.25**), the gauge can be taken over half way round the curve unwaveringly by keeping the fillet and the centre of the stock pressed against the curved edge. The fillet is then transferred to the other edge of the stock and the cutting completed. All the clockwise cuts are made first, and then all the anticlockwise cuts.

Quartered patterns

A veneered pattern, commonly used in decorative work, is the quartered panel of four pieces of veneer with a pronounced striped grain angled to meet on the lines of intersection and form with the lines of figure concentric diamonds. In order to get the precision necessary for the best effect, the four pieces are cut from the consecutive sheets as in the log.

It is convenient if the panel is about 12mm larger each way than its final dimension, so that the cut lines may be seen outside the veneer. This may then be kept in, say, 6mm from the edge. The four pieces are cut and opened out as shown in **Fig. 9.26**, making them about 30mm over size each way. They are then fitted together (butt-jointed) until all the relevant strips of grain meet exactly. Each meeting edge is marked in pencil with parallels 12.5 and 25mm inward.

The centre lines are pencilled both ways on the panel. The first piece of veneer is laid with its 12.5mm lines on the panel centre line. The next is laid lapping 25mm; the cut is made and the waste removed. The third is then laid lapping the second one by 25mm; the cut is made and the waste removed. Finally the fourth

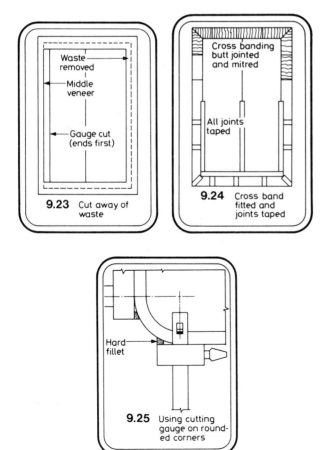

9.23 Cut away of waste

9.24 Cross band fitted and joints taped

9.25 Using cutting gauge on rounded corners

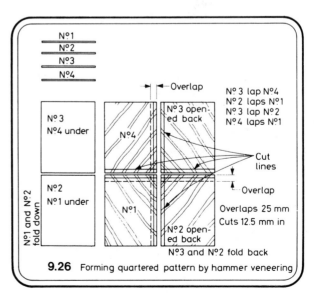

9.26 Forming quartered pattern by hammer veneering

piece is laid lapping the first and third by 25mm. The final cuts are made, the waste removed; then all joints must be rubbed down and sealed with gummed strips.

PATTERN VENEERING UNDER PRESSURE

Patterns more elaborate than those described above, cannot be conveniently formed using the hammer method. The alternative is to fit the veneers to a pattern drawn full size on a sheet of paper, and hold them temporarily with spots of glue. Then tape all the joints, lift the whole assembly off the drawing, glue it, and apply to the grounds under pressure.

Caul veneering
The simplest method of pressure veneering, carried out in the small workshop for occasional small jobs, uses cambered bearers distributed over a stout board (termed a 'caul') through pressure on the face of the veneer. This is exerted by means of G-cramps acting against other bearers under the ground.

The purposes of the camber are twofold. First, pressure is exerted on the middle of the panel, expelling the surplus glue outwards as the G-cramps tighten on the bearers. Second, it ensures that ultimately there is just as much pressure exerted in the centre as there is at the edges. The lower bearers may be straight – in which case they must be heavier, so that they do not bend upwards – or they may have the same camber as the top ones.

Cramping should start in the centre of the length and work towards the end. If animal glue is used, it is applied to both veneer and ground and the caul is heated right through. The transmitted heat softens the glue and allows it to be expelled. It may be necessary to fix the veneer with one or two veneer pins (thin pins about 9mm long) where the pattern dictates that it should be accurately orientated on the panel.

Veneer presses
A step forward from using the method described above is the home-made veneer press (Fig 9.27). It is a stout bench with a 38mm thick top, planed flat and out of wind, over which is set hardwood cross-bearers, cambered about 6mm on the bottom edge.

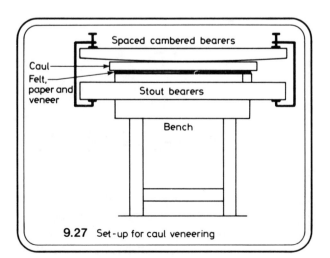

9.27 Set-up for caul veneering

Bolts with T-heads swivel through slots in the top, and swing into end slots in the cross-bearers. These are tightened down by the nuts acting on washers above the slots.

Proprietary hand presses consist of arrangements of metal grillages, by means of which pressure may be applied over a large area from a central screw. Several of these may be combined in one frame, to be used, either separately or in unison (for veneering long panels). Initial adjustments are made rapidly by means of a hand wheel; the final pressure is applied with a long lever acting on a ratchet to turn the screw. In order that pressure may be applied at the centre, each individual cross-bearer in the grillage is attached to the pressure plate (caul) which has a leaf spring to make it flexible in cross-section. This applies pressure in the centre, and afterwards flattens it out. This is generally referred to as a 'cold press', but heat may be applied by using a zinc plate about 6mm thick heated to a suitable temperature. Whether heat should be applied, depends upon the type of adhesive used, its reaction to heat and the need for rapid turnaround.

Where large quantities of veneering are to be carried out, much more sophisticated machinery and equipment is used. This includes such items as multiple presses with tiers of separate platens, hydraulically or electrically operated, and heated by steam or electricity. Heat can be applied individually to each panel.

It is necessary to appreciate the difference between the setting processes of say, animal glue – which melts with heat, stiffens with cooling and actually hardens by evaporating, the process being reversible – compared with the various resin glues which set permanently with heat. Resin glues require the glued surfaces to be brought into tight contact within the close assembly time. This varies with the speed of reaction of the adhesive at the temperature decided upon. Where multiple presses are used, the pressure is uniform overall, and there is no provision for expelling trapped glue. The amount of adhesive used, and its uniformity of spread, is therefore critical. The accuracy of spread is controlled by passing the veneer or ground through a glue-spreading machine. These usually have rubber-faced 'spreading' rollers, which give a generous coating, and 'doctor' rollers, which expel the surplus and feed it back into a reservoir.

CUTTING AND FITTING COMPLICATED VENEERS

As already stated, the patterns are set out full size on a sheet of paper. However it is necessary to give some thought as to how the pieces are to be cut and fitted together.

Where curved or other complicated shapes are formed in single veneers, it is easier to mark out the whole outline on a sheet of some metal, like zinc. This is then cut out, and the template is used to cut out both the pieces which fit in and the opening to receive it. Where the direction of the grain is critical, it is advisable to take a tracing of the initial drawing so that it can be used to observe the grain before marking for cutting.

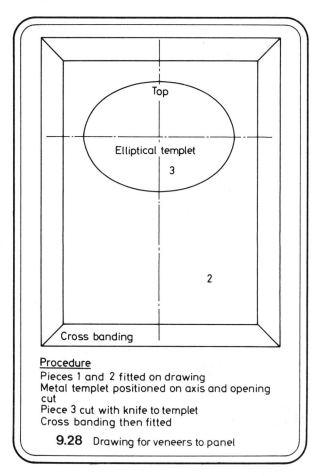

Procedure
Pieces 1 and 2 fitted on drawing
Metal templet positioned on axis and opening cut
Piece 3 cut with knife to templet
Cross banding then fitted

9.28   Drawing for veneers to panel

Fig. 9.28 illustrates the working principles. The joint between 1 and 2 is first shot. The rectangle is fitted on the drawing in line with the vertical centre line and the horizontal axis drawn. The template is drawn and cut out. The veneers are then placed on a flat board and positioned with veneer pins. The template is positioned on the veneers with the axes coinciding, and the ellipse is cut out with a knife. The elliptical veneer is also cut from the same template.

Curved rails

In order to avoid the weakness present in all but the flattest curves in timber, special methods must be used to form the necessary shape. Curved rails may be formed, either by laminating (**Fig. 9.29**), or by building as with bricks.

In the first method, each laminate should be thin

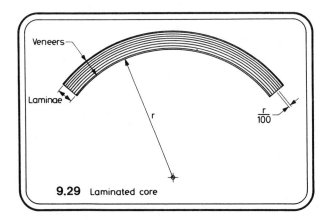

9.29   Laminated core

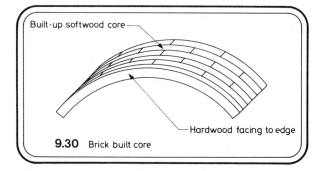

9.30   Brick built core

enough to bend to the shape without fracture. The maximum thickness depends upon the kind of timber, which should in any case be straight grained. But the general rule for thickness is that it should not exceed 0.01 of the radius. It should be assembled between curved formers or cauls. The curve should be slightly sharper than that needed, as some springback must be expected.

In brick building, curved pieces short enough to eliminate cross-grain are glued together to break joint (see **Fig. 9.30**). If they are shaped off the spindle moulder from an accurately prepared template, they should go together satisfactorily without much subsequent correction.

The veneer should be applied under pressure between cauls with paper outside to prevent sticking, and a thickness of felt or thick cardboard to take up inequalities which may be present. Where the width of the member is small, the cauls can be cut from solid timber, both male and female member being cut from the same plank. The radii are adjusted to allow for the thickness of the rail, see **Fig. 9.31**.

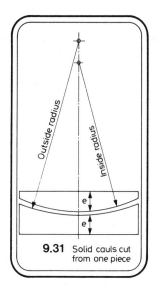

9.31   Solid cauls cut from one piece

Curved panels

Curved panels may be formed from two or more thicknesses of thin plywood bent between formers, the veneer being applied at the same time. All glued joints should be toothed or machine sanded before assembling. To spread the pressure between bearers and limit the number required, they should form a grillage with stiff longitudinal strips, see **Fig. 9.32**. The formers may be lined with plywood to provide a uniform overall surface but, if the strips are narrow and accurate to thickness, that should not be necessary. Pressure on the cauls or formers can be applied by cramps at the ends, or the set-up can be placed in the press. Where G-cramps are used at the ends of bearers, they are subject to bending stresses; therefore the centre of the hollow rib should be as thick as that of the round one (**Fig. 9.32**).

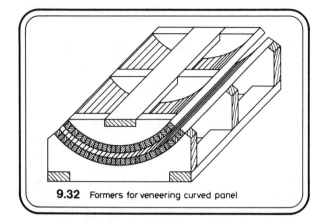

9.32 Formers for veneering curved panel

Specialists in veneering use either a vacuum press or a compressed air press for veneering convex-shaped work; only the male former is needed. In both cases, a rubber sheet is fastened down over the veneered member on its former and secured to the table. In the vacuum press, the air is then withdrawn from under the sheet, thus creating a near atmospheric pressure on the rubber sheet, which pulls down tight on to the work. In the compressed air press, air pressure is applied to the sheet above the table. It is not therefore limited to atmospheric pressure, and may be more easily adjusted.

FINISHING

It is important to keep all veneered work as clean as possible. To clean up the veneered face which should be fully hardened, the paper strips over the joints should be damped as little as possible and scraped off. When the face is completely dry, it should be machine sanded (using a fine grit on a drum), wide-belt sanded, or cleaned up by hand. The best tool to use for this is the cabinet scraper. If the surface is dead flat, a specially-set smoothing plane with a fitted back iron close to the cutting edge can be used. This takes off a shaving the same thickness as that from the scraper. The scraper should be sharp, and used where possible along the grain. A shearing action sometimes helps with difficult wood. The scraping should be followed by, say, $1\frac{1}{2}$, 1 and 0 grade papers. Paper with the grain where possible. Otherwise, concentrate on cross-grain scratch marks by circular movements with the finer grades of paper.

QUESTION FOR CHAPTER 9

Question 22
A veneered panel is to have a central diamond in a quartered panel in which the grain of the diamond is to be horizontal; all the veneers are to have pronounced stripes. Describe how the veneer pattern would be fitted and assembled.

CHAPTER 10

Ecclesiastical Joinery and Fitments

Ecclesiastical joinery and fitments, tied to an historical background and traditional methods, date back to the first days of the craft guilds. Within the overall limits of a general design, each craftsman was given freedom to express his own ideas in all the work he carried out. In early cathedrals, for instance, no two carved bench ends or other identifiable carvings, such as bosses or rosettes, would be identical. Because of age, damp and the death-watch beetle, ecclesiastical buildings are often in need of maintenance. So the modern joiner needs some knowledge of the original construction to carry out repairs, where necessary, in the traditional style.

Either oak or, where economy dictated, pitch pine was used. Both the joiner and the stonemason used tracery in recesses in walls, windows, screens and in general fitments. The work involved simple geometric principles with circles tangent to curves and straight lines, which were then built into triangles, squares or regular polygons.

BASIC SHAPES

The basic semicircular, (or more) curves are known as 'foils'. They represent a conventional leaf form. Three curves in a triangle represent a trefoil (**Fig. 10.4**); four curves in a square are a quartrefoil (**Fig. 10.2**); and five curves in a pentagon are a cinquefoil (**Fig. 10.3**).

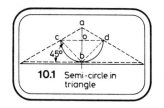

10.1 Semi-circle in triangle

In one case, a semicircle is tangent to the side of the regular figure and meets other semicircles on the bisectors of the external angles of the figure, dividing the figure into identical isosceles triangles (**Fig. 10.1**). In the other case, the semicircles each touch two sides and meet on the bisectors of the sides so that each is drawn within a kite.

In the trefoil (**Fig. 10.4**), section **J–J** is taken through the tracery at the edge and section **K–K** through the middle of the rib. In relating the tracery to the job, half the width of the rib face **R** is marked in from the panel outline and parallels drawn. These now become the basis of all the curves.

After the radii are increased and reduced an equal

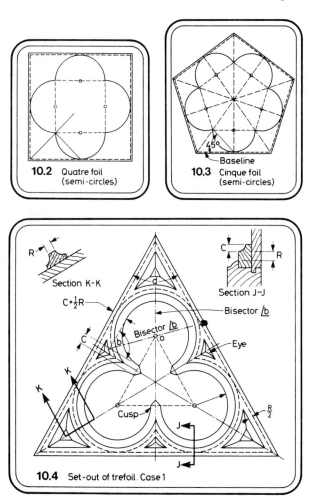

10.2 Quatre foil (semi-circles)

10.3 Cinque foil (semi-circles)

10.4 Set-out of trefoil. Case 1

amount, to give the curve outline for the rib face and again for the hollows in each case, they meet similarly-placed parallels to the straight perimeter base lines.

Shapes based on circles

As an alternative to shapes based on semicircles, the design may start with complete circles nearly tangent to each other. If the circles are made completely tangent (**Fig. 10.5**), the clothing of the circles to form the ribs of the tracery, will continue their full thicknesses into the projecting parts. These are known as the 'cusps', and will then appear clumsy. To avoid this, the set-out must be modified. As already stated, two alternatives are available for tracery with cusps:

1. Each foil touches two sides of the embracing frame; the circle is contained in a kite; or
2. Each foil is tangent to the centre of each side of the frame; each circle is enclosed in a triangle.

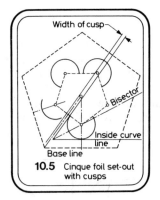

10.5 Cinque foil set-out with cusps

Taking (1) (**Fig. 10.4**), the set-out is as follows. The frame opening, which may be any regular shape, is an equilateral triangle in this case. Half the face width of the rib **R** gives the basic centre lines of the frame. The external angles are then bisected and continued to the opposite side, giving a set-out from which may be taken three kites, each with one bisector.

Now, taking the upper kite, the width **C** is marked centrally on the bisector of the side and parallels drawn, while the width $C + (R \div 2)$ is gauged parallel to the dotted base line.

The angle **b** is a right angle which, bisected to cut the vertical from the apex at **O**, gives the centre for drawing the upper foil. Other centres are on the bisector lines equidistant from the frame centre. The cusp may be made wider or narrower at will by adjusting at **C**. The incised part, where the thickness is not pierced, is known as the 'eye'.

In the case of each foil being tangent to the centre of the containing side, as each foil has to be much smaller, the space at the angles can be filled in with three further completely circular foils.

The initial set-out is as before. But the triangles, and not the kites, are considered as containing the foils. The width of the cusp and the inside curve line are this time drawn in relation to the triangle. The bisector of the inner angle contains the centre for the curves of the lower foil, where it cuts the vertical. The others are equidistant from the main centre of the

frame. This is also the point from which an embracing circle can be drawn. Equilateral triangles formed by tangents to this circle contain the centres for the fill-in foils.

Skeletal modifications before the filling-in of the ribs can be applied to the square and pentagon (**Figs. 10.5** and **10.6**). The basic principle is that a circle can be drawn in any triangle from a centre at the intersection of two bisectors, see **Fig. 10.7**.

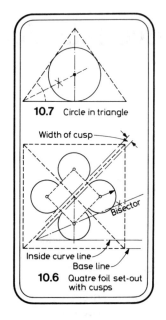

10.7 Circle in triangle

10.6 Quatre foil set-out with cusps

Curved mitres

Where a curved moulded member is intersected with a straight, or one curved to a different radius, the actual mitre between the moulds will be curved and not straight. In small work, that can be judged accurately enough by the eye. But on large and heavy work, it may be long and will need setting-out in order to get the correct intersection.

A method accurate enough for most occasions is shown in **Fig. 10.8**. Strike **m–p** from centre C_1; and **m–q** from centre C_2 to provide the mould edge lines of two curved members meeting at **m**.

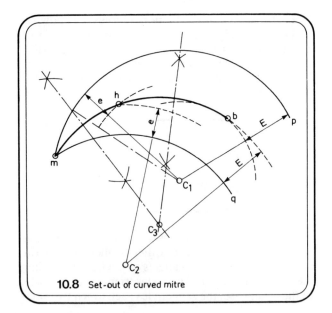

10.8 Set-out of curved mitre

Three points are required through which the mitre curve will pass. From C_1 and its radius minus e, draw a small arc. From C_2 and its radius plus e, draw an arc intersecting the first one at point h. Then h is a point on the mitre.

From C_1 and radius minus E, draw a small arc. From C_2 and radius plus E, draw a second arc intersecting the first at b; then b is a point on the mitre.

Bisect m–h and bisect h–b and produce the bisectors to intersect at C_3. Then a curve from centre C_3 and radius C_3–m will pass through h and b, and will give the line of the mitre to a close approximation.

LINEN-FOLD PANELS

A common form of decoration in church work is the linen-fold panel representing a draped curtain. This also lends itself to modern methods of construction. The surface may first be machined, using moulding cutters on a planer. Then it is shouldered across the ends, with the end of the panel cut in to represent the folds of a cloth as seen in **Fig. 10.9** (elevation).

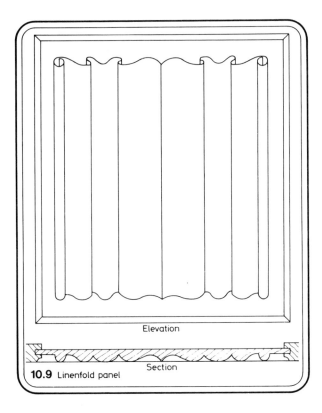

Elevation

Section

10.9 Linenfold panel

To give a realistic look, it is important to cut the inside of the fold as seen at **a**. The bottom should not be finished the same as the top, but should continue the illusion of the hanging folds. The lower curves should be parallel to the upper ones.

CHURCH BENCHES AND PEWS

The design and proportions of church furniture and fittings are largely related to the human form in standing, sitting and kneeling. Church seats, when in the form of benches or pews, should have proportions similar to those of everyday chairs. Some seats in old churches can be uncomfortable, with upright backs and level seats. But seats sloping down to the backs are more comfortable.

Seat backs are framed up from 38mm timber, with muntins (vertical framing panels) about every 900mm, centres and intermediate fillings of vertical matchboard. These are bareface tongued to come flush with the face of the framing. The first and last boards also are tongued to the stile or muntin. Intermediate joints between matchboarding are best made with loose tongues, the boards being grooved centrally on both edges. The loose tongues should be stained before insertion to avoid white lines showing with shrinkage. It is safer to allow for the sum of the widths of the boards to one panel to be a little in excess of that required. When they are finally fitted, each should be planed perhaps one shaving at a time, until they are down to required size.

All exposed dry joints should be made V-shape with mason's mitres at the muntin and stile positions. The end stiles should be fitted between the rails so that the top edge of the back, commonly finished with a mop-stick mound, continues unbroken to give a hand-hold for the infirm.

Bench ends

Bench ends as seen in ancient churches are invariably 50mm or more in thickness with the seat, back and other longitudinal members housed into them. They are often, however, heavily enriched, either with carving or some simpler form of decoration, such as tracery or linen-fold panels recessed into the solid. The front edges of the pews at elbow level may also be heavily moulded with carved stops. Repeating this work today requires the joiner to make maximum use of modern machines and methods without destroying the atmosphere of the original work.

In **Figs. 10.10** to **10.16**, the bench end, instead of being carved from the solid, is built up in three pieces with tongued and grooved joints. The middle part is left out, and a separate tracery plus backing panel inserted in the continuous grooves in the outer parts. Similar grooves are also made in the end grain to receive the panel and tracery ends. If a thin layer of glue is spread on a piece of chipboard and then the tracery is placed back-downwards on it, sufficient glue will be picked up to enable the tracery to be glued to the panel without the glue showing at the face.

All the grain in the bench end, panel and tracery remains vertical, see **Figs. 10.12** to **10.14**. However, there will be a weakness at the top. This is strengthened by making the roll at the top with the grain longitudinal and a stout tongue fitting into a groove (**Fig. 10.15**). If the timber is well-seasoned, no shrinkage problem should occur.

Pellet screwing

The seat is tongued into the bottom rail of the back, see **Fig. 10.11**. It may be secured by pellet screwing. Pellets are usually machine-made on the lathe or router. If possible, more should be provided than required and in different shades of colour, so that each one may be selected to match the surrounding

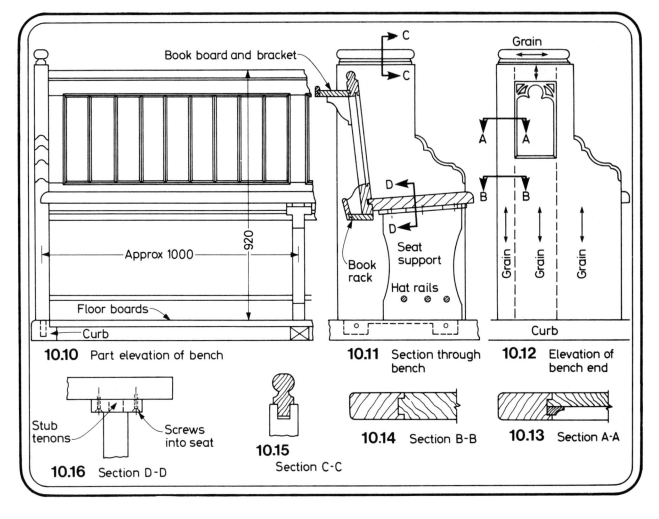

10.10 Part elevation of bench

10.11 Section through bench

10.12 Elevation of bench end

10.16 Section D-D

10.15 Section C-C

10.14 Section B-B

10.13 Section A·A

timber. The direction of grain of the pellet should exactly follow that of the wood around it. The bench ends should also be pellet screwed to the seat and back. Where screws have to be driven into end grain, they should be about 25mm longer, as their holding power will be less certain.

Bench feet and supports
The bench ends may rest on the common floor, or the level of the floor to the pews may be about 75 to 100mm higher than in the aisles. In this case, a continuous curb (**Figs 10.10** to **10.12**) takes the floor boards and is also mortised to take the tenoned feet of the bench ends.

Intermediate supports to the seats are needed at intervals of not more than about 1.5m. But the obvious position for them, design-wise, is under the centre of each muntin. They may be tenoned into wide cleats which may then be screwed up under the seat.

Hat-rails, in the form of round rods or rectangular rails are usually placed under the seat, and keep the seat supports upright.

Horizontal book-boards may be tongued into the top rail at the back, being housed into the bench ends and supported by brackets from each muntin. Additional accommodation may also be provided for books at seat level in the form of racks, also supported by internal brackets (**Fig. 10.11**).

Choir stalls
Choir stalls placed on either side of the chancel are of similar construction to the pews. However the seat backs and book-rests are usually made higher to enable the choir to read from the books while standing.

LITANY DESKS

Litany desks are used by the priest in the kneeling position, see **Figs. 10.17** to **10.19**. They are built up from stout curbs, forming an unequal H-shape in plan. Solid desk ends, 38mm thick, are tenoned into the front arms of the outer curbs; the desk front, also 38mm thick, is tongued into the cross-member. The desk fronts are housed into and pellet screwed through the desk ends (**Fig. 10.19**).

The desk top, 38 to 50mm thick, is supported by a heavy bed mould, tongued into the top. A kneeling-board may rest on the end curbs; it is secured by being screwed from underneath or perhaps housed into them. The top is moulded on the front and ends and tongued into a book stop.

The desk front may be enriched in various ways. It may be open or panelled or have open tracery. This is tongued into the frame, the part facing out being moulded and the back kept plain. The desk ends are also shaped.

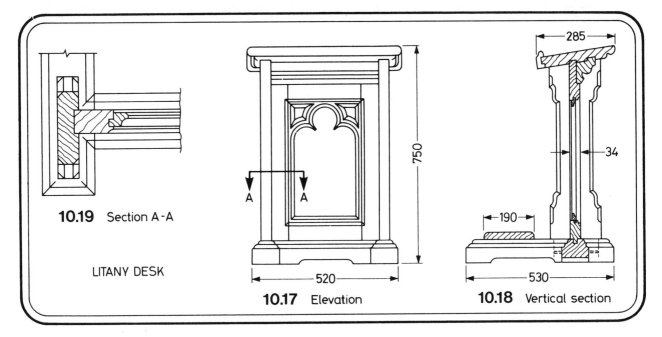

10.19 Section A-A

LITANY DESK

10.17 Elevation

10.18 Vertical section

ALTAR RAILS

The communion or altar rail should be set at a height to suit the kneeling communicants, and may be from 500 to 750mm high. In its simpler form, it is a stout horizontal rail from 100 by 75mm timber, supported by pillars at about 900mm centres. The centre part is removable for access to the altar, but is kept in place when communion is administered.

A more elaborate communion rail takes the form of a low screen with centre gates opening back, see **Figs. 10.20** to **10.22**. It can be framed up with stiles, top and bottom rails and intermediate muntins. Buttresses are fitted against each vertical member, to give the appearance of a greater stability. The two centre bays form gates, and are hinged back through 180 degrees when open.

The screen is kept rigid by means of anchor bolts taken through drilled muntins, embedded in the concrete underfloor and tightened down; the ends of the bolts are covered by the capping. Enrichment is by means of tracery, together with backing panels housed and grooved into the framing.

In order to allow the gates to be hinged right back, it is necessary to use parliament hinges, taking the pivot point outside the widest part of the capping or plinth. The hinge joint in the capping is kept in line with the buttress. The closing joint in the capping and plinth must be especially set out (**Fig. 10.20**). A diagonal is drawn from the hinge centre to the outer corner of the buttress. The closing joint must be at 90 degrees to this. The bottom part of the buttress and framing at plinth level must be cut away to allow the bottom of the gate to swing through.

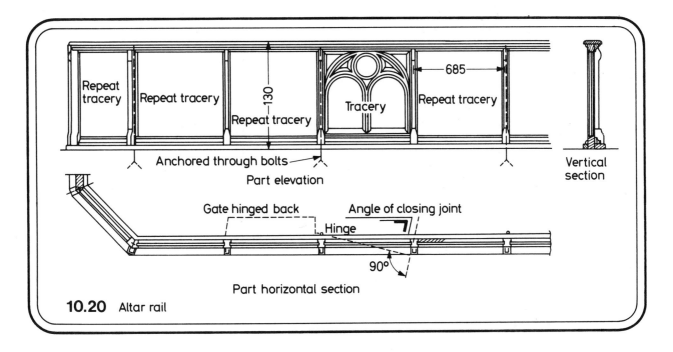

10.20 Altar rail

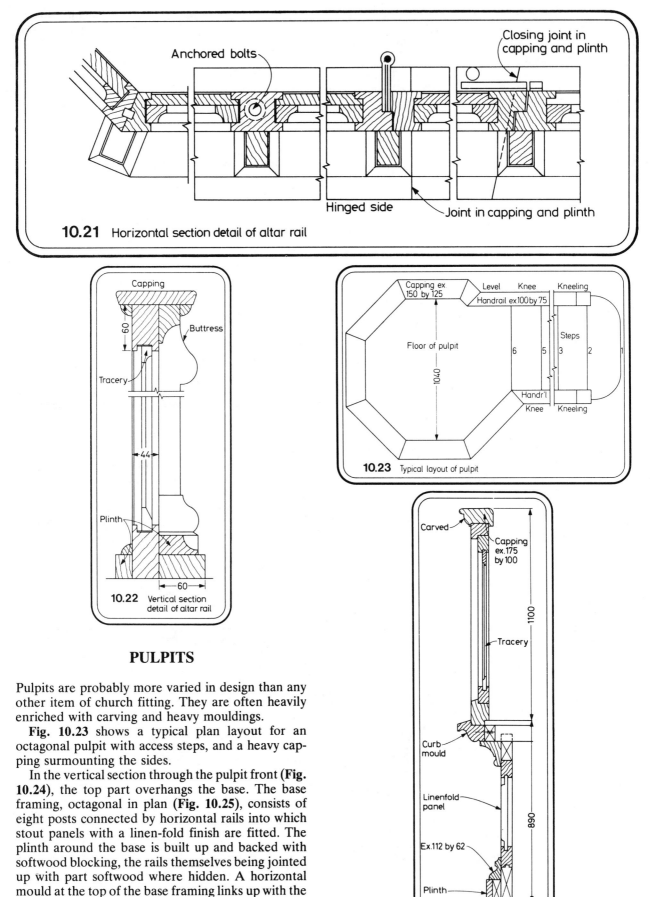

10.21 Horizontal section detail of altar rail

Anchored bolts

Closing joint in capping and plinth

Hinged side

Joint in capping and plinth

Capping

60

Buttress

Tracery

44

Plinth

60

10.22 Vertical section detail of altar rail

Capping ex 150 by 125

Level   Knee   Kneeling

Handrail ex 100 by 75

Floor of pulpit

1040

Steps

6   5   3   2   1

Handr'l

Knee   Kneeling

10.23 Typical layout of pulpit

Carved

Capping ex.175 by 100

1100

Tracery

Curb mould

Linenfold panel

890

Ex.112 by 62

Plinth

10.24 Section through pulpit front

PULPITS

Pulpits are probably more varied in design than any other item of church fitting. They are often heavily enriched with carving and heavy mouldings.

Fig. 10.23 shows a typical plan layout for an octagonal pulpit with access steps, and a heavy capping surmounting the sides.

In the vertical section through the pulpit front (**Fig. 10.24**), the top part overhangs the base. The base framing, octagonal in plan (**Fig. 10.25**), consists of eight posts connected by horizontal rails into which stout panels with a linen-fold finish are fitted. The plinth around the base is built up and backed with softwood blocking, the rails themselves being jointed up with part softwood where hidden. A horizontal mould at the top of the base framing links up with the curb to the upper part.

The pulpit floor (**Fig. 10.26**) is carried by softwood timbers, all 75 by 75mm; with the exception of one

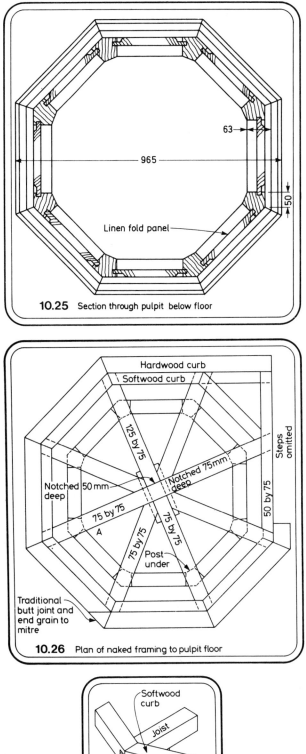

10.25 Section through pulpit below floor

10.26 Plan of naked framing to pulpit floor

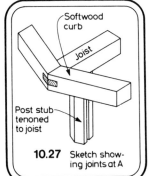

10.27 Sketch showing joints at A

full length joist, 125 by 75mm, which is notched 50mm at the top to take another full-length joist. This is notched into it by 25mm at right angles, so bringing the tops flush. The other four joists are cut to fit in the

angles, and are supported by cleats nailed to the deeper joist. The posts of the base are stub-tenoned up into the joists, which extend over them. The joists are then bridle-jointed to the softwood curbs (**Fig. 10.27**), which carry the edges of the flooring. The outer hardwood moulding completes the curb.

The upper part of the pulpit is assembled in a similar manner to the base with corner posts, and is rebated to receive framed in-fills with open tracery. To keep strictly to tradition, alternate moulded members would be taken through, showing end-grain at the mitres. But a point against this is that any subsequent moisture movement would break the line of the mould.

The steps to pulpits vary considerably in their design. They may be straight or may have curved strings with winders to save space. Construction generally closely follows standard staircase construction, see Chapter 6.

A STYLISTIC POINT

It is not always appreciated by the casual observer that all ancient churches were 'modern' when they were built, and used the best techniques available at the time! Compare Early English style with the Perpendicular style, for instance. It would therefore seem logical to follow this policy in modern times, and discard the methods which seem to be difficult to execute and time-consuming.

CURVED PEWS

Although old churches may have the seating following the traditional rectangular pattern on plan; the new or non-conformist church may have a different layout. One variation may have the seats set out to segmental curves with radii centred on the pulpit, see **Fig. 10.28**. This involves some geometrical develop-

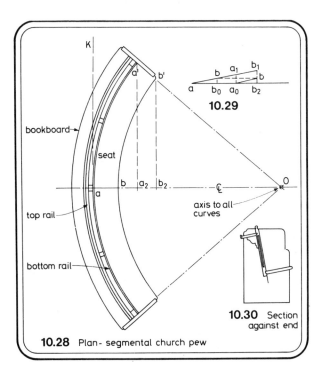

10.29

10.30 Section against end

10.28 Plan- segmental church pew

ment in any curved surfaces – such as backs, seats and book-boards – which are not in a horizontal or vertical plane. All these shapes will be parts of very flat cones with their apexes based on the common axis. This axis is, in effect, a plumb line taken from the plan centre of the seat curves.

Setting out seats and book-boards

In setting out the principles of seat and book-board, constructional details such as exact dimensions of the tongue on the back of the seat would be necessary. The plan curves must include the book-board, top and bottom back rails and seat. The radii of the seat and book-board would be obtained by continuing the inclined lines of each in the central vertical section to intersect the vertical axis rising from the plan centre, see **Fig. 10.31**.

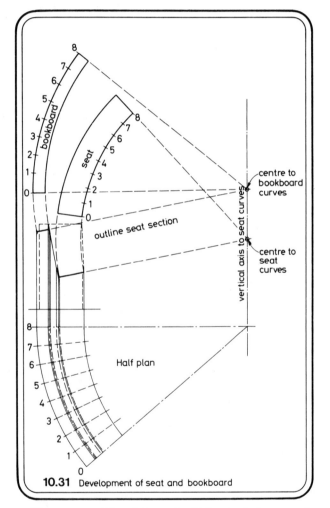

10.31 Development of seat and bookboard

The seat and book-board still have their curved edges horizontal, so their plan lengths are the true lengths. They are transferred from the respective edges of the plan to those in the development by means of a series of short steps so that the chord between points shall not be appreciably shorter than the curve it subtends. The ends in all cases lie on the radii from the curve centres.

Twisting the seat timbers

As stiffness in timber is mainly in the direction of the grain – when a board has to be bent around a cone,

even when that cone is little more than a camber – it will react strongly to what is in effect a twisting stress. It may be necessary to construct the seat of thinner material, supporting the front edge by a curved rail with radial bearers, taken to the back. Additional lining to the front edge will give a more solid appearance.

To find the amount by which a seat must be bent or twisted from the straight, refer to **Fig. 10.28**. Take half the seat (without thickness) as being represented by points a, a^1, b^1 and b which are hinged in a horizontal plane about the axis a–k. Assume that the plane is tilted to correspond with the pitch of the seat given in section in **Fig. 10.29** and that **Fig. 10.30** is a section on line a–o of the plane before and after tilting. Then a, b, a_1, b_1, are the heights above the horizontal in the untwisted plane. Referring to the plan and linear section, a and b stay as they are but a_1 drops the distance a_1–a_0 and b drops the distance b_1–b_0 to bring the seat surface into the necessary curved shape.

In experiments to decide on the maximum thickness of the seat board, always remember that only limited restraint may be available to hold the seat down.

Setting out the back rails

The top and bottom rail of the seat back and, of course, the back panelling will have conical surfaces. But the radii will be so long as to make the centre practically inaccessible. However, the stout section will require that the back rails be cut from the solid (**Fig. 10.32**). They may be formed without any surface development. With the set-out of back rails, the

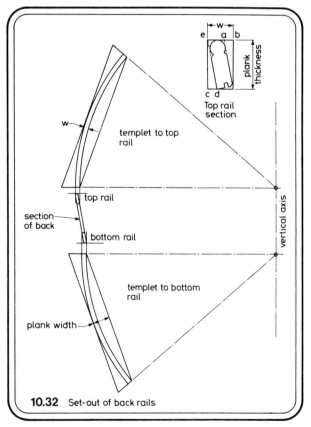

10.32 Set-out of back rails

rectangular raking sections are enclosed in vertical rectangles.

Horizontal radii taken back to the common axis will then give the centres from which the templets for the rails may be marked out and cut. The dimension **a–b** and **c–d** (top rail section) may be gauged around from the top inner and lower outer edges respectively, and the waste removed to this line to give the conical faces needed. Alternatively, the templets may be made to the width, **e–a**, only. The plank would be cut on the bandsaw with the table tilted as required.

PARCLOSE SCREENS

Screens used in churches usually form symbolic barriers only, and are generally left open at the top – hence the name 'parclose' (partly closed) screens. They are often enriched with carving and elaborate patterned tracery. There may be an impressive head and cornice, equally spaced mullions and a dado rail about 1m above the floor. The top is usually open with tracery filling, while the bottom may be panelled.

Fig. 10.33 shows the elevation of a parclose screen in which the enrichments have been kept to a minimum. A central opening is provided, the design being continued through with pendant members. The lower part is filled with panels backing the tracery. **Figs. 10.34** and **10.35** give sectional details to a larger scale.

The cornice

In medieval churches, all members were heavy and monolithic. But the construction, liable to distortion

with moisture movement, is no longer economically viable. So built-up construction is used today, with concealed cores of softwood.

The cornice in **Fig. 10.33** would consist of a number of members tongued together. The top moulding under the capping is formed separately, so that the cutaway necessary to give the dentil ornament may be taken straight through without stopping. The curved ribs in the open part could be grooved to include some open tracery. Half round beads, applied overall, cover the various joints and give a surface uniformity of finish. The moulding of the ribs should match the general framing.

The basic framing should be assembled dry, ensuring that the widths of all the bays are exactly the same. Templets may then be made to assist in marking and cutting the joints. The ribs and framing to one bay are set out full size including the curved mitre intersections. A templet is then made in one piece for marking the exact intersections for fitting both ribs in one bay (**Fig. 10.36**). This is done with the frame accurately dry assembled. The joints are tested by passing the templet through the thickness.

A box should be made into which each rib may be fitted separately, one after the other, after shouldering first to length (**Fig. 10.37**). The joints are marked, cut and fitted, again using loose templets (**Fig. 10.38**). The order of construction is as follows:

1. Make the frame templet and check that it lines up with all the bays in the frame.
2. Make the box with the blocks for positioning the ribs and fit two ribs into it.

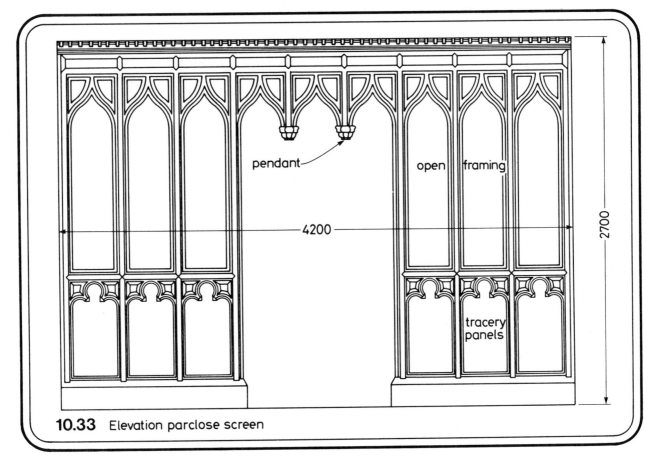

10.33 Elevation parclose screen

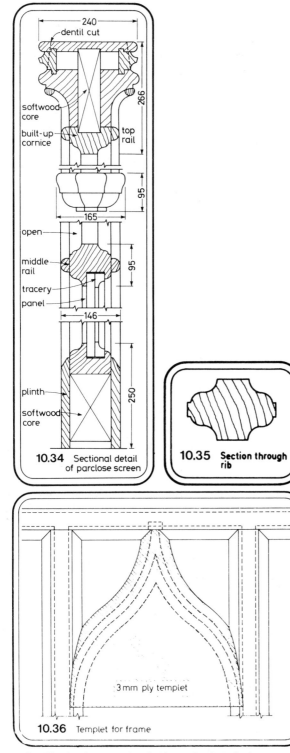

10.34 Sectional detail of parclose screen

10.35 Section through rib

10.36 Templet for frame

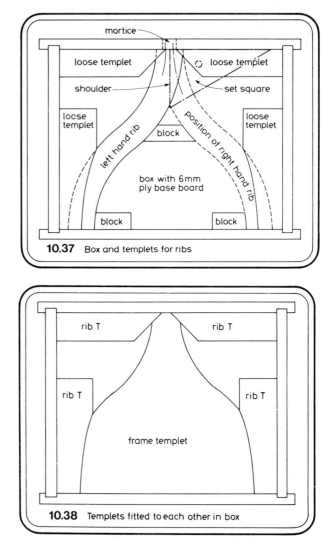

10.37 Box and templets for ribs

10.38 Templets fitted to each other in box

3. Fit the frame templet into the box in its correct position in relation to the ribs.

4. Fit all rib templets to it in the box.

If now all these templets fit together to give perfect joint lines, and the ribs and frame members are cut to fit their respective templets, the assembly should be right first time.

CHURCH DOORS

Church doors are generally fitted into solid frames both for inside and outside work. They are mostly either framed, ledged and braced, or of a panelled construction. Main characteristics include heavy ornamental wrought-iron hinges and curved heads shaped to suit masonry arches of Norman (semicircular) or gothic (pointed) types of various proportions.

A typical pair of panelled gothic church doors (**Fig. 10.39**) would have the joints to the bottom rail of standard construction, with twin tenons usually pinned. But the bottom rail is commonly weathered, instead of being moulded, even when not exposed to the weather (**Fig. 10.40**).

Panels are bareface tongued into the framing to show the panelled effect on the face side. The hanging stiles may be bridle-jointed or hammer-headed tenoned to the top rails. Due to the cross-grain in a tenon cut from the solid rail – with the joint between the curved rail and the closing stile – it is better to use a loose tenon, glued and set first into the rail: see **Fig. 10.41**.

In making the frame, the curved heads may be hand rail-bolted or hammer-head tenoned to the jambs. The heads could also be hand rail-bolted together, dovetail-keyed or hammer-head keyed. But considering the durability and strength of modern resin adhesives, double loose tenons (**Fig. 10.42**) would give the greater strength needed to resist, for example, the slamming of a heavy door in the wind.

With the horizontal sections through the jamb, door stiles and muntins **(Fig. 10.43)**, face widths as seen from the most important side of the door should be uniform.

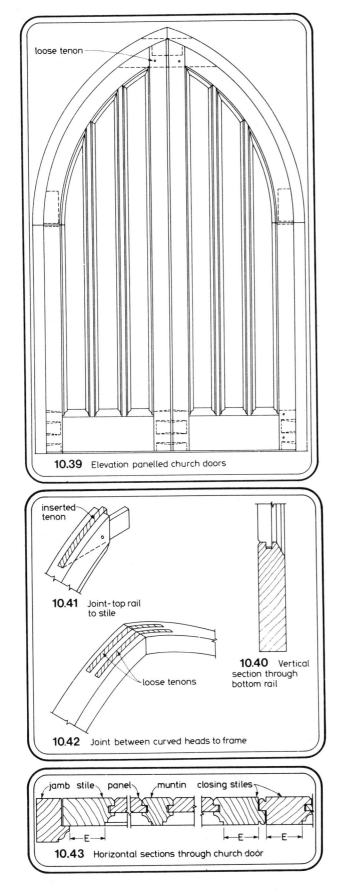

10.39 Elevation panelled church doors

10.41 Joint-top rail to stile

10.40 Vertical section through bottom rail

loose tenons

10.42 Joint between curved heads to frame

10.43 Horizontal sections through church door

GALLERIES

The provision of a gallery in some non-conformist churches introduces a problem in construction and design. In an old church, the floor is likely to be carried by a timber binder. However, in the example given here, it is presumed that a BSB has been used. The gallery front is not likely to be subject to the type of sudden surges one might expect from a football crowd. But it would be under considerable pressure in the event of a fire, and needs to be solidly constructed.

The main support is shown to come from 75 by 75mm vertical softwood posts, hook bolted to the top of the BSB, and retained by cradling at the lower end **(Fig. 10.44)**. The posts should be spaced at intervals of about 1.5m, and should be carefully plumbed and lined, with packing where necessary. Bottom rails are then cut between the posts and a continuous top rail, weathered to the slope of the book-board, notched over them.

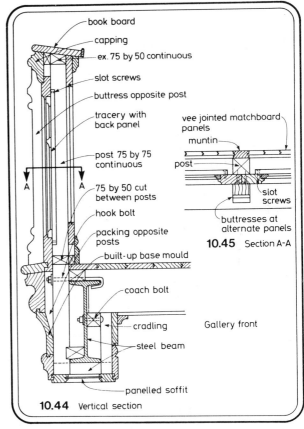

10.45 Section A-A

10.44 Vertical section

Front panelled frames with tracery or other decorative forms are used. They are fitted with joints on the centre of each post outside. Simple panelled frames with perhaps matchboarded panels are butted together on the inside **(Fig. 10.45)**. Cradling, which also retains the bottoms of the posts, is fitted along the BSB at about 75mm centres, with bearers to transfer the weight of the floor and balustrade to the BSB. The base of the front could be finished with a heavy, built-up mould; packing is used to reduce the amount of show timber used.

Alternative methods of finishing the soffit and back of the beam are possible. The top of the balustrade is

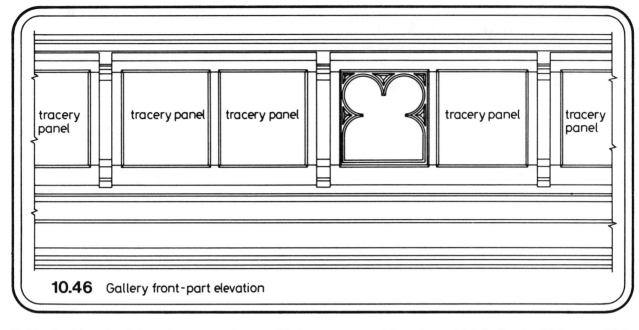

10.46 Gallery front-part elevation

(tracery panel, tracery panel, tracery panel, tracery panel, tracery panel)

finished with a book-board surmounting moulded cappings.

Buttresses opposite each post cover the joints between the outer panelled frames. With the face of the balustrading or gallery front (**Fig. 10.46**), the tracery panels are often traditionally of varying designs.

FONT COVERS

A particular type of ecclesiastical work not met with elsewhere is the cover fitted to the stone font. Both are often octagonal in plan. This is generally heavily enriched with carving and other decorative work. This is largely omitted in **Fig. 10.47** (the elevation and section of an octagonal font cover) in the interests of simplicity. The construction is light compared with that of most ecclesiastical work – a necessity when it may have to be man-handled.

Briefly, the font cover would consist of an octagonal base into which is fitted a high pyramidal cap surmounted by the cross. Working from the bottom, an octagonal base frame is mitred and dowelled together and moulded to the sections given, see **Figs. 10.48, 10.49** and **10.50**. This is attached by screwing to the prismatic body.

The body is constructed from eight posts with eight top and eight bottom rails tenoned into them. The posts line through to the centre. This framing is filled with open tracery panels backed by solid panels screwed to the posts and rails. The parts of the bottom rail, extending beyond the tracery, are mitred with solid blocks moulded on three sides and housed into the posts. They are then continued and finished with pinnacles. Shaped (and possibly carved) cresting is cut between the posts and tongued into the top rails.

The pyramid constituting the upper part of the cover is formed with eight near-triangular boards, mitred and tongued together, the joints being covered with suitably shaped moulds. The bottom edges of the boards forming the pyramid are bevelled to fit neatly inside the vertical boards to the base and securely screwed. The top part of the pyramid is filled with a softwood core, made in four pieces, see **Fig. 10.51**. It is finished with a capping, and surmounted by a cross (**Fig. 10.52**). The cover may be suspended from the ceiling, when lifted, with cords or chains from a pulley with counterbalance weights. An eye must be securely fixed to the cross, which must itself be taken through the core and secured with a wedge.

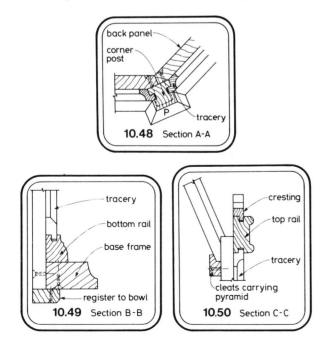

back panel
corner post
P
tracery

10.48 Section A-A

tracery
bottom rail
base frame
register to bowl

10.49 Section B-B

cresting
top rail
tracery
cleats carrying pyramid

10.50 Section C-C

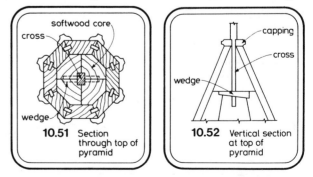

softwood core
cross
wedge

10.51 Section through top of pyramid

capping
cross
wedge

10.52 Vertical section at top of pyramid

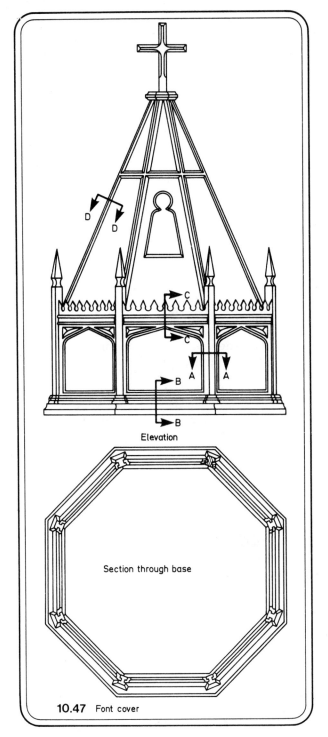

Elevation

Section through base

10.47 Font cover

QUESTIONS FOR CHAPTER 10

Question 23
A small church is being renovated. It is to be fitted with pews of traditional design.

    a. Draw a cross-section through one pew indicating the main dimensions and timber sizes. Scale 1:10.
      b. Sketch constructional details of
        (i) the back, and
        (ii) the fixing of the seat and back to the pew end.
      c. State, with reasons, the timber recommended.

Institute of Carpenters, Associate Examination, 1971.
Time allowed: 30 minutes.

Question 24
A small modern church, the main features of which are laminated portal frames of pine, is to be fitted with pews which will match the decor.

    a. Draw a cross-section through a pew indicating the main dimensions and size of members.
    b. Sketch details of how the back and seat are joined to the pew end and how the whole would be fixed to the floor.
    c. State how the pews would be prepared for a natural finish.

NOTE: Although this is another question on church pews, this one is for a non-traditional church. Wood carvings and solid monolithic construction would be out of place here and there is an opportunity for some original thought.

City & Guilds of London Institute Examination, Purpose-Made Joinery, 1975. No. 5.

CHAPTER 11

Answers

All answers given are the author's own. They are not authorised by the examining bodies concerned.

CHAPTER 1

Answer to question 1
Name four different types of bit for use in the swing brace. Give the use and limitation of each and state how they should be sharpened and maintained. Answers must be brief.

PRELIMINARY THOUGHTS: In setting about this question, you cannot expect to think up the correct answer right away. You may have, say, 12 minutes to answer the question, but the writing should not take more than five minutes. I suggest the following approach.

List the brace bits you know of, say, expansion bit, Irwin bit, Russell Jennings pattern bit, brass countersink, screwdriver bit, wood countersink, wood reamer, centre bit, shell bit, Gedge pattern bit, spoon bit, morse twist drill.

Then look at the list and pick out four different ones that you know well. Note that you were asked for bits, not just drills. Some of these have the same function, such as the countersinks and the Russell Jennings bit and the Irwin bit. The morse twist drill belongs to the wheel brace. Say then that the ones you have selected are the following. Write the name of each one and then the few words about each which are required.

ANSWER: **Russell Jennings pattern bit:** Used for boring clean and accurate holes. Sharpened with a fine file on the inside of the cutters. Protect from contact with other tools.

Centre bit: Used for boring large holes, not suitable for deep holes. Maintain by keeping point sharp and sharpening from the inside.

Gedge pattern bit: Specially suited for boring end grain. Not suitable for side grain. Sharpen from the inside with fine rat-tail file.

Shell bit: Not accurate and only suitable for screw holes. Sharpen on the outside with fine file.

When you have finished, firmly cross out all the preliminary work and the examiner will ignore it. It always pays to make one or two preliminary notes before writing the answer.

Answer to question 2
Specify a suitable adhesive for the following purposes and give reasons for your choice together with any safety precautions to be observed.

a. Interior softwood joinery;
b. Stressed skin panel for roof;
c. Fixing plastic laminate sheeting in workshop with press available;
d. Fixing plastic laminate sheeting on site.

PRELIMINARY THOUGHTS: What is required of each adhesive? What adhesive fills the bill in each case? What risk is there for the operator; or of the failure of the work?

ANSWER: a. Either animal glue or pva woodworking glue. It is cheap, easy to use and strong in dry positions. There are no special risks.

b. Resorcinal formaldehyde. This is water- and boil-proof, gap-filling and stronger than the timber itself. If, however, the panel is to be kept dry, then casein glue, which is also strong and gap-filling, could be used.

c. PVA general-purpose glue or urea formaldehyde. They are both adhesive to wood and laminated plastic and are both moisture resistant; this is necessary where the working surface may have to be washed.

d. The obvious choice for this is impact adhesive which holds on contact. Precautions:

1. Wear rubber gloves when using resin glue;

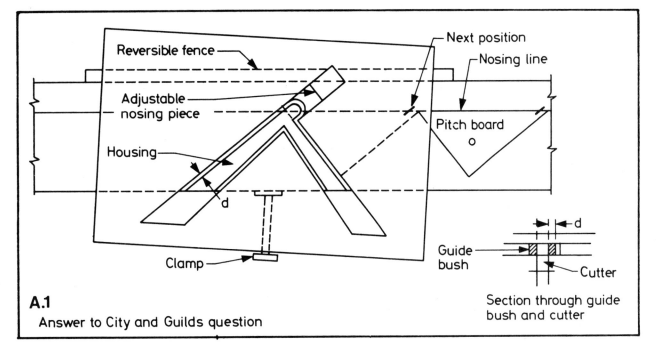

A.1
Answer to City and Guilds question

Labels in figure: Reversible fence — Adjustable nosing piece — Housing — Clamp — d — Next position — Nosing line — Pitch board — o — Guide bush — Cutter — d — Section through guide bush and cutter

2. Keep naked lights away from impact adhesive which is inflammable;
3. Follow maker's instructions when using all proprietary makes of adhesives.

Answer to question 3
a. Why is it important that the moisture content of the timber is appropriate to the conditions in which it is to be fixed?
b. State a suitable moisture content for:
   1. Window frames:
   2. Wall panelling in a centrally heated building.

PRELIMINARY THOUGHTS: (a) What happens to timber of average moisture content if it is taken outside in winter? It will not only swell but may also warp or distort and the heart side will go hollow.

If it is taken into a heated room it will shrink and the heart side will go rounded. Panels which swell may buckle or burst off shoulders and stiles which shrink may open at the joints.

b. Window frames are going to be exposed to weather. Wall panelling is going to be continuously warm. If you do not know the British Standards, make an intelligent guess.

ANSWER: a. The moisture content of timber should be taken precisely to that at which it would be likely finally to settle, so that there shall be no swelling or shrinkage or distortion. This might happen if it were to gain or lose moisture after it was fixed.
  b. 1. 10 to 12 per cent
    2. 17 to 18 per cent.

CHAPTER 2

Answer to question 4
A number of closed stair strings are to be cut out to house the steps. Describe how this operation can be carried out using the portable powered router.

PRELIMINARY THOUGHTS: What are the requirements for the housing of the string? They will have to be in pairs, left- and right-hand; the housings will have to agree with the pitch board; and there will be a specified margin. The housings will also have to allow for the nosing and the wedges.

Next consider the machine. What are the essentials? It is only necessary to show the projection of the cutter below the templet, not forgetting the guide bush as this controls the width of the housing. For the metal templet: all that is needed is the housing outline, the fence and means of fixing. Show as much as you can by sketches.

ANSWER: The sketch of the jig (**Fig. A.1**) shows its position on the string in relation to the pitch board. The templet is turned over and the fence reversed to do the other string.

The size of the guide bush governs the reduction in thickness of the housings.

The router is fed forward and back so that the cutter revolves against, not with, the guiding edge.

Answer to question 5
A number of short rails 600 by 60 by 30mm have to have stop rebates run on one edge as shown in **Fig. 2.23**. Sketch a safe method of performing this operation at the vertical spindle.

PRELIMINARY THOUGHTS: The question reminds the candidate that the rail is short, and introduces the term 'safe'. Is a jig necessary to keep the hands a safe distance from the cutters? What is the danger of 'dropping on' and how is this combated? Are the rails going to be worked face down or face up? If face up, a saw guard will have to be used to keep the rail firmly on the table or the job will be spoilt. Also, the cutter block will be exposed above the wood and will have to be guarded separately. If the rebate is worked face down, the actual working will be concealed. Finally, the ends are stopped to a very small radius; does this dictate the type of cutter to be used?

ANSWER: It is better to work the rebate face down, being simpler and safer. The obvious cutter block to use in order to get the small radius, is the French head. To give the maximum protection, a faceboard should be used, nailed to the wooden fence. Stops should be nailed to the faceboard both for the start and finish of the cut. With the small projection of the cutter through the faceboard, and the protection afforded by the saw guard, a jig should not be necessary. If, however, a large number of rails had to be machined, a jig would be worthwhile for convenience.

Only the method has to be sketched, so the drawing can be simple. Also, only a sketch is asked for, not a written description. However this should be fully labelled. **Fig. A.2** is an example of the type of sketch which would constitute a complete answer.

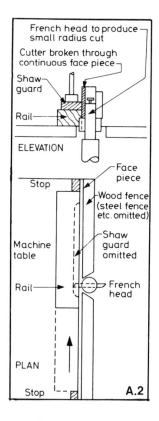

CHAPTER 3

Answer to question 6
The outline of the top corner of a glazed panel with a shaped top rail is shown in **Fig. 3.83**. Sketch details of the joint between top rail and stile.

PRELIMINARY THOUGHTS: Complete the elevation by putting in the mould line because this will give the position of the mitre.

Where will the tenon come in the thickness and how will this affect the width of the mortise? Obviously it will be one-third thickness and it will be central. The mortise can only come to the back of the

rebate. Will there be short grain in the rail at the mitre? Yes, it is better to take the shoulder line back.

Would it be advisable to have a double tenon? No, because the haunches and tenons would be too narrow. If the tenon is made about half the available width, will the bulk of it be opposite short grain on the shaped rail? Not in this case. These are only thoughts.

ANSWER: See **Fig. A.3**.

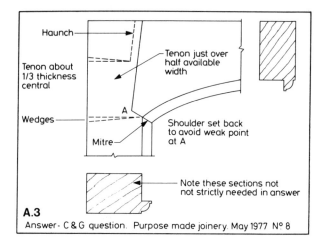

A.3
Answer- C & G question. Purpose made joinery. May 1977 Nº 8

Answer to question 7
A fire report on a public building calls for both half hour and one hour fire check flush doors and frames constructed to BS459, Part 3. Sketch horizontal sections to show the construction of both types of doors and frames.

PRELIMINARY THOUGHTS: This is a specific question to which you either know or do not know the answer. Note that only a sketch is asked for; but there is no need why it should not be drawn to scale, good proportion thus being ensured. The examiner is looking for knowledge of certain values on the candidate's part. I do not think the candidate would be penalised if he did not keep to the letter.

The one hour fire check flush door also contains all the parts of the half hour door and I suggest that one sketch would do for the two but a little explanation becomes necessary. It is therefore important that the sketch (**Fig. A.4**) should be fully labelled. Perhaps the most important thing to remember is that all rebated joints must have 25mm cover on face.

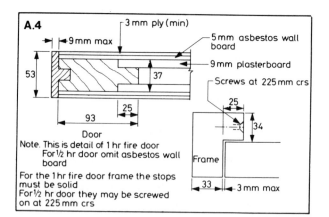

NOTE: For possible examinees. This is all the information asked for. Other details such as hinges, fastenings, preservative treatment, etc, are not required and will not earn extra marks or be accepted as substitute information.

ANSWER: **Fig. A.4** should provide the complete answer.

Answer to question 8
A segmental headed door to a bank is 1200mm wide and ex 50mm thick with a height of 1900mm at the springing line and 250mm rise. The framing has solid stuck mouldings and is arranged to take five horizontal raised and fielded panels.

 a. To scale of 1:10, draw an elevation of the door and indicate the joints;
 b. Specify a suitable timber;
 c. Draw, to a scale 1:1, a section through the jamb, stile and part of the panel.

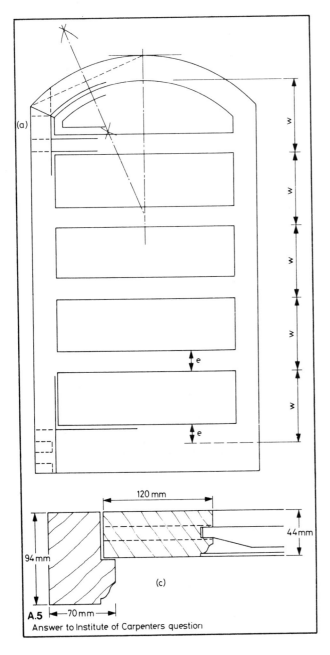

A.5 Answer to Institute of Carpenters question

PRELIMINARY THOUGHTS: This is a drawing question and there is quite a lot to do in the time allotted. Avoid time-wasting repetition. Draw just enough to show the examiner that you know what is required.

 a. Draw the elevation first. Some very simple geometry is needed to set out the head as most candidates should know. Leave the construction in; do not rub it out. No section sizes are given but, as it is a solid job for a bank, make the stiles 126 to 150mm wide and the bottom rail 250 to 275mm wide. Keep to nominal sizes on the scale drawing.

Draw the curved top rail and wide bottom rail and decide on the width of the intermediates, say 100mm. Add this on to the distance in the clear and divide by 5. Next, mark off rails one side of each division (see **Fig. A.5**). Now come the joint (shoulder) lines; a good ruler is necessary for this. Always put in mouldings, rebates, etc, first in the elevation; then the backs of these lines are the shoulders. Outlines of tenons should be dotted. Remember that plough grooves reduce tenon widths.

 b. The timber recommended needs to be hardwood, good-looking, weather-resisting and stable. The candidate should be prepared for this type of query which is frequently included in examination questions in carpentry and joinery. If you cannot think of anything else, oak, mahogany or teak will generally fill the bill.

ANSWER: a. **Fig. A.5** is sufficient to satisfy the examiner.

 c. Full-sized detail: This cannot be shown here but remember your drawings will be measured. Always remember to draw to finished sizes, not nominal sizes. Thus 50mm becomes 44mm, 125mm becomes 120mm and so on.

CHAPTER 4

Answer to question 9
A works office adjacent to an airport has a casement window of 100 by 75mm rebated frame and 44mm moulded sash as shown in **Fig. 4.97**. Draw a horizontal section through the jamb to show any recommended modification to reduce the passage of sound when:

 a. The existing window is retained,
 b. A new window is inserted. (Scale half full-size).

PRELIMINARY THOUGHTS: What are the requirements for sound insulation? They are:

 1. A space of at least 50mm within the double glazing,
 2. Two different thicknesses of glass to cut out sympathetic resonance, and
 3. A surface of glass exposed to sound waves disconnected from the main structure.

It is not possible to fit a second window outside the existing one as an obstruction would be formed. A second inside window will be needed. The inner window will not need to be weather resisting.

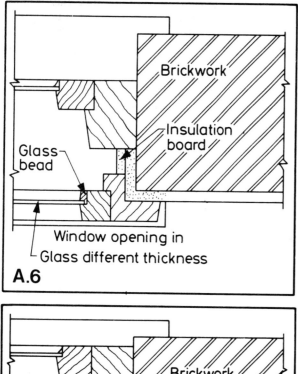

A.6

Brickwork

Insulation board

Glass bead

Window opening in

Glass different thickness

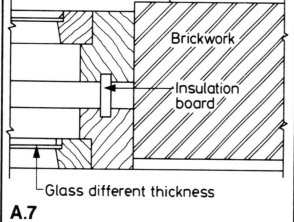

A.7

Brickwork

Insulation board

Glass different thickness

ANSWER: a. The above points have been considered in the section shown in **Fig. A.6**. The second window is extended into the room to give a wide insulated space.

b. The double glazing is formed within the wall thickness, see **Fig. A.7**.

Answer to question 10

During alterations to a large country house, it is discovered that although the hardwood sills are sound, the lower part of the pulley stile and outer linings of a number of boxed frames are decayed. State the repairs necessary.

PRELIMINARY THOUGHTS: Is the decay dry rot or cellar fungus? Presumably it is the latter, in which case it is primarily a matter of finding the cause of the decay: i.e. the entry-point of water between timber and brickwork. Painting may have been neglected.

Consider the construction of the casing, pocket piece to pulley stile. Is the pulley stile tongued to the lining or is the lining merely nailed on? The outer lining should be easily removable. The back lining would have to be left in.

ANSWER: The outer lining could be removed and replaced or a new piece could be spliced on the bottom. The pulley stile could be spliced above the pocket piece, assuming the pocket piece is still sound (see **Fig. A.8**).

Fresh wedges would be needed to secure the pulley stiles in the sills. It would be advisable to brush the inside of the casings with a colourless organic solvent preservative, such as clear Cuprinol. All the new work and adjacent old work should be well painted. The joints to the brickwork should be made good with a suitable mastic.

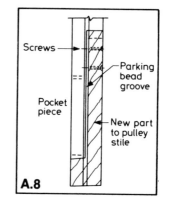

Screws

Parking bead groove

Pocket piece

New part to pulley stile

A.8

Answer to question 11

Describe the problems associated with fitting of lights in the roofs of buildings and, with the aid of simple sketches, state how they may be dealt with.

PRELIMINARY THOUGHTS: This is a general question. Simple sketches are asked for, so only the constructional detail related to the question need be shown.

What kinds of lights are fitted to roofs? What are to common problems? They are all greatly exposed to the weather, wind and rain. They will all have condensation problems. Those on pitched roofs with tiles or slates must be proofed against water flowing around them.

The candidate should not make his answer too prosy. He only has to show that he knows it and a detailed description is unnecessary. There is not time for it.

ANSWER: The problems and their solutions are as follows:

Condensation: Due to the warm humid air striking the cold glass, excessive condensation will always occur and it must be allowed to flow away. In pitched lights it is allowed to run out over the bottom rail (**Fig. A.9**). In vertical lights, it is connected in a gutter and piped away (**Fig. A.10**).

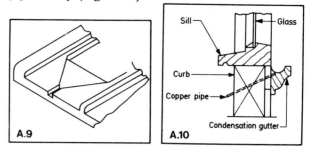

A.9

Sill

Glass

Curb

Copper pipe

Condensation gutter

A.10

Water-proofing: Rain is likely to run back on undersurfaces and to be driven in by the wind. This is prevented by drips and tongued joints (**Figs. A.11(a)** and **A.11(b)**). The joint between the roof covering and the roof light needs special consideration as the normal waterproofing, by the overlap of tiles is destroyed.

At the back of the light a gutter is formed in lead or other suitable material. The light is kept above the roof on a curb and the lead is dressed over the curb, under the light and up under the roof tiles (**Fig. A.12**). The water flowing off the roof light is taken away by a lead flashing dressed up under the light and over the tiles.

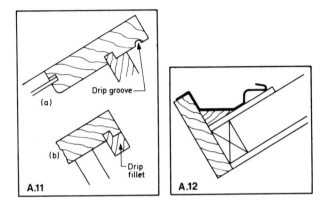

On a flat roof water gets away very slowly and the impervious roof covering must be taken up the curb and its top edge covered by flashing (**Fig. A.13**).

The joint between the curb side and the tiles may be made either by means of a gutter (**Fig. A.14**) or by using soakers bonded in with the tiles and covered with lead flashing.

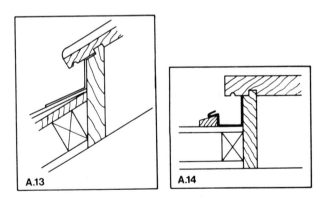

CHAPTER 5

Answer to question 12
Fig. 5.56 shows the dimensions of a public inquiry counter and screen in an office. The hardwood screen is 94mm thick. The counter is formed with 18mm thick chipboard and the top is covered with plastic laminate. The screen and counter are to be made in the shop.
  a. Draw a section through the transom. Scale 1:2.
  b. Sketch a vertical section through the counter showing the method of construction.

PRELIMINARY THOUGHTS: The glass and the chipboard panel would look best if they both came centrally in the thickness of the frame, but the job would be easier to machine if the back of the glass rebate coincided with the side of the panel groove. If this is so shown, it is as well to state the reason.

The counter appears to be fitted against the wall. In this case, access to the interior would appear to be from the customer side. Either show doors and shelves reached from this side or assume there is space for access from the back. It is as well to state why this is being done. As the chipboard used is 18mm thick, very little intermediate support will be needed for the chipboard front.

The sketch of the counter section can quite easily be set out to some scale. Keep this as large as reasonably possible. The laminate on the counter top could lap a similar edging or could be rebated into a hardwood edging. The sketch will not be scaled so any sizes should be written in.

ANSWER: See **Fig. A.15**.

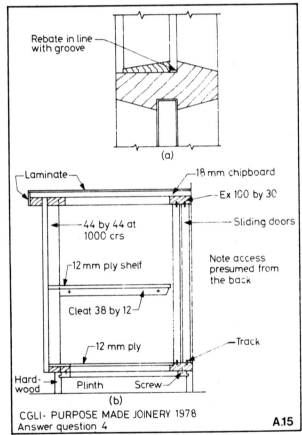

Answer to question 13
A manager's office is required to be panelled out in polished 6mm veneered plywood and finished with moulded mahogany trim as indicated in **Fig. 5.57**.
  a. Draw scale 1:1, sections at A–A, B–B, C–C, D–D and E–E showing construction and fixing.
  b. Explain how the mouldings would be cleaned up by hand suitable for finishing with French polish. Give reasons for the methods described.

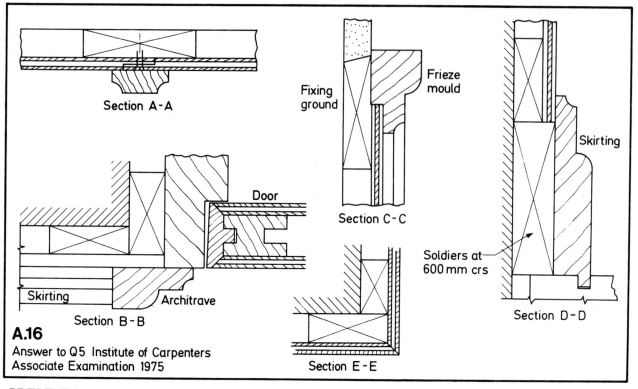

Section A-A

Fixing ground

Frieze mould

Section C-C

Door

Skirting

Section B-B   Architrave

Skirting

Soldiers at 600 mm crs

Section D-D

Section E-E

A.16
Answer to Q5 Institute of Carpenters
Associate Examination 1975

PRELIMINARY THOUGHTS: The moulding
has to be French polished and the panels are also
polished, so it is expected that a well-designed
highly-finished job will be required. This will mean
that the frieze mould, skirting, architrave and cover
mould between the panels will have some uniformity
and where they intersect they should do so on a mitre:
i.e. the mould on the top edge of the skirting and the
bottom member of frieze mould should be the same.
Secret fixing is difficult with thin plywood panels but
the panels may be fixed under the moulds; then the
moulds are pinned on and the pin holes are stopped in
with coloured wax. It is a requirement of French
polished work that the most of the polishing should be
done before assembly.

ANSWER: a. The sections, as asked for, are shown
in **Fig. A.16**. The panels will be screwed to grounds
underneath the mouldings which are pinned with
holes stopped in with coloured wax.

b. The mouldings should be cleaned up with glasspaper wrapped around a shaped moulding-rubber so
as not to destroy the shape or round the arised of the
moulding. Coarse paper should be used at first to
remove machine marks; finish with finer paper. The
moulding should then be damped to raise the grain
and finally rubbed down with flour paper.

CHAPTER 6

Answer to question 14
An open newel stair is shown in **Fig. 6.80**. The stair is
for private use.
   The total rise is 2340.
   Newel posts 100 by 100mm.
   Strings 38mm thick.

Treads 32mm thick.
Risers 15mm thick.
a. Calculate the step rise and determine a suitable
step going.
b. Draw an elevation in the direction of the arrow
of the bottom three steps, showing the joint between the string and the newel post. Scale 1:5.
c. Set out the four faces of the newel post to show
positions of treads, risers and mortises for the
string.
d. Sketch the construction of the bullnose step.

PRELIMINARY THOUGHTS: What part of the
question must be influenced by the Building Regulations? The going of the lower flight is not given but
the step going is the same throughout to comply with
the Regulations. The total number of risers is 13 but
only 11 treads (four in top flights).
   No scotia mould is specified to the nosing so it need
not be given. The question does not say whether the
string is open or closed – the closed string is the
simpler to draw.
   The bullnose step could be built up with a veneer
riser or could be of preformed plywood. The latter
does not however make sense of d.
   The string is only 38mm thick so it should preferably be barefaced tenoned to the newel posts to allow
the step housings to clear the tenon. The newel post is
given at 100 by 100mm. This is normally a nominal
size but the question does not state this; so draw it 100
by 100mm and state that this is not usual.
   In setting out the newel post, although not asked
for, it helps to draw the plan before doing the set-out
of the faces. Both drawings can then have identifying
numbers.

ANSWER: a. Step rise = $\dfrac{\text{total rise of stairs}}{\text{no of risers}}$

$$= \frac{2340}{13} = 180\text{mm precisely.}$$

Step going: take the top flight. This has four treads covering 900mm: therefore step going

$$= \frac{900}{4} = 225\text{mm.}$$

Note: There is no point in checking against Building Regulations.

ANSWERS: b, c, and d; These are all drawings, see **Fig. A.17.**

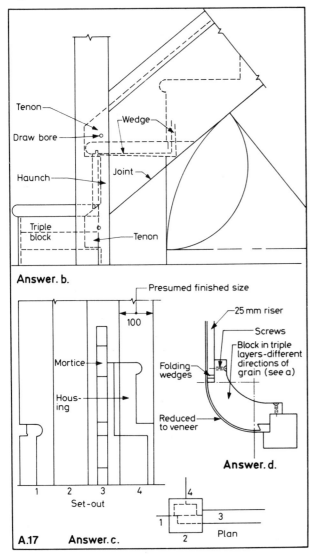

A.17   Answer. c.

Answer to question 15
Fig. 6.81 shows the plan of a geometrical stair. The wreathed string is cut and bracketed. Given that the width of the fliers is 300mm, and the width of the tapered steps at their narrow ends is 125mm, draw a development of the wreathed string when the rise is 190mm. Scale 1:20.

PRELIMINARY THOUGHTS: What effect will the fact that the string is bracketed have on the answer? It will have none; but a subsequent question refers back to it and the information will have some bearing on the answer to this question.

As all horizontal dimensions are given in figure in the script, the only need for the drawing provided **(Fig. A.18)** is to give the numbers of winders and fliers. The joint in the wreath comes back on the end of the adjoining flier above and below.

Count the number of treads and the number of risers and calculate overall dimensions.
There are 10 risers, so 10 × 190 = 1900mm
There are 8 winders, so 8 × 125 = 1000.

Using convenient unit dimensions on the scale rule, set out the goings and the storey rod as shown and complete the drawing.

ANSWER: See **Fig. A.18.**

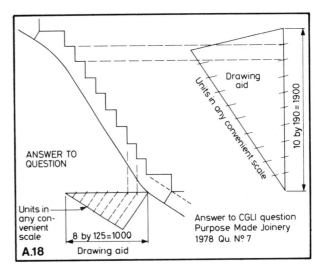

Answer to question 16
To a scale of 1:20, draw the development of the well string in **Fig. 6.55** and indicate the joint lines.

PRELIMINARY THOUGHTS: As the development is asked for, this means the lower wreathed part of the string. As the fliers are obtained from the elevation, the bottom step would preferably be joined to the string at the second rise, the block of the curtail step having an extension to stiffen the joint. These details are not required here.

Reading the relevant text, the goings of the winder on the string are all the same. The going of each winder in the plan quadrant will be the stretch-out divided by 7, so the total goings on the 9 risers will be 800 × 9. Using a simple calculator, this equals 1616mm.

The total rise of the wreath, including 2 fliers = 12 × 156 = 1872mm.
As all the winders are the same, the nosing line will be a straight line. Starting at the joint to the curtail step, the step outline may now be set out.

ANSWER: **Fig. A.19** shows a simple way of doing it, holding the scale rule to form the hypotenuse of a right-angle triangle to read the required number of whole graduations. Any convenient scale (in this case 1:20) may be used. The pitch of the winders will be different from that of the fliers. The soffit lines should join in a smooth curve. The rest of the drawing should be self-explanatory.

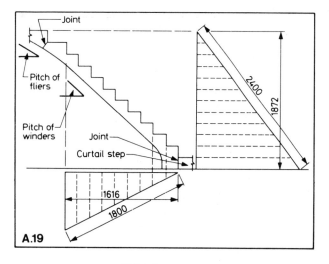

A.19

CHAPTER 7

Answer to question 17
A handrail wreath is to be set out to suit the conditions given in **Fig. 7.53.**
   a. Determine the shape of the facemould, and
   b. The twist bevels and thickness of plank required.
Scale 1:10.

PRELIMINARY THOUGHTS: No height is given for the handrail over the landing, so this may be assumed to be adjusted to suit the handrail. Therefore the upper tangent will be level, the centre-line plane will be a rectangle, and there will be only one pitch bevel to the top tangent which will govern plank thickness. The lower end of the wreath will be the actual handrail width.

With this knowledge it would be possible to give the information asked for without drawing the plan or step outlines but, unless you are pushed for time, it is better to proceed in the traditional way, see **Fig. A.20.**

ANSWER: The setting-out procedure is

   1. Put down the plan,
   2. Draw the elevation of the steps folded back, project up to give shank widths and draw tangents and centre-line plane,
   3. Draw axes, complete facemould and set out twist bevel and thickness of plank.

Answer to question 18
Taking the example on normal sections given on page 114, but assuming that both tangents are pitched at 38°, obtain the twist bevels only.

PRELIMINARY THOUGHTS: Taking this as an examination question, saving time is important. So, with a little thought, it will be realised that only the elevation of the tangents and the plan to the centre line, with selected points of normal sections, are necessary to start with. As the pitches are equal, the lower trace of the upper tangent coincides with the opened back lower trace so that the horizontal trace will be at 45 degrees to the **X–Y** line.

Note that to obtain each twist bevel, we start off with the plan of the tangent to the normal section and

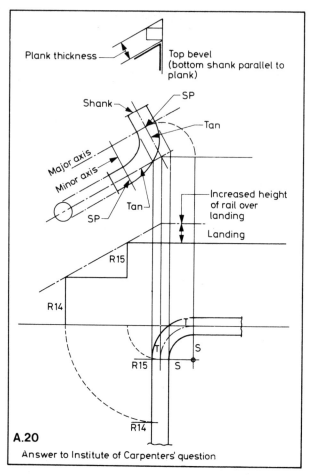

A.20
Answer to Institute of Carpenters' question

then the horizontal trace of the plane containing the twist bevel is square to this. The actual twist bevel is formed by the intersections between the vertical-tangent plane, the plane containing the twist bevel and the centre-line plane. As the normal section at **c** is parallel to the main horizontal trace, it will also be parallel to this plane. Therefore the twist bevel will be a right angle. However, the procedure of obtaining

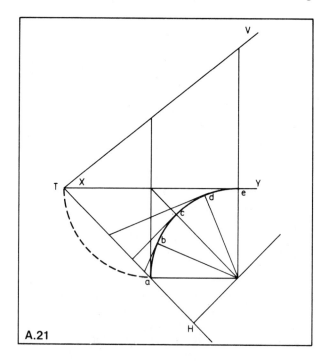

A.21

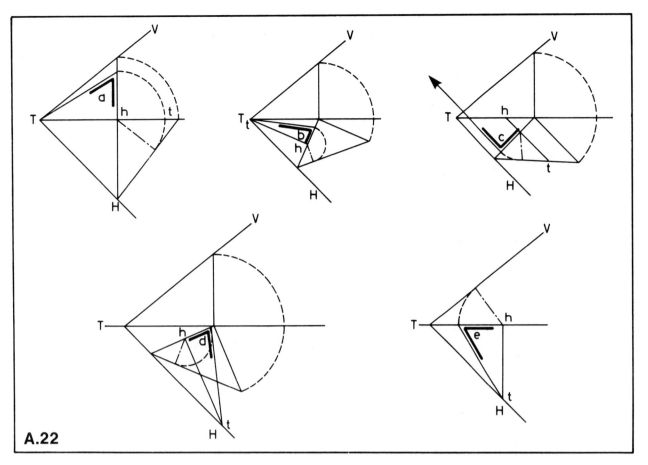

A.22

the bevel has been followed through to make it a little plainer to the reader. By referring back to Chapter 7, pages 114–16, the answer should now be clear to him.

ANSWER: See **Figs. A.21** and **A.22.**

Answer to question 19
A staircase with upper and lower outer strings approaching at an angle of 60 degrees, is formed with the turn wreathed at 200mm radius. The step rise is 170mm and the going to fliers 240mm. Set out the wreathed string in outline, designed so that the position of fliers and winders give a rake to rake handrail of equal pitches without easings.

PRELIMINARY THOUGHTS: Although not specifically asked for, the model answer to this question has included the shape of·the centre-line plane with the centre line of handrail. To provide the complete answer in practice, it would be necessary to comply with the Building Regulations. There is, however, not sufficient information given as to stair width, etc, for this to be done. The question is purely a test of the candidate's knowledge of staircase geometry.

The requirement is that, when the prism is opened out, the going to and from the corner **b** of the prism must equal the going of the flier. This is so that the upper and lower nosing lines will meet on this corner

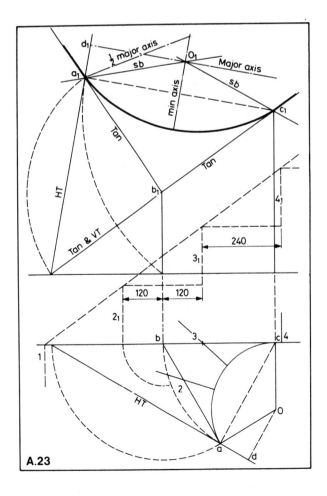

A.23

irrespective of whether the handrail is of uniform height above all the nosings.

It is the points where the riser lines cut the tangents that matter; with the proviso that the actual angles of the winders do not affect the design of the wreath. Therefore, in the drawing (**Fig. A.23**) the sum of the distances of risers **2** and **3** on plan must equal 240mm.

ANSWER: The plan of the centre-line plane in **Fig. A.23** is **a–b–c–0**; and a_1–b_1–c_1–0_1 is its true shape. As the handrail is rake to rake, equal pitches, the centre-line plane is symmetrical. An appreciation of this helps the setting-out. The drawing should be self-explanatory.

CHAPTER 8

Answer to question 20
Straight glued laminated beams, 6m long, 120mm wide and 400mm deep, are to be made up for use in a works kitchen.
  a. What is the maximum thickness of laminates recommended?
  b. Sketch two types of longitudinal joints which may be used in the laminates.
  c. What type of adhesive would you recommend?

PRELIMINARY THOUGHTS: As the beams are straight, the laminates will not have to be bent, so they can be full recommended thickness. The thicker the laminates, the fewer cramps will be needed. If the beams are simply supported, the top laminates will be subject to compression. The scarfs can therefore be made shorter, saving money.

The beams are to be placed in a works kitchen. So there may be considerable amounts of rising steam. The examiner may consider that this warrants an expensive WBP gap-filling glue.

ANSWER: a. The laminates should not be more than 50mm thick.
  b. Two possible scarf joints are shown in **Fig. A.24**.
  c. As the beam will be exposed to considerable moisture, resorcinal formaldehyde gap-filling resin glue, although expensive, is the best adhesive. Alternatively, casein glue would be satisfactory in dry conditions as this is also strong and gap-filling.

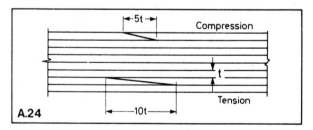

A.24

Answer to question 21
  a. What is meant by stressed skin construction?
  b. Sketch details of a stressed skin panel, noting the important points of construction.

PRELIMINARY THOUGHTS: Take the individual words: 'stressed' means under load: 'skin' means a thin sheet, say plywood. However, stressed skin construction really refers to that in which the plywood is loaded within the plane of the sheet. A box beam would have its plywood flanges under shear. So this could be called stressed skin.

However, a lead is given in the question which refers to a stressed skin panel. So, what is being asked for relates to a floor or roof panel in which the plywood sheeting is under stress within its thickness.

Therefore, the top sheet will be under compression; the bottom sheet, if there is one, will be under tension; and the joists or bearers will be under shear. The important points to note are that the length of the sheeting must be without weak points. The joints between the plywood and the bearers must be fully shear resistant, either being close nailed or glued to full strength.

ANSWER: a. Stressed skin construction is that which uses plywood to act as a component of the moment of resistance, in a box beam or floor panel. In the case of the box beam, the plywood web is under shear. In the case of the floor panel, the plywood acts as flanges. The top sheet is in compression and the bottom sheet is in tension.
  b. See **Fig. A.25**.

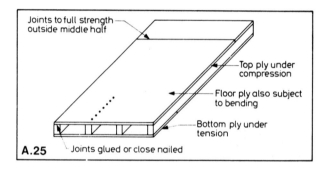

A.25

CHAPTER 9

Answer to question 22
A veneered panel is to have a central diamond in a quartered panel in which the grain of the diamond is to be horizontal; all the veneers are to have pronounced stripes. Describe how the veneer pattern would be fitted and assembled.

PRELIMINARY THOUGHTS: As the emphasis is on the striped grain, it is certain that the direction of grain is important both in the diamond and the background. It would look best if the direction of the grain exactly followed the lines of the diamond. The grain in the diamond should have one line exactly from corner to corner.

ANSWER: The quartered panels should be cut from four consecutive veneers in the plank, checking that lines of grain match before cutting. Set out the pattern full size (**Fig. A.26**). Shoot the diamond to size and pin in position on drawing. Cut all the quartered veneers together, allowing a little for fitting. Fit them together on board and tape the joints. Finally glue up the whole in a press.

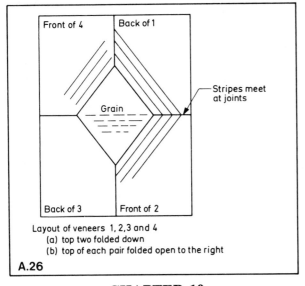

Layout of veneers 1, 2, 3 and 4
(a) top two folded down
(b) top of each pair folded open to the right

A.26

CHAPTER 10

Answer to question 23

A small church is being renovated. It is to be fitted with pews of traditional design.

 a. Draw a cross-section through one pew indicating the main dimensions and timber sizes. Scale 1:10.

 b. Sketch constructional details of

 (i) the back, and

 (ii) the fixing of the seat and back to the pew end.

 c. State, with reasons, the timber recommended.

PRELIMINARY THOUGHTS: If the drawing for question a. is made with sufficient care in the smaller detail, it can also include some of the information for the answers to b. Of course, the careful production of these sketches can be time-consuming in exam conditions. The examiner will accept suitably labelled, ruled sketches in orthographic projection.

 Drawings must be well-proportioned. For example, a tenon should be about one-third the total thickness of the mortised member. And it is as well to write in such details.

ANSWER: a. and b. See **Fig. A.27.**

 c. The other fittings in the church will almost certainly be oak, but could be pitch pine. The seats could be of the same timber. Either is suitable, being strong and durable. They both have a good appearance, and clean up well.

Answer to question 24

A small modern church, the main feature of which are laminated portal frames of pine, is to be fitted with pews which will match the decor.

 a. Draw a cross-section through a pew, indicating the main dimensions and size of members.

 b. Sketch details of how the back and seat are joined to the pew end and how the whole would be fixed to the floor.

 c. State how the pews would be prepared for a natural finish.

PRELIMINARY THOUGHTS: As the seats have to match the decor they will have to be simple in

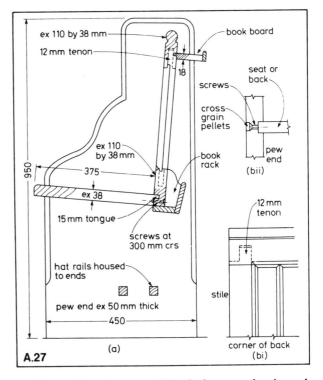

A.27 (a) (bi) (bii)

outline and perhaps could include some laminated members in the construction. The seat and seat back must be a standard size and solid. A book-board also will be necessary. There is no time to ponder over intimate details of design.

ANSWER: a. Put in the seat and overall standard sizes (see dotted lines in **Fig. A.28**). Draw in the seat and back. Put in the framework necessary to contain these. Put in book-board and rack and a sole piece for fixing to floor.

 b. This involves pellet screwing. Avoid pictorial sketches: you have only to show that you know, not make someone understand.

 c. Surfaces to be given a natural finish must be finished smoothly without scratches. The work should be glasspapered, starting with coarse paper and finishing with fine, and with the grain always. If it is damped to bring up the grain and then papered down, the grain will not rise again in a humid atmosphere.

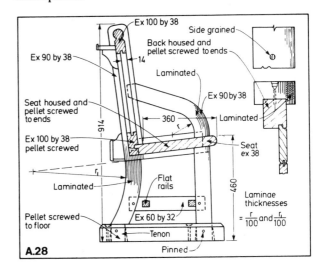

A.28

Index